Pitt Press Series

M. ANNAEI LVCANI

DE BELLO CIVILI

LIBER VIII

T0381944

M. ANNAEI LVCANI

DE BELLO CIVILI

LIBER VIII

Edited by

J. P. POSTGATE, Litt.D., F.B.A.

Fellow and sometime Senior Classical Lecturer of Trinity College, Cambrid
Professor of Latin in the University of Liverpool

Cambridge
at the University Press
1917

CAMBRIDGE
UNIVERSITY PRESS

University Printing House, Cambridge CB2 8BS, United Kingdom

Cambridge University Press is part of the University of Cambridge.

It furthers the University's mission by disseminating knowledge in the pursuit of education, learning and research at the highest international levels of excellence.

www.cambridge.org
Information on this title: www.cambridge.org/9781107487178

© Cambridge University Press 1917

First published 1917
First paperback edition 2015

A catalogue record for this publication is available from the British Library

ISBN 978-1-107-48717-8 Paperback

PREFACE

THIS edition of the second of what may be called the
'Pompeian' books of Lucan's *Civil War* follows
that of the first in the same series after a long interval
and on a more ample scale. For this there are various
reasons, one of them the opinion expressed by several
competent critics that the difficulties of Lucan stood in
need of some fuller elucidation. To supplement the
presentation of the subject in the Eighth Book two
extracts have been added from the Ninth with the bare
minimum of annotation. The due discussion of matters
appertaining to the text has necessitated a longer Introduction and more than one Excursus. As to some of
these matters, circumstances have prevented the editor
from obtaining all the intelligence that he desired. The
more grateful is he to the scholars who have assisted him
upon other points of detail, that is to say, to the following:
Mr J. G. Anderson, Professor W. B. Anderson, Professor
J. B. Bury, Sir F. W. Dyson, Dr P. J. Enk, Dr W.
Warde Fowler, Mr T. R. Glover, Professor A. E. Housman,
Mr H. Stuart Jones, Mr E. H. Minns, the Rev. Dr J. H.
Moulton, Lieut. H. A. Ormerod, Mr A. G. Peskett,
Dr L. C. Purser, Professor J. S. Reid, Lieut.-Col. Hugh
Stewart, and in an especial degree to Mr F. Ll. Griffith
and Dr T. Rice Holmes. Amongst previous works he

owes most to the commentary of Cortius published posthumously by C. F. Weber, to Mr Heitland's Introduction to Haskins' edition of Lucan and to the second edition, by P. Groebe, of Drumann's *Geschichte Roms*. Lastly he would express his sense of indebtedness to the care and skill of all at the University Press who have cooperated in the production of the book.

J. P. POSTGATE.

The University,
    Liverpool.
        January 1, 1917.

CONTENTS

ADDENDA TO INTRODUCTION

p. xiv l. 13.   Between 'that' and 'Sextus' insert : in the version of the source.

p. lxiv n. 1.   After '(p. 760)' add : σῆμα might of course be conjectured.

ADDENDA TO NOTES

l. 122.   Add : **si** is doubled also in a set form of prayer in Livy 7. 26. 4 'precatus deinde *si* diuus, *si* diua esset qui sibi praepetem misisset, uolens propitius adesset.'

l. 249.   On **compensat** add : Perhaps it is simpler to interpret it in the sense of 'gaining,' or 'saving a loss' as in Ov. *Her.* 3. 51 'tot tamen amissis te *compensauimus* unum.'   Here what is 'gained' or 'saved' is the time needed for the winding coast route.

HISTORICAL INTRODUCTION

THE LAST DAYS OF POMPEY THE GREAT

CHAPTER I

THE AUTHORITIES

§ 1. *Lucan*

The Eighth Book of Lucan's *Civil War* has more than one claim upon our attention. As internal evidence may be adduced to show, it was written when the shadow of imperial disfavour had fallen across his path, and youth and vanity spurred him towards the mad adventure which was to bring him to an early and dishonoured grave. This book with the foregoing one constitutes, we may say, a single chapter in the annals of Roman destiny. For with Pompey, as Cicero foreknew[1], death followed inexorably upon defeat. But the interest of the two books is not the same. In the Seventh it is mainly political and historical, in the Eighth rather personal and biographical. Inasmuch however as this book has an apparent claim to be the fullest and most detailed of extant records of the last days of the Roman general, upon whom his countrymen had conferred the proudest title of an Alexander, it is a natural, and indeed a necessary part of our task to inquire how far the presentations of its author are likely to rest on a solid basis of fact.

Seventh and Eighth Books of Lucan.

---

[1] Cic. *ad Att.* 11. 6. 5 'de Pompei exitu mihi dubium numquam fuit.'

That Lucan is to a certain extent an authority for the events which he narrates, most, if not all, modern writers would agree; but the question how far he should be trusted is matter for cautious and delicate appraisement. I have touched upon this subject in the *Historical Introduction* to my edition of book VII[1], where I have cited the opinion of Baron Stoffel that 'Where it is a question of recording facts—we do not say, a question of passing judgment upon them—the poet of Corduba shows himself one of the most veracious among historians.' M. Pichon, the author of a meritorious monograph on the sources of Lucan[2], does not go so far as his countryman. Examination of the poem in detail obliges him to admit that there is much in it that is unhistorical; but his attitude throughout his essay is that of an unwilling critic (if not an apologist) towards an artist whom he admires, as may be gathered from such expressions as that on p. 1 'The *Pharsalia*...is by no means the invention of an ingenious artist, sporting in pure fiction, but in truth a work of solid reality,' or that on p. 161 'Lucan shows himself always eager for exact reality,' and from the naive and novel suggestion that it was Lucan's abstinence from inventions of his own that 'caused the critics of antiquity sometimes to refuse him the name of poet' (p. 158).

Marginal note: Credibility of Lucan. Opinions of Baron Stoffel and M. Pichon.

I see no reason, and I think those who consider the evidence, even as it is presented in M. Pichon's pages, will see no reason either, for any qualification of the judgment which I expressed in 1896, and with which that of the Italian scholar, Prof. V. Ussani[3], substantially agrees.

Some of Lucan's lapses from the principles of precise accuracy which are supposed to have animated him may be

---

[1] Pp. ix—xii.

[2] *Les Sources de Lucain*, par René Pichon, Paris 1912.

[3] In his monograph *Sul valore storico del poema Lucaneo* (1903). Not less decided is the view of M. Lejay in the Introduction to his excellent edition of Book I (1894), p. xxxii, 'The most sensible defect of the *Pharsalia* is the extreme freedom which the author has taken with his subject.'

ascribed to artistic considerations ; and they are so ascribed by M. Pichon, who has invented for them the not inconvenient name of 'synthetic concentrations.' Thus sooner than admit that in the account of the murder of Scaeuola before the altar of Vesta, II 126—129, Lucan has confused the younger with the elder Marius, M. Pichon holds that we have one of ' ces concentrations synthétiques comme nous en trouverons plus d'une dans son récit de la guerre civile,' p. 16. With the motive of these compressions we are not at present concerned ; and each example must be judged by itself. But that they are found and that they impair Lucan's credit as a narrator of facts is incontestable[1].

Lucan's 'Synthetic Concentrations.'

In the *Historical Introduction* to my edition of book VII[2] I pointed out in detail how little scrupulous Lucan was in dealing with the facts when they conflicted with his partisan proclivities or his notions of poetical and rhetorical composition ; and the phenomena of book VII are by no means absent from book VIII. Lucan's work is in form a historical poem but in substance it is rather a political pamphlet whose object is 'the glorification of the cause that was lost at Pharsalia'; and no one would be more astonished than its author if we sought in it anything beyond the accuracy of a poet or a politician. It is the *iniuria fati* (VIII 763), the accident of circumstances through which its sources have been lost, that has raised it to its bizarre and precarious position as an independent historical authority.

Lucan's historical importance an accident.

Of these sources the chief or perhaps the sole one[3] was

---

[1] For instances see below, pp. xxvii n. 2, xxx n. 3, xlix.

[2] Pp. ix sqq.; for the sake of brevity this will be cited as *Hist. Introd.*

[3] 'So far as I know, no evidence is forthcoming that Lucan did actually draw from any other source,' *Hist. Introd.* p. xiii, and M. Pichon's conclusion is the same as mine, p. 107. The first apparently to promulgate the view was G. Baier in his treatise, *De Livio Lucani in carmine de bello civili auctore* (Breslau 1874), a scarce dissertation of which M. Pichon gives a summary, pp. 59—63.

the lost *Civil War*[1] of Livy. In feeling both the historian

Livy's *Civil War* his chief source, now lost. and the poet were heartily 'Pompeian[2],' and in the account of the last days of their hero this bond of sympathy would count for much. Hence in the Eighth Book not only do we find actual borrowings from Livy specifically attested[3], but the influence

Color *Liuianus* in book VIII. of Livy, a *color Liuianus*, may be traced in more than one passage, softening and for the moment even submerging, as it would seem, the writer's own peculiarities[4].

In conclusion a word is necessary on the way in which the construction of the poem has affected its substance. Ancient

Liberties of Historical Epic. Epics, and Historical Epics like the rest, were not composed as wholes but put together in parts which were written for private or public recitation[5]. An Historical Epic then must be regarded as a succession of scenes in which the events are freely handled and their course diversified by episodes.

In claiming this liberty an epic poet is unquestionably within his rights. He asks in fact no more than is readily conceded to the historical novelist or play-writer.

All that we may claim from him in return[6] is that he should

---

[1] That is the eight books 109...116 of the complete *History*, not the *Abridgement* or *Epitome* which cannot be proved to have been made by Lucan's time. See below, p. xx.

[2] For Livy's eulogies of Pompey see Tacitus, *Annals* 4. 34, quoted in *Hist. Introd.* p. xiii n. 5.

[3] See below, p. xxx n. 4.

[4] This is a matter for feeling, not argument. Still I shall be somewhat disappointed if an unbiassed reader does not find in much of book VIII a restraint and pathos which he misses in Lucan elsewhere. Upon this I would refer to what I have written in the *Quarterly Review*, July 1916, pp. 42 sqq.

[5] M. Lejay, op. cit. p. xlvii, rightly emphasises this feature in the poem. Lucan's junction of the different parts, he observes, is often very clumsy.

[6] We do not ask more from the author of the *Jerusalem Delivered*,

confine his deviations from the record, whether by addition or by subtraction, to what is neither impossible nor inappropriate.   To take an example, the conversation between Pompey and the master of the vessel upon navigation ‘and astronomy[1] is no doubt an invention of the poet's own.   But there is nothing intrinsically improbable in Pompey's thus seeking relief from his anxieties ; and the questions which he asks the skipper are strictly relevant to his situation.   The literal-minded may urge that he would have given his instructions before leaving Mytilene and not have waited till the moment when the ship must change its course.   But the poet has with justice employed a device which sets the confusion of his hero in the clearest light; and the incident, if not history, at any rate is art.   We cannot however say the same of the mission of King Deiotarus to the Parthian court, a fabrication which it is as difficult to excuse as it is easy to explain[2].

Legitimate and illegitimate deviations from fact.

A word about the inconsistencies, of which there is no lack in Lucan.   Some of these are defensible on the ground that there has been a change in the person or in the point of view[3].   Some again are due to the lapses of memory from which imaginative literature of any kind can hardly ever escape.   But more appear to be the direct effects of his training in the schools of public speaking which, provided arguments were ingenious, never troubled if they happened to be incompatible.

Inconsistency in Lucan.

When an inconsistency relates to matter of fact, its detection and explanation have a special importance, as they may throw much needed light on Lucan's historical materials and procedure. I will take a couple of examples from our book.

as events have not thrust Torquato Tasso into the position of being an authority upon the Crusades.

[1] Lines 159 sqq., below, p. xxxii.

[2] 209 sqq., below, p. xxxiv.

[3] See e.g. 88, 388, 529, notes.

In lines 202—5 :

ostendit terras Titan et sidera texit ;
Occurrit in   sparsus ab Emathia fugit quicumque procella,
VIII 205.   adsequitur Magnum; primusque a litore Lesbi
occurrit natus, procerum mox turba fidelis,

offence, and not unreasonable offence, has been caused by
occurrit; and *accurrit* has been conjectured. If, as Lucan's
words at first sight suggest, Pompey was still in full flight from
Lesbos, how could he be 'met' by his son who was following him
from that island ? The truth is that Lucan here, as elsewhere,
has curtailed the narrative without regard either to fact or
intelligibility[1], and that Pompey touched at some point in Ionia,
which Lucan does not name, and that Sextus 'met' him when
he again put to sea[2].

In lines 595—612 Lucan is describing how Pompey passed
from the warship into the little boat which he was never to leave
alive.

transire parantem   595
Romanus Pharia miles de puppe salutat
Septimius, qui, pro superum pudor, arma satelles
regia gestabat posito deformia pilo, etc.

iam uenerat horae   610
Ablatus in   terminus extremae, Phariamque *ablatus* in alnum
VIII 611.   perdiderat iam iura sui. tum stringere ferrum
regia monstra parant e.q.s.

More readers of Lucan than one must have been puzzled by
ablatus, and some, I daresay, have wished to read 'Pharia—in
alno.' A comparison with the account of Plutarch *Pomp.* 78
clears everything up. Septimius had greeted his ancient chief
before the boat was alongside his trireme (ἐν τούτῳ δὲ
πελαζούσης τῆς ἁλιάδος φθάσας ὁ Σεπτίμιος ἐξανέστη καὶ Ῥωμαιστὶ
τὸν Πομπήιον αὐτοκράτορα προσηγόρευσεν), Achillas had saluted
him in Greek and apologised for the smallness of the craft that
was to convey him to the shore (Lucan 565—7), Pompey had

---

[1] An example from book VIII, 35 sqq., is noted below, p. xxvii n. 2.
[2] See more below, pp. xxix, xxxiii.

said farewell to his wife Cornelia (Plutarch, Lucan 579 seq.) and bidden his four companions precede him, when Achillas came forward to welcome him and assist him into the boat, δεξιουμένων αὐτὸν ἤδη τῶν περὶ τὸν ᾿Αχιλλᾶν ἐκ τῆς ἀλιάδος. This natural and not superfluous act of attention[1] is what is behind the *ablatus* of Lucan, that to the unwary carries a suggestion of violence, all appearance of which (is it necessary to say?) it was the design of the assassins to avoid.

With a writer like this no general formula is of service. Inutility of a general statement. Each item in his work must be separately scrutinised, and our judgment represent the sum of our observations. I shall be satisfied if, in regard to the book before us, my presentations in this Introduction and the Commentary with their supplements provide the material for a fair and reasonable estimate[2].

§ 2. *Other Authorities*

Lucan apart, the fullest account of the closing scenes of Pompey's life is that of his biographer PLUTARCH, Authorities for the period. a younger contemporary of the poet, of which that by the Byzantine compiler Zonaras x 9—10 is a mere repetition. CAESAR in his *Commentarii de bello ciuili* book III 102 sqq., supplies additional information on a number of points; but his narrative is neither full nor continuous. CICERO again is for this period almost a blank. Of the 112th book of LIVY we have little beyond the meagre *periocha* or table of contents, supplemented by the statements of later writers known to have used his history or some abridgement of it[3]. The rapid sketch of VELLEIUS PATERCULUS, written in 30 A.D., devotes one chapter, II 53, to this period. His contemporary

---

[1] Pompey was not in robust health at the time. He takes the hand of his freedman to rise from his seat in the boat (τῆς τοῦ Φιλίππου λαμβανόμενον χειρὸς ὅπως ῥᾷον ἐξανασταίη).

[2] These references are collected in Index IV.

[3] On this question see below, pp. xix sqq.

VALERIUS MAXIMUS in his collection of *Notable Deeds and Sayings* adds something to our knowledge. So does the Greek Geographer STRABO, circa 20 B.C. Of later Greek writers APPIAN, circa 160 A.D., and DIO CASSIUS, about 50 years later, are the most important[1]. Among Latin works the Compendium of EUTROPIUS, circa 370 A.D., and the History of the Christian presbyter OROSIUS just deserve a mention. The scattered notices in SENECA and other Roman writers call for no special remark.

A doubt overhangs the witness of FLORUS. This author

Florus.

of a summary of Roman history, more lively than accurate, has generally been supposed to have taken his epitome from Livy. If this were so, his agreements with Lucan, which are not inconsiderable, would have the special value of assuring us that the statements now traceable only to a rhetorical poet were derived from a professed and capable historian. But a German scholar, E. Westerburg, in the *Rheinisches Museum*, vol. 37, pp. 34 sqq., has made out a strong case for the view that such agreements are not due to the epitomator and the poet having both made use of the historian but to the summarizer having taken his summary

---

[1] Prof. V. Ussani, *Sul valore storico del poema Lucaneo*, Rome 1903, pp. 9 sqq., has striven to show that Appian, Dio Cassius and Orosius have borrowed from Lucan. This would of course impair their value as independent authorities. But the evidence, as M. Pichon (*Les Sources de Lucain*, pp. 81 sqq.) has maintained, is extremely weak. So far as Appian goes, the most striking argument is that already adduced by Mr B. Perrin (*American Journal of Philology* 5. 326 sqq.), the agreement of Appian 2. 74 and Lucan VII 326 sqq. in attributing to Caesar a remarkable order for the demolition of the defences of his camp before the battle of Pharsalia ; see my note on VII 326 and *Hist. Introd.* p. xxvi n. and p. xxxviii *Addenda*. At all events there is no trace of the influence of Lucan in Appian's account of the events covered by book VIII ; and Appian's substitution of Σεμπρώνιος for Σεπτίμιος (below, p. lv n. 1) is strong evidence the other way. Ussani's proofs (op. cit. p. 14) that Dio borrowed from Lucan in his account of the weeping of Caesar over the head of Pompey are quite unconvincing.

from the poet. It does not admit of question that Florus used other sources than Livy. It is not less certain that he had read Lucan and fallen under his influence. The coincidences of expression and style accumulated by Westerburg, to which more might be added, put this beyond all doubt[1] They are far more numerous and striking than the similar correspondences between Florus and Livy where both are extant for the comparison.

It seems a hard saying—it certainly seemed so to me before I read Westerburg's article and when I wrote the note on p. xiii of the *Historical Introduction*—that a historian should go to a poet for his facts. And there is force in M. Pichon's objection that some of the alleged coincidences presuppose misunderstandings of Lucan by Florus too gross to be lightly assumed. But the matter wears a different aspect if we regard these as due to confused recollection, of which there are other instances in Florus, e.g. *Scaeuolae* for *Scaeuae* 4. 2. 40, *Metellus* for *Ateius* 3. 11. 3[2].

However this may be, it is at present hazardous to assume that Florus is an independent witness in places where, after all, his *ultimate* authority may only be Lucan.

I will take one passage by way of illustration. Florus 4. 2. 30 sqq. deals with the events described by Lucan IV 401 sqq. The passage from Florus is as follows : 'aliquid tamen *aduersus absentem ducem ausa Fortuna est* circa Illyricam et Africam oram quasi de industria prospera eius aduersis radiaret. quippe cum fauces Adriani maris iussi occupare Dolabella et Antonius, ille Illyrico, hic Curictico litore castra

---

[1] The strength of Westerburg's case lies in its presentation as a whole. M. Pichon, who rejects his view (pp. 70 sqq.), attacks it in detail—an easy but fallacious proceeding.

[2] Westerburg however goes too ar, fas is pointed out by W. Judeich, *Caesar im ¦Orient* (1884), pp. 11 seq., when he says that the section of Florus on the civil war between Caesar and Pompey is in substance not infrequently taken word for word from Lucan and that in other parts also Lucan is transcribed. The influence of Lucan upon Florus is predominantly literary.

posuissent, iam maria late tenente Pompeio, repente legatus eius *Octauius Libo* ingentibus copiis classicorum utrumque circumuenit. deditionem fames extorsit Antonio. missae quoque *a Basilo* in auxilium eius rates, quales inopia nauium fecerant *noua Pompeianorum arte Cilicum* actis sub mari funibus captae quasi per indaginem.' In this passage we may note (1) a striking resemblance in the turn of expression to Lucan's words 'non eadem belli *fortuna* per orbem | constitit, *in partes aliquid* sed *Caesaris ausa est*'; (2) a confusion of the two Pompeian commanders *Octauius* and *Scribonius Libo*, the latter of whom is not mentioned by Lucan; (3) a discrepancy in regard to the action of Basilus : according to Lucan 415 sqq. Basilus did not send rafts to the aid of Antonius and his troops but the latter built them to escape to Basilus 'ut primum aduersae socios in litore terrae | et Basilum uidere ducem, noua furta per aequor | exquisita fugae'; (4) an agreement in words and a disagreement in fact with Lucan 448 sqq. 'at *Pompeianus* fraudes innectere ponto | *antiqua* parat *arte* Cilix.' The disagreement—*antiqua arte* Lucan, *noua arte* Florus,—Westerburg sought to remove by reading *nauium* for *noua*, M. Pichon by reading *nota*. But neither change is necessary. The *noua arte* of Florus is simply a confused reminiscence of the *noua furta* of Lucan.

There is a similar doubt about the authority of a paragraph found in an anonymous work entitled *De Viris Illustribus* and often cited under the name of AURELIUS VICTOR. Immediately after the author's account of Pompey, c. 77, which concludes as follows :

'De Viris Illustribus.'

> In Pharsalia uictus ad Ptolomaeum Alexandreae regem confugit. eius imperio ab Achilla et Potino satellitibus occisus est,

comes a more detailed narration, which is omitted by a number of the manuscripts, is out of proportion to what corresponds in the remaining biographies, and contradicts the account of the matter that has just been given :

> Huius latus sub oculis uxoris et liberorum a Septimio Ptolemaei praefecto mucrone confossum est. iamque de-

functi caput gladio praecisum quod usque ad ea tempora fuerat ignoratum. truncus Nilo iactatus a Seruio Codro inustus humatusque est inscribente sepulcro *Hic positus est Magnus.* caput ab Achilla, Ptolomaei satelliti, Aegyptio uelamine inuolutum cum anulo Caesari praesentatum est ; qui non continens lacrimas illud plurimis et pretiosissimis odoribus cremandum curauit.

It too contains more than one confused reminiscence of Lucan and must, I fear, be rejected as a late addition to the text, whose value is sufficiently indicated by *positus* for *situs* and the non-classical *praesentatum* in the sense of 'presented.'

No proof is needed that the value of non-contemporary statements must in the first instance depend upon the sources whence they are drawn ; nor is it less evident that it will differ according as they derive from original work or from an abbreviated redaction. It is necessary therefore to say something upon the 'EPITOME' OF LIVY or *Historia Romana* as it appears sometimes to have been called.

The 'Epitome' of Livy.

The 'Epitome' as early as MARTIAL.

That an abbreviated Livy existed in the time of MARTIAL is placed beyond all doubt by an epigram in his fourteenth book :

Titus Liuius in membranis.

Pellibus exiguis artatur Liuius ingens,
  quem mea non totum bybliotheca capit.   (14. 190.)

It is true that *artatur* here might refer to merely physical compression. It is true also that, by the use of parchment and minute characters, a work might be got into much less space than it would occupy if written on papyrus rolls. But that in the present connexion the verb need not so be limited is shown by Velleius, who applies it to his own Abridgement of Roman history 'in hoc transcursu tam *artati operis*,' 2. 86. 1. And that under no circumstances could Livy's hundred and forty books and more be crowded on to 'pelles exiguae' is plain to any one who will reflect how much room is taken by the thirty-five books that remain. But, in addition to this, the second line, (Livy) 'whom my library will not hold *in his entirety*,' is intelligible only if some thing *not* 'entire' is referred to.

That this *Epitome Liuiana* was used frequently, perhaps even exclusively, by the later writers has been held, and not without reason, by numerous scholars from Niebuhr onwards[1]. The vast work of Livy was not for every one. As years rolled on and Roman letters declined, the *Epitome* supplied a more popular because a mere restricted pabulum. But this should not blind us to the fact, not sufficiently taken into account by some who have written on this subject, that, the nearer we approach to the age of Livy, the less likely is it that professed historians and biographers should have neglected the great History of Rome for a jejune and unauthorised compendium.

We have concluded from Martial that an 'Epitome' of Livy—we may say *the* 'Epitome' since 'entities are not to be multiplied beyond necessity'—existed in his time. A further inference seems permissible. The articles, for which the distichs of book 14 were composed, were designed to ac-
company *Apophoreta*, 'Christmas presents' as we might call them, and so, in the case of books, presumably novelties. If this be so, then in 85 A.D. our *Epitome* had not long appeared. If however Mr Sanders[2] is to be believed, the *Epitome* was known to Seneca, Lucan and Valerius Maximus, and, if we follow Ussani, to Velleius Paterculus as well. This would throw the composition of the *Epitome* and consequentially the *periochae*, also supposed to derive from it, back into the reign of Tiberius, that is at least some fifty-five or sixty years before the epigram of Martial.

But not as early as Tiberius.

The evidence adduced for all this is of the flimsiest character.

---

[1] See the section under T. Liuius in Schanz, *Geschichte der römischen Literatur* II i, § 324, and Henry A. Sanders, *Die Quellencontamination im* 21 *und* 22 *Buch² des Livius*, pp. 18 sq.

[2] *Op. cit.* p. 21.

I will cite some specimens, premising only that the *Epitome* is

Weakness of the counter-arguments. held not to have been a straightforward abridgement of the longer *History* but to have included additions from elsewhere. Because Valerius Maximus (5. 3. 2) has 'Sp. Maelium regnum adfectantem' and the *periocha* of book 4 the same words, and because Augustine (*Ciu. D.* 3. 17), who is supposed to have used

Valerius Maximus did not use the 'Epitome.' the *Epitome*, writes 'Sp. Maelius crimen regni affectati incurrit,' whereas the phrase 'adfectare regnum' does not occur in the longer Livian account, it is argued that Valerius used the *Epitome*, he being thus presumed incapable of summing up the treasonable ambitions of Maelius in the Latin phrase which most obviously described them. I will take another instance where the evidence is misrepresented. On the strength of 'Val. Max. 5. 6. 2' (in his account of Q. Curtius's self-sacrifice) 'urbem virtute armisque excellere...praecipitem in profundum se egit. Augustin. *civ. d.* 5; 18 viris armisque se (Romanos) excellere...in abruptum hiatum terrae praecipitem se dedit' by 'Livius 7, 6, 5 equo exornato armatum se in specum immisisse[1]' it is argued that, since Augustine *did not* use Valerius Maximus in the *Ciuitas Dei*, a negative proposition more easy to assert than to establish, and since he *did* use the *Epitome*, 'we have no choice left but to assume that the Epitome Livii is earlier than the publication of the Dicta et facta memorabilia.' It would have been well if the writer had endeavoured to set before himself what it was that *did* stand in the text of the *Epitome* and *did not* stand in the text of Livy. Had the 'Epitome *uirtute* (Valerius) or *uiris* (Augustine)? Had it *in profundum* (Valerius) or *in abruptum hiatum terrae* (Augustine)? Had it *egit* (Valerius) or *dedit* (Augustine)? If the discrepancies are to be neglected, why should we respect the agreements? The extract from Livy, as quoted, presents, it is true, no verbal similarity to the other quotations; but it is not all that we find

[1] I reprint these quotations exactly as they appear in Sanders, op. cit. p. 47.

in the *History*. In § 3 we read 'tum M. Curtium, iuuenem bello egregium, castigasse ferunt dubitantes an ullum magis Romanum bonum quam *arma uirtusque* esset': another reduction in the private property of the *Epitome*. The size of the *Epitome* can only be a matter for conjecture. But if anyone troubles to compare the length of the narrative in Valerius, alleged to be thence derived, with the length of the narrative in Livy, he will see that on the same scale this 'Abridgement' would have occupied the space of at least *seventy* books of the *History*. In fine, there is no reason against supposing that, when Valerius consulted Livy, it was in all cases, as admittedly it was in most[1], the *History*, not an 'Epitome' that he consulted.

So too with Velleius Paterculus. The parallels, of varying

Nor
Velleius
Paterculus.
degrees of closeness, between Velleius Paterculus and Lucan which Prof. Ussani cites[2] do not constitute a proof that either writer drew from an 'Epitome.'

Seneca has the Annaean inaccuracy[3]. And he was quite

Nor
Seneca.
capable of misrepresenting the position of the armies at Cannae (*N.Q.* 5. 16. 4 compared with Livy 22. 46. 8) without the help of an 'Abridgement.' He quotes Tibullus but once and gives the quotation

---

[1] 'Viel öfter dagegen hat Valerius Maximus, was allgemein bekannt ist den völlstandigen Livius benutzt,' Sanders, op. cit. p. 48.

[2] Op. cit. pp. 19 sqq. M. Pichon rightly rejects Ussani's conclusion (p. 91) though he does not discriminate properly between faint and strong resemblances.

[3] Compare below, p. lvii n. 4. Neither in names nor in dates can he be trusted. From even three books of the *Dialogi* (10—12, ed. J. D. Duff) a plentiful crop of errors may be gathered: 10. 1. 2 (Aristotle instead of Theophrastus), ib. 5. 5 ('cum conlegis'), 12. 12. 6 ('Scipionis filiae ex aerario dotem receperunt'), 11. 15. 1 (Pompeia daughter of the triumvir confused with Iulia), 12. 16. 6 ('Corneliam ex duodecim liberis *ad duos* fortuna redegerat'), 12. 13. 7 (Aristides instead of Phocion). Perversions of historical sequence: 10. 4. 5, 11. 1. 2, 12. 9. 8.

to Ovid[1]. It is fortunate that he has done so only once, or some *Quellenforscher* would have discovered that the philosopher did not possess a separate copy of Tibullus but quoted from an Anthology in which his elegies were fathered upon Ovid.

The settlement of the obligations of the foregoing writers is a matter of only incidental importance. Our chief concern is with *Lucan*. It is not contested that the division of Livy's great work which had the special title of the *Civil War* was accessible to our poet. Is it no slur then on his intelligence or his industry to suggest that he would not take the trouble to read the five books of the *Civil War* which covered the period of which he was to write, but preferred to have recourse to an Abridgement? This would place him for both below his scholiast, who, commenting on III 181 sqq. 'exhausit totas quamuis delectus Athenas, | exiguae Phoebea tenent naualia puppes, | *tres*que petunt ueram credi Salamina carinae' draws from the fountain head 'Liuius in *primo libro belli ciuilis* ait "nam Athenienses de tanta maritima gloria uix duas naues effecere."' Schol. Bern. ad loc.[2] And the same may be said of the scholiasts on X 471 'ut T. Liuius meminit < in > libro quarto' and X 521 'ut meminit Liuius in libro quarto ciuilis belli.'

Nor Lucan.

[1] *N.Q.* 4a. 2. 2 'quare non cum poeta iocor et illi *Ouidium suum* impingo qui ait "nec Pluuio supplicat herba Ioui,"' Tibullus 1. 7. 26.

[2] The discrepancy between Lucan and Livy, *tres*, *duas*, is easily explicable by the supposition that instead of II Lucan had, or thought he had, III in his copy of Livy. I have given, and M. Pichon has repeated, a similar explanation of the numerical mistake in VII 219, IIII for III; see *Hist. Introd.* p. xi n. 4. The conflict of testimony as to the number of Marians slaughtered in the massacre of Sulla (Lucan II 196 sqq.): Florus 3. 21. 24 (4000), Strabo 5. 4. 11 (3000 or 4000), Orosius 5. 21. 1, Plutarch, *Sulla* 30 (6000), Seneca, *Clem.* 1. 12. 2 (7000), Firmicus Maternus 1. 8 (7000), Livy *per.* 88 (8000), Appian *B.C.* 1. 93 (8000), Seneca, *Benef.* 5. 16. 3 (2 legions), Schol. Bern. on Lucan l.c. (2 legions), Valerius Maximus 9. 2. 1 (4 legions), probably arose in the same way. These all appear to come from IIII, misread either as III or VII, the latter by further misreadings becoming VI or VIII.

Before dismissing this subject I would set out precisely what is meant when it is said, as it will be said more than once in the sequel, that a statement relating to the Civil Wars goes back to 'Livy.' If the authority for the statement is *Plutarch* or an earlier writer, it means that it was derived from the lost *History* of Livy. If a later writer, that it was derived from the lost *History* of Livy *or* from the lost *Epitome* of Livy. So far as substance is concerned, it is probable that in few cases would this make any difference. But whether it make a difference or not, it is outside the province of a sane inquiry to determine the mutual relations of two objects, both of which have disappeared.

Conclusion.

POSTSCRIPT.   Much of the difficulty concerning the relation of Florus' narrative to Lucan's would be removed by the assumption, to which there is no evident objection, that the *epitomator* of Livy made use of *Lucan* and that *Florus* used the *Epitome*.

CHAPTER II

The Events. Pharsalia to Mount Casius

When the manœuvre of Pompey which was to win him the

Flight of
Pompey
after
Pharsalia.

battle of Pharsalia had been foiled by the counter-stroke of Caesar[1], the beaten commander sought shelter in his camp, dispirited and incapable of further effort but weakly hoping against hope. He was not to stay there long. At the first sign of the victor's assault upon the camp, he flung off his general's cloak, and with but four friends[2] to attend him took horse to Larisa.

He did not deem it safe to accept that city's tendered hospitality, counselling it to transfer its allegiance to the conqueror[3], who in fact was in Larisa on the following day. At Larisa he was joined by a few more of his followers, his whole company mustering some thirty horsemen. Full of

---

[1] For an account of the battle of Pharsalia and the events immediately preceding or connected with it see the *Historical Introduction* to Book VII.

[2] Appian, *B. C.* 2. 81. Judeich, *Caesar im Orient*, p. 41, would have it that the four were the two Lentuli, Fauonius and king Deiotarus. The three Romans may well have shared his flight from the outset; not so the king who was not with Pompey when the merchantman picked them up. See below, p. xxvii. Velleius Paterculus 2. 53. 1 quoted in n. 4, p. xxix below, which see, gives the first three together with Pompey's son Sextus as sharing his flight.

[3] Lucan VII 712 sqq. with my note. Dio Cassius 42. 2. 3 adds that he did not even enter the city, φοβηθεὶς μή τινα αἰτίαν ἐκ τούτου ὄφλωσιν.

fears and foreboding, of shame for the present and regrets for
the past, he pursued his way towards the Vale
of Tempe and the sea.   It was a bitter aggrava-
tion of his disgrace if, as our poet avers, he
encountered a number of volunteers, who, still ignorant of
what had happened, were on their way to join the camp of
Fortune's favourite[1].   To add to his distress, his horse which
he had urged beyond its strength collapsed in the forest[2], and
he was forced to finish his journey on foot.   Thirst too oppressed
him, and his biographer tells us that, when he reached the
Peneus, he threw himself on his face and drank
greedily from the stream.   It was late at night
when he arrived at the river's mouth[3], and found
shelter and rest in a friendly fisherman's hut.

Past Larisa through Vale of Tempe.

He reaches the coast.

When day broke, he dismissed all in his company, except
the freemen, bidding them go to Caesar and have no misgivings about their treatment.   With the rest he embarked on
a small river boat[4] in which he coasted along the shore until he
sighted a large corn vessel[5] about to put to sea, commanded
by one Peticius, a Roman who was not an intimate of Pompey
but knew him well by sight.   This Peticius, we are told, had
had a dream, in which Pompey seemed to be holding converse
with him, not as he had known him in the past, but humble
and dejected.   He was in the very act of telling his dream to
his fellow-voyagers when one of them observed the river boat
rowing away from land and its occupants making signals to
them, waving their cloaks and stretching out their hands.

---

[1] There is nothing impossible in this.   For his way for some distance
beyond Larisa lay along the direct route to Macedonia where, as we
shall see, Pompeian influence was strong.

[2] Lucan (VIII) v. 3, Plutarch c. 72 ἐβάδιζε διὰ τῶν Τεμπῶν.

[3] Caesar, B. C. 3. 96. 4 'nocturno itinere non intermisso';
Plutarch l.c.

[4] ποταμίου πλοίου, Plutarch l.c. ; 'ratis...flumineis uix tuta uadis,'
'exiguam...alnum,' Lucan 35 sqq.

[5] εὐμεγέθη φορτηγόν, Plutarch; *nauem frumentariam*, Caesar l.c.

Thereupon Peticius stopped his ship, and saw the Pompey of

Picked up
by a mer-
chantman. his dream. Striking his head in anguish, he gave orders for the ship's boat to pick up Pompey and his party. Pompey brought with him the two Lentuli and M. Fauonius, a senator and ex-praetor; and the vessel resumed its course. It had not gone far when a boat, carrying Deiotarus, the old king, or tetrarch, of Galatia, was seen to be hurrying towards it. He too was taken on board[1] and the vessel proceeded on its way to Amphipolis[2].

When the dinner hour approached, an incident occurred

Fauonius
and Pompey. which shows the consideration that Pompey after all retained among his followers and which stands out amid sombre surroundings to cast a favourable light on ancient Roman manners and the character of Fauonius. In the past the Senator had been an unsparing critic of the

---

[1] In Lucan (210) Deiotarus takes pains to pick up his leader's tracks and join him in Ionia. The reason for this infidelity to history is clear. The desertion of his leader by this ‘faithful’ Pompeian prince, upon which see below, p. xxxiv, would appear in a still worse light if it should transpire that that leader had stopped in his course to save his follower from the enemy's pursuit.

[2] Lucan, crushing events and voyages together in a ‘synthetic concentration’ (p. xi above), omits all reference to the merchantman and Amphipolis and leaves his readers to suppose that Pompey crossed the sea to Lesbos in an open river boat. The constancy of this boat is remarkable, if, as it seems, it reappears in Cilicia, ‘parua puppe,’ 258. It would also appear to be the ‘nauicula’ of Florus, 4. 2. 51, ‘ut una *nauicula* Lesbon applicaretur,’ for the independence of that writer a very damaging coincidence. See the whole passage quoted below p. xxxviii n. 2.

Dio Cassius, 42. 2. 3, does not mention Amphipolis, saying that Pompey took what he needed from Larisa and came down to the sea coast from which ‘he sailed on a merchantman to Lesbos for his wife Cornelia and son Sextus’: nor does Orosius 6. 15. 27 ‘Pompeius fugiens in ostio Penei amnis onerariam nauem nanctus in Asiam transiit.’ From which Judeich, op. cit. p. 15, unconvincingly argues that there was no mention of Amphipolis in Livy.

aims and conduct of Pompey[1]; but when he saw his leader reduced to perform for himself the humble offices for which Romans of even moderate social position employed the service of slaves, he hastened to his assistance, unlaced his boots and anointed his body and for the rest of the voyage tended him as though he had been his private valet[2].

Pompey made no long stay at Amphipolis. He remained at anchor in the river for only a single night. But he caused a proclamation to be issued that all the men of military age in the province of Macedonia, Romans and Greeks alike, should repair to that city and enrol themselves for service. Caesar, who tells us of this[3], observes that its object was uncertain. It might have been a ruse of Pompey to conceal a design of further flight or it might have indicated his intention, if left undisturbed, of making a fresh stand in Macedonia. If it were the latter, Pompey was quickly undeceived. Caesar had arrived at Larisa on the day after Pompey left it for the coast; and his first object was immediate pursuit. Nothing was further from his thoughts than allowing his beaten adversary time to recover. He at once set out for Macedonia with his cavalry, giving orders for one legion to follow in support[4]. Moving with all possible rapidity, he was presently within reach of Amphipolis; and Pompey was apprised of his approach. The latter had been supplied by his

Pompey at Amphipolis.

---

[1] It was Fauonius who had cried 'Stamp, Pompey!' in derision of the boast that if he stamped his foot armed men would rise from the soil of Italy (Plutarch, *Pomp.* 60).

[2] Plutarch l.c.

[3] *B.C.* 3. 102. 2, 3.

[4] 'Caesar *omnibus rebus relictis persequendum* sibi *Pompeium* existimauit quascumque in partes se ex fuga recepisset ne rursus copias comparare alias et bellum renouare posset et *quantumcumque itineris equitatu efficere poterat, cottidie progrediebatur*, legionemque unam *minoribus* itineribus subsequi iussit,' *B.C.* 3. 102. 1. So Lucan IX 950 seq. quoted on 210.

On Mark Antony's statement to the opposite effect in Dio C. 44. 45 see below, p. xxxviii n. 1.

friends in Amphipolis with money for immediate necessities;
and he at once weighed anchor for Lesbos, where
were his wife Cornelia and Sextus, his younger
son. At the beginning of the war Pompey had
placed Cornelia in Lesbos[1], which was bound to
him by strong ties of gratitude and affection, inasmuch as, at the instance of Theophanes, he had restored its chief
town Mytilene to the position of 'free state' which it had for-
feited by siding with Mithridates[2]. That Sextus was in Lesbos
we know from Plutarch[3]; but when or why he went there we
do not know[4].

Takes ship to Lesbos to pick up Cornelia and Sextus.

The voyage to Mytilene was accomplished in a few days[5],
and, as soon as the vessel was in port, Pompey despatched
a messenger to Cornelia to acquaint her with his arrival and
defeat. After her husband's victory at Dyrrhachium and subsequent pursuit of Caesar, as to which she had been kept well

---

[1] Lucan v 723 sqq. 'summa uidens duri Magnus discrimina Martis |
iam castris instare suis seponere tutum | coniugii decreuit onus Lesboque
remotam | te procul a saeui strepitu, Cornelia, belli | occulere.'

[2] Plut. *Pomp.* 42 ; Vell. 2. 18.

[3] *Pomp.* c. 74 *init.* 'And so he sailed along to Amphipolis and
crossed from thence to Mytilene to pick up Cornelia and his son' (βουλό-
μενος τὴν Κορνηλίαν ἀναλαβεῖν καὶ τὸν υἱόν) ; cf. Dio Cassius l. c. above
p. xxvii n. 2. (On Lucan's account, 204 sq., see p. xiv above.)

[4] Lucan had mentioned Sextus in book VI 419 sqq., 827 sq. where
he is made to consult the Thessalian witch Erichtho as to the issue of
the war and, seemingly, to return to the camp on the eve of the battle
of Pharsalia. But the interview is clearly poetic fiction, and with Lucan
a natural inference is hazardous. It might be thought from Velleius
2. 53. 1 'Pompeius profugiens cum duobus Lentulis *Sextoque filio* et
Fauonio praetorio quos comites ei Fortuna segregauerat,' that Sextus
accompanied his father from the first; but the implication is not
necessary, nor can Velleius be wholly trusted. See below, p. liv n. 3.

[5] As we learn from the summary of events in Caesar l.c. § 4 'ipse ad
ancoram unam noctem constitit et uocatis ad se Amphipoli hospitibus et
pecunia ad necessarios sumptus conrogata cognito Caesaris aduentu ex
eo loco discessit et Mytilenas paucis diebus uenit.'

informed by a stream of well-meaning messengers[1], Cornelia
expected nothing but good news[2]; and she fainted at the
shock. Recovering herself at last she hastened down to the
Meeting   shore, where Pompey met her and folded her in
with   his arms[3]. At the sight of her husband's forlorn
Cornelia.   and weary face, she burst into a passion of self-
upbraiding[4], to which he replied in a strain of cool and austere
reflexion, designed to restore her to her self-control[5].

Stress of weather forced Pompey to stay two days in
Pompey at   Lesbos[6]; but, as at Larisa and Amphipolis, he did
Mytilene.   not enter the city, despite the friendly entreaties
and protests of the Mytileneans, whom he advised

---

[1] Plut. *Pomp.* 66.

[2] Plutarch l.c. The description of her forebodings and anxious
watch upon the cliffs (Lucan 44 sqq.) is but elegant poetic fiction.

[3] The account in Lucan (54—70) is another 'synthetic concentration.'

[4] The substantial agreements in the speech of Cornelia as given in
Plutarch l.c. and Lucan (87 sqq.) might of themselves have induced us
to infer a common source. But we have in addition the direct witness
of the scholiast, who tells us on *v.* 91, 'hunc locum poeta *de Liuio* tulit
qui Corneliam dicit dixisse Pompeio: "uicit, Magne, felicitatem tuam mea
fortuna. quid enim ex funesta Crassorum domo recipiebas nisi ut
minueretur (MSS minueret) magnitudo tua?"'

[5] Sentiment has found the speech of Pompey cold-blooded, and
Lucan has been reprehended accordingly. A portion of the charge
rests upon a questionable punctuation of 85 (see the Critical Apparatus
on this line). Apart from this I see no sufficient ground for censure.
The tone adopted in the speech was the one most suited to attain its
object : and it may well have been as true to nature as it was to art.
Pompey was naturally cold-blooded, though he was, for all that, an
affectionate husband and one who inspired real devotion in his wives.
It may be recalled that the death of his previous wife Iulia was directly
due to a shock induced by the belief that her husband had been killed
in a tumult, Valerius Maximus 4. 6. 4. We must however add that the
appropriateness of Pompey's speech is no proof of its authenticity, and
it has nothing in common with the one that Plutarch puts in his mouth.

[6] Caesar, cap. cit. § 5 'biduum tempestate retentus.'

to make their peace with the conqueror[1]. Before he left he received a visit from one of the Greek professors whom it had always been part of his practice to court, the philosopher Cratippus. Pompey engaged him in a discourse upon the ways of Providence, in the course of which his complainings drew from the philosopher the pertinent but not over-considerate question, 'What proof have you, Pompey, to convince us that you would have used your victory better than Caesar[2]?"

At Lesbos he appears to have received a small accession of force in the shape of some four small swift-sailing craft (*naues actuariae*)[3]; and, wife and son aboard, with the good wishes of the islanders[4] he set sail in fair weather and with a fresh wind from the north-east[5]. His

Leaves Mytilene.

[1] His partisans naturally ascribed this conduct to magnanimity. But with men in such plight a more powerful motive is fear. Pompey did not disguise to himself the risks that he would run by being too confiding. See Lucan 144 sqq., a passage of particular significance. Also id. 5—12.

[2] Plutarch l.c.

[3] Caesar l.c. § 5, who does not however give their number or tell us whence they came. Appian, *B.C.* 2. 83, is more specific, calling them 'triremes from Rhodes and Tyre.' Tyre was certainly friendly towards the fugitives, n. on 662. But what about Rhodes? see below, p. xxxvi.

[4] Lucan's description of the farewell scene (109—158) seems true to life; in particular the representation of the affection that the Lesbians cherished for Cornelia. Cornelia, as Plutarch tells us, was unspoiled by the higher education. ' The girl had many charms apart from her physical attractiveness. She had been admirably trained in literature, music (περὶ λύραν) and geometry, and she had been a constant and intelligent attendant at lectures on philosophy. But her disposition showed no trace of the disagreeable and meddlesome spirit (ἀηδίας καὶ περιεργίας) which such studies are wont to induce in young women' (*Pomp.* 55 init.).

[5] This is an inference which every reader can make who considers with due attention the indications afforded by the account of Lucan, especially those of *vv.* 193 sqq., 246 sq. In the narrative of Pompey's voyage Lucan appears on the whole to be closely following his authority. Exceptions will be noted as they occur.

plans for the future were as yet undetermined; but four possi-

The four choices before him. bilities were present to his anxious thought. He might rally to his side the 'free' and 'federate' cities of Ionia and Asia, the chief of which was the great State of Rhodes, or he might apply for aid to one of the monarchs of Numidia, Egypt and Parthia[1]. Whatever course he might adopt was immaterial until he arrived at a point where the choice would affect the direction of his voyage; and Lucan accordingly, using a poet's liberty, has selected this as the place for the skipper to ask and Pompey to give the necessary instructions. A glance at a map will show that, unless Pompey was to return on his path, or to make at

Passes south between Chios and the Oenussae islets. once for the mainland of Asia, his course, after clearing the island of Lesbos, must lie towards the S.W., whatever were his ultimate destination. This course was pursued until the island of Chios was sighted, shortly after sunset on the day of his departure from Mytilene[2]. Here, as the poet says, in the only simile to be found in this book, the steersman, like a practised charioteer negotiating a turning post, put the ship about, changing its course from S.W. to S., and passed through the narrow channel to the east of the island[3].

---

[1] These various alternatives are clearly presupposed in the paragraph of our poem which describes Pompey's anxious reflexions and his conversation with the master of the ship (159 sqq.). In 162–4, 162 refers to the *ciuitates foederatae*, *regum* are the kings of Numidia and Egypt, and the *inuia mundi arua* are the distant empire of Parthia. In the skipper's speech again the three ultimate alternatives may be discerned in the background, *Syriae* (Parthia) 181, *Pharon* (Egypt) and *Syrtim* (Numidia) 184.

[2] The indications of time here and in 201 are not, it would appear, idle insertions of the poet, but have been taken over from his source.

[3] There is no doubt that this is the meaning, though *Asinae* (195) still lacks both explanation and defence. See the Critical Apparatus.

After passing the OENUSSAE islets Pompey continued his
flight towards the south; but some uncertainty
hangs over its details. The biographer tells us in
general terms that he only stopped where necessary
to take in water and provisions[1]. But something more can be
gleaned from the poet. On the day after leaving Mytilene
Pompey touched at a place on the coast of Ionia, whose name
Lucan has omitted to give us where he should[2], but which may
be reasonably conjectured to have been EPHESUS or some
spot in its immediate neighbourhood.

Pompey in Ionia.

The reasons for thinking that this shore was at Ephesus, or
near it, are briefly as follows. *Ephesus* is the place
mentioned next after Chios (195) in Lucan's account
of the route pursued by Pompey, 'ipse per Icariae
scopulos, Ephesonque relinquens | et placidi Colophona maris,
spumantia paruae | radit saxa Sami'; for the order *Icariae—
Epheson—Colophona* is simply that prescribed by the verse[3].
Pompey had to pass Colophon (Notium) before he passed
Ephesus. Secondly, with the exception of Smyrna, which is out
of the question, it is the most convenient landing-place for any
one who wished to go to Galatia. Thirdly, as we infer from the

At or near Ephesus.

---

[1] Plutarch c. 76 init. ἀναλαβὼν δὲ τὴν γυναῖκα καὶ τοὺς φίλους
ἐκομίζετο προσίσχων ὅρμοις ἀναγκαίοις ὕδωρ ἢ ἀγορὰν ἔχουσιν.

[2] That is in 205. In 243 he says vaguely *in litore*. Compare
supra p. xiv.

[3] On the tense of 'relinquens,' 244, see the explanatory note ad loc.
The verb itself deserves some attention. This 'leaving' may well
import that Lucan found in his source that Pompey either stopped or
tried to stop at the place in question. The first is clearly the case in
456 'liquere' (Cilicia) and 460 'deseruit' (Paphos). We must take
the same view of IX 1003 'pelagoque Rhodon spumante *relinquit*' of
Caesar in his pursuit of Pompey. We know from Appian 2. 89 that
Caesar *did* stop at Rhodes, but the only trace of this in Lucan's account
is that he has not dropped the stopping place from the itinerary. On
the time taken by Caesar for the whole of this voyage see the judicious
discussion of Judeich, *Caesar im Orient*, p. 60. For the 'relinquit' of
247 see below, p. xxxvi n. 1.

events recorded by Caesar, c. 105. 1, it was strongly held in the Pompeian interest[1].

Here it was that Pompey received a lesson not to put his trust in princes. Deiotarus had gladly given him his company on his passage to the East; but once on the terra firma of Asia the attractions of a safe return to his tetrarchate were too strong for his loyalty to a beaten cause; and the monarch of Galatia slipped away into the interior.

Desertion of King Deiotarus.

This defection did not succeed in propitiating the anger of Caesar[2]; but it brought the tetrarch into deep discredit with his former friends. Cicero speaks of it as a 'lamentable occurrence[3],' and Lucan has got rid of it in characteristic fashion. It was insupportable that the 'most trusty of monarchs[4]' should leave his leader at the first convenient opportunity. So he is despatched on a dangerous and yet futile mission to Parthia, of which of course nothing further is heard. But, as I have written before[5], 'it must not be supposed that, if a narrative of Lucan cannot be accepted as it stands, it is therefore destitute of all foundation. Exaggeration, suppression and distortion are in general easier modes of perverting than sheer fabrication; and a close and critical examination may sometimes discover, even in the wildest improbabilities, the vestiges of truth.' So here too. Pompey *did* send a senator, Lucilius Hirrus, as envoy to the king of Parthia, and the envoy was thrown into prison (Caesar *B.C.* 3. 82. 4, Dio C.

His fictitious mission to Parthia.

---

[1] I am glad to see that Mr Duff, *Journal of Philology* l.c. below, makes the place intended by Lucan 'somewhere near Ephesus.'

[2] See Cicero, *pro Deiotaro* 9 sqq., where 'Pharsalico proelio facto a Pompeio discessit' is not quite exact, as *de Diuin.* 2. 79 shows.

[3] *De Diuin.* 2. 79 'fugit e proelio cum Pompeio; graue tempus! discessit ab eo; luctuosa res! Caesarem eodem tempore hostem et hospitem uidit; quid hoc tristius?'

[4] 'fidissime regum,' 212 n. Methinks our poet doth protest too much. He should have remembered what he had written in v 54 sq. 'fidumque *per arma* | Deiotarum,' that is, not 'fidum *per fugam.*'

[5] *Hist. Introd.* p. xi.

42. 2. 5). And while it is hard to divine why the king should dress up as a slave (239 sqq.) for the purpose of this mission to Parthia, he may yet have found some disguise a convenience to screen his departure from the eyes of the Pompeians at Ephesus[1].

Pompey might not unnaturally hope for support in a part of the world where but fifteen years ago he had distributed benefactions and mandates with the hand of an autocrat[2]. But the news of Pharsalia was everywhere; and the past was obliterated[3].

Effect of the news of Pharsalia in Asia.

At CNIDUS it would appear this was first brought home to the fugitive. Cnidus offered the attraction of excellent harbours, and no place owed more to Pompey for his successful termination of the Piratic War[4]. But, no doubt at the instance of their countryman Theopompus (the mythographer), a powerful friend of Caesar's, the Cnidians refused to entertain him[5].

At Cnidus.

[1] It is not necessary to examine the story in detail. It has forgery on its face. And Burman long ago and Mr Duff recently (*Journal of Philology* 32. pp. 128 sqq.) have done well to reject it.

[2] As Dio Cassius says, 37. 20. 2 τά τε πλείω ἔθνη τῶν ἐν τῇ Ἀσίᾳ τῇ ἠπείρῳ τότε αὐτοῖς ὄντων νόμοις τε ἰδίοις καὶ πολιτείαις κατεστήσατο καὶ διεκόσμησεν ὥστε καὶ δεῦρο αὐτοὺς τοῖς ὑπ' ἐκείνου νομισθεῖσι χρῆσθαι.

[3] Cicero, writing to Atticus shortly after Pompey's death, bears witness to this, 'de Pompei exitu mihi dubium numquam fuit. *tanta* enim *desperatio rerum eius omnium regum et populorum animos occuparat* ut, quocumque uenisset, hoc putarem futurum,' *ad Att.* 11. 6. 5.

[4] Strabo 14. 2. 15, p. 656 Κνίδος δύο λιμένας ἔχουσα ὧν τὸν ἕτερον κλειστὸν τριηρικὸν καὶ ναύσταθμον ναυσὶν εἴκοσι. It had been captured by the pirates, as Cicero tells us, *pro lege Manilia* 33, 'Cnidum aut Colophonem aut Samum nobilissimas urbes innumerabilesque alias captas esse commemorem?'

[5] This is inference, but probable inference. One of the first things that Caesar did on his arrival in Asia Minor was to confer autonomy on Cnidus (Plut. *Caes.* 48). This was no doubt in a sense 'a favour to Theopompus'; but Theopompus must have had something to go upon when he asked it, and what had the Cnidians done for Caesar? The 'fugit' of Lucan, 247, may well be significant.

He fared no better at RHODES, as we learn from a letter of

At Rhodes. one of Cicero's correspondents, P. Lentulus the
younger, written five years after the event, in which
he complains of the conduct of the Rhodians in refusing to
receive his father (P. Lentulus), L. Lentulus, Pompey and other
distinguished optimates[1].

From Rhodes Pompey took a straight course across the sea
outside the bay of Telmessos and thence pursued his voyage
in the direction of Pamphylia[2]. According to Lucan, whose
statement there seems no reason to doubt, his first stopping-
place was PHASELIS, a town in Lycia on the borders of

Pompey at Pamphylia, once of considerable importance, but
Phaselis and dismantled by P. Seruilius Vatia (Isauricus) in the
Attalia. war with the Pirates and now almost empty of inhabitants and so incapable of doing any mischief even to so small
a force as Pompey's[3]. After a brief rest here, he followed the
coast to ATTALIA, passing the celebrated Climax, an offshoot of
the range of Mount Taurus, which borders the sea, and the
remarkable torrent or cascade which is called *Dipsus* in Lucan
and *Cataractes* by Strabo[4].

---

[1] Cic. *Fam.* 12. 14. 3 'qui tum fugientem *patrem meum*, qui
L. Lentulum, qui *Pompeium*, qui ceteros uiros clarissimos *non receperunt.*' This should be compared with Caesar's fuller account of the
treatment of the two Lentuli, c. 102. 7 'idem hoc L. Lentulo qui
consul superiore anno fuerat et P. Lentulo consulari ac nonnullis aliis
acciderat Rhodi, qui, cum ex fuga Pompeium sequerentur atque in
insulam uenissent, oppido ac portu recepti non erant missisque ad eos
nuntiis ut ex his locis discederent, contra uoluntatem suam naues
soluerant.' As Pompey is not mentioned here, it may be argued that
he did not even venture to approach the city. In any case Lucan's
'relinquit,' 247, appears to be a significant euphemism. Compare
'fugit' n. 5 p. xxxv above.

[2] Lucan 248 sqq.

[3] Lucan 250 sqq.

[4] Excursus B pp. lxxxii sqq. Plutarch says Attalia was the first city
that Pompey entered. Perhaps he did not reckon Phaselis as such. But
the discrepancy may be due to deliberate contradiction of the other

At Attalia Plutarch tells us that he was met by triremes from Cilicia and joined also by some sixty of his surviving adherents in the Senate[1]; and before long he had collected the nucleus of a military force. This alleviated his despondency a little and encouraged him to proceed to the scene of his ancient

Pompey in Cilicia.

triumphs, CILICIA, and we find him ultimately at SYHEDRA, now *Sedra*, and SELINUS, *Selindi*, about 15 miles further along the coast. He stayed some time on the Cilician sea-board, and, in person or by his emissaries, delivered requisitions on the cities in the neighbourhood, exacting what he could from them both in money and men[2]. The money was obtained by compulsory levies on the associated tax-farmers, an old device of Pompey, and by private borrowing from friends. The men were either drawn from the employees of the associations or selected from among the servants of the Roman financiers in the province. By these measures, as Caesar tells us[3], he found himself at the end in the possession of a considerable war chest and as many as 2000 men. As a guard this was a respectable force; but a couple of Caesar's cohorts would sweep it away.

There was no longer any reason for remaining in Cilicia; in fact to do so was not safe. Caesar had Asia Minor at his feet,

account, such as we find in Lucan's description of the Enipeus VI 373 which is a 'pointed contradiction' of Ovid's *Met.* 1. 579; see *Hist. Introd.* p. xxxvi and infr. 460 sqq. (p. lxxxvii n.), 638 n., 662 n.

[1] Plutarch c. 76, who also tells us that the news they brought that the fleet was still intact and that Cato with a considerable force was crossing to Africa was the signal for Pompey to break into fresh lamentations and regrets that he had been forced to fight on land.

[2] Plutarch l.c. ἐπὶ τὰς πόλεις περιέπεμπε· τὰς δ' αὐτὸς περιπλέων ᾔτει χρήματα καὶ ναῦς ἐπλήρου.

[3] Caesar c. 103. 1 'pecunia a societatibus sublata et a quibusdam priuatis sumpta et aeris magno pondere ad militarem usum in naues imposito duobusque milibus hominum armatis, quos partim ex familiis societatum delegerat, partim a negotiatoribus coegerat quos ex suis quisque ad hanc rem idoneos existimabat.'

he was now aware of Pompey's movements[1], and his arrival

Council of War at Syhedra. was only a matter of days. Vacillation must end, a plan be formed and a refuge sought. At Syhedra[2] Pompey summoned a council of his principal followers and put the situation before them.

As will have been gathered from the foregoing narrative, he had long been brooding in secret over the idea of

Pompey would seek aid from Parthia. an application to Parthia; but not till now did he venture to disclose a design so repugnant to Roman sentiment[3]. In his speech, whose substance is given

[1] Caesar had for long been as uncertain of Pompey's intentions as Pompey himself. This is indicated by *coniectans* c. 106 (below, p. xl n. 3); and implied in the somewhat improbable story in Plutarch, *Brutus* c. 6, that the idea of Pompey's taking refuge in Egypt was suggested to Caesar by Brutus 'when no one could tell in what direction Pompey was flying and they were all at a loss.' It is confirmed by what Dio says in 42. 6. 1 that Caesar 'pursued Pompey with all haste as far as Asia, but had to stop there, as no one knew in what direction he had sailed.'

Mark Antony in his funeral oration over Caesar, Dio C. 44. 45, ingeniously twists Caesar's involuntary delay into a proof of his clemency towards his enemy. 'This is shown by his not pursuing him at once but allowing him to fly at his leisure (κατὰ σχολὴν εἴασε φυγεῖν).'

[2] So Lucan 259, with whom Florus agrees. The source of both may be Livy. Unfortunately however the passage of Florus (4. 2. 51 sq.) bears so many traces of the influence of Lucan that it is unsafe to treat it as independent evidence. It will be best to quote it in full : 'superstes dignitatis suae uixit (= Lucan 28 sq. uita superstes imperio) ut cum maiore dedecore per Thessalica Tempe equo fugeret, ut una nauicula Lesbon applicaretur (above, p. xxvii n. 2), ut Syhedris in deserto Ciliciae scopulo fugam in Parthos Africam uel Aegyptum agitaret, ut denique Pelusio litore imperio uilissimi regis, consiliis spadonum et, ne quid mali deesset, Septimii desertoris sui gladio trucidatus sub oculis uxoris suae liberorumque moreretur.'

Plutarch on the other hand appears to make the council held in *Cyprus*; on this see below, p. xlii n. 1.

[3] Appian's statement is as definite as words can make it, c. 83. 'He concealed the project until he was in Cilicia, when he reluctantly

by Plutarch in a few bald sentences but expanded by Lucan into sixty-two lines of vivid and vigorous declamation, Pompey dwelt with emphasis on the greatness of the Parthian power and urged that in it alone would they find an ally able to protect them for the present and provide them with resources for a future renewal of the struggle.

He met with little support. Some of those present thought that they should repair to Numidia, whither Cato had already gone with the fleet; but the majority inclined to Egypt. According to Plutarch, the chief advocate of this view was THEOPHANES, a Greek sophist of Lesbos, Pompey's inseparable companion and domestic historian. This is not the version of Lucan. To our poet it would have been an indecorum had the chief part on so momentous an occasion been assigned to a Greekling when a Roman of high station was available[1]. Accordingly L. LENTULUS, the consul of the previous year, who, at the beginning of book V 15 sqq. was selected to propose Pompey as generalissimo, is here again put forward to

divulged it to his friends' (τὸ ἐνθύμημα ἐπέκρυπτε μέχρι περὶ τὴν Κιλικίαν μόλις ἐξέφερε τοῖς φίλοις).

[1] Mr Duff, *Journal of Philology* l.c. p. 131, suggests two reasons for Lucan's alteration of the name. His first differs little from that given above. ' I suspect,' he says, ' that Lucan had two reasons for attributing this speech to the wrong person. First it seemed proper that a patriotic argument should be spoken not by a Greek and man of letters but by a Roman and a senator.' The second motive suggested (that it was impossible for him to introduce into his verse the name of Theophanes, ' even if he had contracted it into Theuphanes, few of the cases would be admissible'), if it operated at all, must have been quite subordinate. *Theu-* (Θευ-) was a recognised equivalent of *Theo-* (Θεο-): cf. Θευδώροιο, Anth. Pal. 7. 426. 3 ; Θεύδοτος, ib. 7. 596 (Ovid, *Ibis* 466) ; Θεύγενες, Callimachus, *Oxyr. Pap.* 1362. 21, Anth. Pal. 7. 543 ; Θευδόσιος, ib. 9. 682. And a versifier of much less dexterity than Lucan would have found it quite easy to introduce the word in the genitive, as for example

eminuit questus uox inter Theuphanis omnes,

or even in the ablative.

oppose him[1]. In both places the sentiments he expresses are the poet's; and here, as well as there, he carries his audience with him. Both in Lucan and Plutarch the length of Pompey's speech is much exceeded by that of the reply, and this together with a general similarity in treatment suggests that they both derive from a common source, doubtless the lost history of Livy. The speaker urged that the Parthians were not a war-like but a treacherous race and that Cornelia would not be safe in their hands[2], and that it was a deep disgrace to a Roman to have dealings with Parthia until the Crassi had been avenged, while on the other hand there was every reason to believe that in Egypt, a kingdom whose natural advantages and obligations to Pompey were insisted on[3], he would find powerful and loyal assistance[4]. The views of the speaker proved to be those of the assembly; and, as on the eve of Pharsalia, the general capitulated to his followers[5].

The Council decides for Egypt as advised by Theophanes.

From Cilicia[6] they moved due south to CYPRUS[7], whence Pompey hoped to obtain further reinforcements. As they were putting into PAPHOS, Pompey observed a magnificent building on the shore and asked the

Pompey at Paphos in Cyprus.

[1] A little phrase in the lines that introduce his speech, ' *dignas*que tulit *modo consule* uoces,' 330, lets the cat out of the bag.

[2] According to Plutarch this argument weighed heavily with Pompey.

[3] These two considerations were present to Caesar's mind when he heard that Pompey had been seen at Cyprus (c. 106. 1) 'coniectans eum Aegyptum iter habere propter necessitudines regni aliasque eius loci opportunitates.'

[4] Plutarch c. 76; Lucan 351—453.

[5] 'uicta est sententia Magni,' Lucan; ἐνίκα φεύγειν εἰς Αἴγυπτον, Plutarch c. 77.

[6] Probably from Selinus which, to judge from the mention in the *Stadiasmus Maris Magni* 204, would be the port of departure for Cape Acamas, that is for Paphos in Cyprus. On Lucan's obscure reference to it, 260, see note ad loc.

[7] Lucan 456; Caesar c. 102. 5; Plutarch c. 77; Valerius Maximus (1. 5. 6) 'cursum in insulam Cyprum, ut aliquid in ea uirium contraheret, classe derexit.'

steersman what it was called. The steersman answered, 'The Palace Below[1].' The ominous name struck a chill into Pompey's heart. It seemed to sound the knell of all his hopes. He turned his head away from the sight, and a groan burst from his breast.

Before long he had another shock. He received intelligence

Hostile attitude of Antioch.

from ANTIOCH that the inhabitants of the great capital, upon which he had himself conferred autonomy when he constituted the province of Syria, had agreed with the Roman commercial community to seize the citadel with the object of excluding him from the place, and that the Pompeian refugees in the neighbouring places had been warned that they would approach Antioch at the peril of their lives[2]. It would appear that the idea of taking refuge in Parthia was still fermenting in Pompey's mind; but now he realised that it was altogether impracticable[3]. And

---

[1] Valerius Maximus l.c. 'adpellensque ad oppidum Paphum conspexit in litore speciosum aedificium gubernatoremque interrogauit quod ei nomen esset. qui respondit κατωβασίλεια uocari. quae uox spem eius quantulamcumque comminuit, neque id dissimulanter tulit: auertit enim oculos ab illis tectis ac dolorem quem ex diro omine ceperat gemitu patefecit.' It may be observed here that this 'Lower Palace' had no doubt belonged to the Ptolemy whom Clodius had ejected from Cyprus, now annexed to Cilicia.

[2] Caesar c. 102 § 6 'Ibi cognouit consensu omnium Antiochensium ciuiumque Romanorum qui illic negotiarentur arcem captam (arma capta *Forchhammer*, *Meusel*) esse excludendi sui causa nuntiosque dimissos ad eos qui se ex fuga in finitimas ciuitates recepisse dicerentur ne Antiochiam adirent; id si fecissent, magno eorum capitis periculo futurum.'

[3] Caesar says 'deposito adeundae *Syriae* consilio.' It should in fairness here be added that some writers of antiquity disbelieved that Pompey had ever formed such a design. Dio Cassius, 42. 2. §§ 5, 6, argues against the story as wholly incredible, and Velleius Paterculus, 2. 53. 1, says '*aliis* ut *Parthos*, aliis ut Africam *peteret* in qua fidelissimum partium suarum haberet regem Iubam *suadentibus*, *Aegyptum petere proposuit*, memor beneficiorum quae in patrem eius Ptolemaei

he announced to a meeting of his council[1] that he would proceed to Egypt without delay.

Embarking in a 'Seleucid trireme[2],' and attended by the **Pompey sets sail for Egypt.** greater part[3] of the vessels, some warships and others transports, that he had collected, he followed the coast of Cyprus to the south as far as the promontory of Curias and thence struck across the open sea[4]. His objective was ALEXANDRIA[5]. But there was a strong **Is carried to Pelusium.** west wind blowing ; and when he made the Egyptian coast he found himself at PELUSIUM, the port on the easternmost branch of the Nile.

qui tum puero quam iuueni propior regnabat Alexandriae contulerat.' But these dissents (especially Dio's in view of 41. 2. 3) are of little weight against the concurrent testimony of Caesar, Lucan, Plutarch and Appian.

[1] This seems the natural explanation of the apparent discrepancy between Lucan and Plutarch already referred to. Drumann indeed, *Geschichte Roms* (2nd ed.) 3. 466, n. 7, argues that the council in question must have been held at Syhedra 'because the crossing to Cyprus proves that it had already been resolved to go to Egypt.' But the argument is not conclusive. Pompey had other reasons for going to Cyprus ; and the island, as a glance at the map will show, was very little out of his way to Syria.

[2] Plutarch c. 77. What particular kind of trireme this was is not known. Perhaps it was a cross between a warship and a merchantman (an 'armed liner' as it were), since Velleius l.c. § 2, speaks of Pompey's ship as an 'oneraria.' Lucan's description (564 sqq.) implies that it was a warship.

[3] This qualification is necessary as L. Lentulus followed him later. See below, p. lxiii.

[4] So Lucan, 461 sq., perhaps putting Curias *due South* of Paphos. Dio C. 42. 3. 1, takes him straight from Cilicia to Egypt. This, while strictly incorrect, confirms the conclusion that the formal decision was taken in Cilicia and not in Cyprus, p. xxxviii above.

[5] This explains why Eutropius says 'fugatus *Alexandriam* petiit' (2. 21. 3). All other authorities (Caesar 103. 1 ; Plutarch c. 77 ; Dio C. l.c.) agree with Lucan in making him go to Pelusium. Lucan alone has the credit of adding the reason.

Egypt was itself in the throes of civil war. Ptolemy XI,
surnamed Auletes or 'the Piper,' expelled by
his subjects in 57 B.C., had, with the countenance
of Pompey[1], been forcibly reinstated by A. Gabinius,
proconsul of Syria. A large Roman force· which Gabinius
left behind for his protection maintained him on the throne
till his death. By his will, in which he had ad-
jured the Roman people in the most solemn terms
to enforce its dispositions, he left his kingdom to
his eldest son and eldest daughter, who were to
marry and reign in common[2]. The Roman people was explicitly
constituted their guardian[3]. Two copies of the will were made.
One was left under seal at Alexandria; the other was sent to
Rome to be deposited in the Treasury. But the state of public
affairs prevented this being done; and it was placed for safe
custody with Pompey.

This is all that Caesar says upon the subject, nor was it
incumbent on him to tell us any more. But it must be borne in
mind that Ptolemy owed his restoration in the first instance to
the interposition of Pompey; nor was this likely to be forgotten
when safeguards were being considered for the settlement in his
will. From 55, the date of the king's restoration, to 51, the date
of his death, Pompey was paramount in Rome, and there seems

Affairs in Egypt.

Restoration and Will of Ptolemy Auletes.

---

[1] Hence Lucan writes of Pompey and the young Ptolemy IX.
1028 sq. ' hospes auitus erat; *depulso* regna *parenti* | reddiderat.' On
the deposition and restoration of Ptolemy see the special section in the
Introduction to vol. 2 of Tyrrell and Purser's *Correspondence of Cicero*,
pp. xxix sqq.

[2] Caesar l.c. c. 108 'in testamento Ptolemaei patris heredes erant
scripti ex duobus filiis maior et ex duabus filiabus ea quae aetate ante-
cedebat. haec uti fierent, per omnes deos perque foedera quae Romae
fecisset, Ptolemaeus populum Romanum obtestabatur,' *Bell. Alex.* 33
init. 'Caesar Aegypto atque Alexandria potitus *reges constituit* quos
Ptolemaeus testamento scripserat atque obtestatus erat populum Romanum ne mutarentur.'

[3] Dio Cassius 42. 35. 4 τὸν δὲ δὴ τῶν Ῥωμαίων δῆμον τὴν ἐπιτροπείαν
σφῶν ἔχειν ἐγέγραπτο.

good grounds for believing the statement of Eutropius[1], confirmed by the expressions of Livy, Lucan and Seneca[2], that, in virtue of the powers conferred upon the Roman people by the will of the king, the Senate appointed Pompey guardian of his young son, who at the time was hardly more than ten[3]. All this was in strict accordance with what had happened on the death of Ptolemy IV (Philopator) when M. Aemilius Lepidus was sent to Egypt to exercise the rights of guardianship as the representative of the Roman people[4]. Pompey, though glad enough to secure such an addition to his titles, can have done but little for his ward, though he may have been consulted when THEODOTUS, a Greek professor of rhetoric from Chios, or according to Appian from Samos, was chosen as preceptor to the king[5]. Events in Rome demanded all his attention, and Egypt was left to itself.

Pompey appointed guardian of the young Ptolemy.

[1] Eutropius 6. 21. 3 'Ipse fugatus Alexandriam petiit ut a rege Aegypti, *cui tutor a senatu datus fuerat* propter iuuenilem eius aetatem, acciperet auxilia.'

[2] Livy, *periocha* 112 'Cn. Pompeius, cum Aegyptum petisset, iussu Ptolemaei regis, *pupilli* sui, auctore Theodoto praeceptore, cuius magna apud regem auctoritas erat et Pothino occisus est ab Achilla, cui id facinus erat delegatum, in nauicula antequam in terram exiret'; Seneca, *Ep.* 4. 7 'de Pompei capite *pupillus* et spado [Pothinus] tulere sententiam'; Lucan 449 (cf. 518 sq., 558 sqq.). Ovid, l.c. on 594, calls him Pompey's *cliens*.

[3] At the time of Pompey's death he was 13, ἐπὶ τρισκαίδεκα ἔτη μάλιστα γεγονώς, Appian 2. 84. His sister was born in 69 and would need no guardian in 51.

[4] Valerius Maximus 6. 6. 1 'cum Ptolemaeus rex tutorem populum Romanum filio reliquisset, senatus M. Aemilium Lepidum pontificem maximum, bis consulem, ad pueri tutelam gerendum Alexandrini misit'; cf. Justin 30. 2. 8 'legatos Alexandriam ad Romanos misere orantes ut tutelam pupilli susciperent (this implies a testament) tuerenturque regnum Aegypti'; ib. 3. 4 'mittitur et M. Lepidus in Aegyptum qui tutorio nomine regnum pupilli administret.' Cf. id. 31. 1. 2.

[5] Plut. c. 77, id. *Brutus* 33, who uses in both places the same phrase, ἐπὶ μισθῷ ῥητορικῶν λόγων διδάσκαλος; Appian 2. 84.

It was otherwise when the civil war broke out. The govern-
The
Egyptians
side with
Pompey
against
Caesar. ment of Alexandria were reminded of the ancient
obligations which, although our poet has concealed
the fact[1], they were not backward to honour. Not
only were large supplies of corn despatched from
the Egyptian granaries, but a force consisting of
50 ships of war and 500 men from the Gabinian guards was
sent to the seat of war under the command of the elder son of
Pompey[2].

Presently they had something to ask in return. The old
king's scheme of a dual rule was not long in breaking down.
The boy king was a puppet in the hands of his ambitious
ministers, the chief of whom was POTHINUS, a eunuch, who had
charge of his person and was the head of the civil administration[3]. But his sister was not so pliable. As often happens in
a decadent stock, the female was the stronger strain; and
Revolution
in Egypt.
Cleopatra
dethroned
and banished. in address, capacity and daring CLEOPATRA was
another Berenice. She stoutly resisted the en-
croachments of the Regents. But they were too
strong for her; and late in 49 or early in 48 she

---

[1] Not only is Egypt omitted from the roll of Pompey's auxiliaries
to which 125 lines of book III (171 sqq.) are devoted, but Pothinus is
allowed both to state and to imply the direct opposite of the truth,
VIII 519, 531 and notes.

[2] Caesar, B.C. 3. 5. 1; 4. 4; 3. 1; 111. 3, where it is stated
that the naval force returned to Alexandria after the battle of Pharsalia. The incidental observation of Lucan that Septimius was *not*
at Pharsalia, 601 sq., suggests that he knew that other Gabinians
were.

[3] Caesar 112. 11 'Pothinus nutricius pueri et procurator regni';
cf. ib. 108. 1 'erat in procuratione regni propter aetatem pueri nutricius
eius, eunuchus nomine Pothinus.' How little the king counted for, may
be seen from the high-handed actions of Pothinus as described by
Caesar 108. 2 'deinde, adiutores quosdam consilii sui nactus ex regis
amicis, exercitum a Pelusio clam Alexandriam euocauit atque eundem
Achillam cuius supra meminimus omnibus copiis praefecit.' The caustic
phrase of Lucan, 536—8, is fully justified.

was deposed and banished, with the assent of her brother the king[1].

The situation thus created would naturally be referred to Pompey; and it seems that it was so referred. But a change so fundamental in the dispositions of the old king could hardly be valid without the sanction of the Senate, the majority of whom, together with the two consuls of 49, were amongst the adherents of Pompey. We need not consider too curiously whether from the standpoint of constitutional jurists such a body was a Senate, a quasi-Senate, or simply a *consilium*. To Pompey and the aristocrats it was a Senate in right and fact—it, and not the upstart assembly that met in Rome[2]. It was this Senate that

Application of the Egyptian Regency to the Pompeian 'Senate' and decision in favour of Ptolemy.

---

[1] Caesar c. 103. 3 'quam paucis ante mensibus per suos propinquos atque amicos regno expulerat'; cf. Strabo 17. 1. 11. The charge upon which she was brought to trial and condemned ('damnatae—sorori,' Lucan 500) was no doubt one of treason. Iohannes Malalas, a late and illiterate annalist, says, *Chron.* 9. p. 279, that Cleopatra was banished to the Thebaid. As he makes the statement twice, it is probably not an oversight and may conceivably be true. But of what its author is capable may be judged by what he has made of a passage in the 8th book of 'the most accomplished Lucan,' as he calls him. 'Caesar,' he says, 'surprised Pompey and killed him in Egypt,' καταφθάσας αὐτὸν ἀνεῖλεν αὐτὸν εἰς τὴν Αἴγυπτον χώραν καθὼς περὶ αὐτοῦ ὁ σοφώτατος Λουκανὸς συνεγράψατο (ib. 276). He has got this out of Cornelia's speech (641); or was he thinking also of 629?

[2] I agree with Mr Heitland, *Roman Republic* 3. 296 n., in his dissent from Mommsen, *Staatsr.* 3. 925 sqq. (where other *soi-disant* senates are discussed). The description of the meeting in Epirus, Lucan v 7 sqq., bears obvious traces of being based on fact though it would be rash to conclude that it must in all respects correspond to reality, and Mommsen, l.c., may be right in maintaining that the election of Pompey as commander-in-chief by this quasi-senate is an invention of Lucan's. Attentive reading of Dio 41. 43 shows that the Pompeians took all pains to give a constitutional appearance to their proceedings, even going the length of consecrating a piece of ground in Thessalonica for the purpose of taking the auspices (§ 2), and it is incredible that they

in the exercise of its just or arrogated powers received the envoys of the Regents and pronounced in favour of the accomplished fact in Egypt. This step must have been taken on the initiative of Pompey; and our poet therefore seems to have fair warrant for the repeated assertions[1] that to him did the young prince owe his throne.

Cleopatra was quick to meet force with force; and presently she was on the Egyptian frontier with an army that she had raised in Syria and Arabia to assert her rights[2]. The Council of Regency on their part put large forces in the field to oppose her, of which the young king was in nominal command; and at the moment of Pompey's arrival the two armies were facing each other on Mount CASIUS, now *El Katieh*, a sandy waterless ridge running out to sea about 33 miles beyond Pelusium[3].

Civil War in Egypt.

It was still afternoon when Pompey cast anchor off Pelusium, and learned where the young king was encamped. If there is

should have failed to challenge the pretensions of the Caesarian 'senate.' Caesar's silence on the subject is intelligible, whether as accident or design. It is true that Dio (unlike Plutarch, *Pomp.* 65) does not use the term βουλή in this connexion, but from his expression (ἦρχον l.c. § 5) we may infer that both bodies, Pompeian and Caesarian alike, claimed the sovereign powers of a senate.

[1] v 58 sqq. 'et tibi, non fidae gentis dignissime regno, | Fortunae, Ptolemaee, pudor crimenque deorum | cingere Pellaeo pressos diademate crinis | permissum. saeuum in populos puer accipit ensem, | atque utinam in populos! donatast regia Lagi. | accessit Magni iugulus regnumque sorori | ereptumst soceroque nefas'; VIII 448 'sceptra puer Ptolemaeus habet tibi debita, Magne'; 518 sq. 'quod nobis sceptra senatus, | te suadente, dedit'; 560 'qui tibi regna dedit'; 572 sq. 'si regia Magno, | sceptrorum auctori, uera pietate pateret.'

[2] Appian 2. 84 init. στρατὸν ἀμφὶ τὴν Συρίαν ἀγειρούσης: cf. Strabo l.c. It should be remembered that Syria was without a governor, as Scipio had left for Europe some time before the battle of Pharsalia, *Hist. Introd.* p. xv.

[3] From Strabo 16. 2. 33, p. 760. In § 28 he gives the distance as 300 stades. (Plutarch c. 77 wrongly makes the king encamped in Pelusium.)

any truth in a story of which the historian Dio makes mention, the very name of the mountain might have bidden him take heed. The prevalent pronunciation of the word Casius was with a single *s*; but there was another one, of which there are traces both in Latin and Greek, in which the *s* is doubled[1]. Pompey had been warned by an oracle to beware of *Cassius*.

Pompey
arrives at
Mount
Casius.

He had looked with suspicion on all the Roman bearers of the name; but the far-off promontory of Egypt had never entered his thoughts[2].

Pompey now turned to the east. With the changed direction the wind was fair astern[3]; and by the next day's dawn he would arrive at his destination. He was guided to the exact spot by the sight of the king's troops who were plainly visible from the sea[4].

Meantime a mounted scout had ridden at full speed along the coast and apprised the court of his coming. It was filled with consternation; and a council was hastily summoned to consider how the unbidden guest should be received[5]. Before it met, envoys arrived from Pompey to plead his cause before the court. They urged on his behalf the bonds of friendship and hospitality which had united the young king's father and himself[6], and asked that in this hour of his need he should be

---

[1] Apart from Dio, l.c. below, the spelling *Cassius* (Κάσσιος) is found in the best MSS of Vitruuius (8. 3. 7), in MSS of Ammianus, Solinus, Ptolemy, Hierocles etc. Pliny, like Lucan, has the single *s*.

[2] ἐς πάντας τοὺς πολίτας τοὺς Κασσίους ἐκ χρησμοῦ τινος ὑποπτεύων πρὸς μὲν ἀνδρὸς Κασσίου οὐδενὸς ἐπεβουλεύθη παρὰ δὲ δὴ τῷ ὄρει τῷ τὴν ἐπίκλησιν ταύτην ἔχοντι καὶ ἀπέθανε καὶ ἐτάφη, Dio C. 42. 5. 6.

[3] Lucan 470 sq. So Appian says, 2. 84, 'As Fate would have it, the wind carried Pompey down to Mount Casius (ἐς τὸ Κάσιον τὸ πνεῦμα τὸν Πομπήιον κατέφερε).'

[4] Appian l.c. 'Observing a large force on the land he halted in his course, guessing rightly that the King was there.'

[5] Lucan 472 sqq.

[6] Caesar 103. 3 'ad eum Pompeius misit ut pro hospitio atque amicitia patris Alexandriam reciperetur atque illius opibus in calamitate tegeretur.' So more shortly Appian c. 84 πέμψας τε ἔφραζε περὶ ἑαυτοῦ

accorded the shelter of Alexandria and the protection of the Egyptian king.

When they had delivered their message, the envoys showed themselves so ill-advised, or so ill-instructed, as to enter into intimate conversation with a number of Roman soldiers who were serving in the Egyptian army and to urge them 'to do their duty to Pompey and not to despise his low estate[1].' This conduct did not perhaps amount to tampering with the loyalty of the troops, but it came dangerously near thereto; and it was easy to represent it as part of a design 'to make Pompey master of Alexandria and Egypt[2].'

Indiscretion of his envoys to the king.

It is significant that there is not a word of this mission in Lucan. From 560 sq. one would suppose that instead of Pompey's dropping anchor for the night as soon as he arrived off Mount Casius his sails were furled and his vessel rowed towards the shore. Another synthetic concentration!

The meeting was without doubt a small and a secret one. The king would of course preside. Besides him we know of only four who were present; Pothinus, the head of the regents, Achillas, the king's commander-in-chief[3], Theodotus, his tutor in rhetoric, and if

Meeting of the king's Council.

καὶ τῆς τοῦ πατρὸς φιλίας, and Plutarch c. 77 ἐκεῖ (κατὰ Πηλούσιον) κατέσχε προπέμψας τὸν φράσοντα τῷ βασιλεῖ καὶ δεησόμενον. Cf. Ovid, *Pont.* 4. 3. 41 sq. quoted on 594. According to Dio C. 42. 3. 2 Pompey asked for definite assurances; see below, p. liv n. 2.

[1] Caesar l.c. § 4 'qui ab eo missi erant, confecto legationis officio, liberius cum militibus regis conloqui coeperunt eosque hortari ut suum officium Pompeio praestarent neue eius fortunam despicerent.'

[2] Caesar 104. 1 'amici regis qui propter aetatem eius in procuratione erant regni, siue timore adducti, ut postea praedicabant, sollicitato exercitu regio, ne Pompeius Alexandriam Aegyptumque occuparet siue desperata eius fortuna ut plerumque in calamitate ex amicis inimici existunt,' e.q.s.

[3] Caesar 104. 2 'Achillam praefectum regium singulari hominem audacia.' His *audacia* was hardly greater than that of Pothinus; see supra, p. xlv n. 3.

we may trust our author so far, the venerable high-priest of Memphis.

The name that Lucan gives to this priest is ACOREUS[1], which is hardly Greek, as are Ἀχιλλᾶς and Ποθεινός, and may be native Egyptian. Prof. H. Diels in his paper *Seneca und Lucan* discusses the question, citing Parthey's *Verzeichnis Ägyptischen Personennamen*[2] and referring to a communication of G. Steindorff. In Syncellus (ed. Dind. I 179) we have Ἀγχορεύς[3] given as the name of the 9th king of Egypt[4], with which may be compared that of Οὐχορεύς (possibly a corruption of Ἀχορεύς) who, according to Diodorus I 50, was the founder of Memphis. The meaning however of the name is obscure.

Acoreus high priest of Memphis.

Now it so happens that the high priest of Memphis at the time of Pompey's landing in Egypt is known to us from elsewhere. An inscription in Brugsch's *Thesaurus Inscriptionum Aegyptiacarum*[5], Part V, Introd. p. viii and 941—944, gives a detailed account of his life and distinctions. In respect of neither of these is there discordance between what we find in the inscription and what Lucan tells us of his Acoreus.

According to Bouché-Leclercq's determination of the regnal chronology[6], the high priest would be born on Nov. 5, 93 B.C. ; according to Strack's[7], which Mr Griffith thinks more probable, on Nov. 4, 90: and he was made high-priest by Ptolemy Auletes (Neos Dionysos) at the age of 14, that is on the first reckoning in 79 and on the second reckoning in 76. In July 48 he would therefore be in his 45th year, according to

[1] Or *Achoreus*; see *Crit. App.* on 475 below.

[2] In *Abhandlungen der königl. Akademie der Wissenschaften zu Berlin* for 1885, p. 6.

[3] Goar's Ἀχορεύς is probably one of that editor's many mistakes.

[4] The names here seem to be connected with the kings of the historical 18th dynasty.

[5] For my knowledge of this inscription and other help in the matter I am indebted to Mr F. Ll. Griffith, Reader in Egyptology in the University of Oxford.

[6] *Histoire des Lagides* II 381 sqq.   [7] *Dynastie der Ptolemäer*, p. 163.

Bouché-Leclercq, and in his 42nd according to Strack and Mr Griffith. As Egyptians are often 'old at forty,' either date would agree excellently with Lucan's description of Acoreus as 'iam placidus senio fractisque modestior annis' (476); it also agrees with the further indication of time that during his priesthood there had been more than one of the Sacred Bulls ('non unus Apis,' 479), as of course there would have been, seeing that he had held that office for at least 28 years; see my note on the line. Furthermore the numerous distinctions of the high-priest rehearsed in the inscription show that it relates to a person of high consideration and favour in the court; and such we know was the Acoreus of Lucan[1].

But we are now faced by a contradiction. The name of the priest in the inscription is not Acoreus or anything like Acoreus. It is *Pshemptaḥ*, a compound of *P-shêre-n-Ptaḥ* = 'the-son-of-Ptaḥ.' Inasmuch as the *re* was slurred in pronunciation, this would be given in Greek by *Ψεμφθας. If Lucan found in his authority a name that he would have to Latinize as *Psemphthas*, he may well have been alarmed and have cast about for a substitute; and if, as seems not impossible, the high priests of Memphis claimed to be the successors of the reputed founder of the city, just as all the kings of Parthia bore the name of *Arsaces* and as *Caesar* is the title of every 'emperor,' then the substitute chosen was a very natural one. Whatever the source of the appellation, it is clear that here too Lucan has deliberately deviated from fact.

The petition of Pompey for assistance might have been answered by a simple *Yes* or *No*; and such it seemed at the outset would be the probable issue of the debate. Some of these present—amongst them Acoreus, who, by right of his age

Doubt about the name.

---

[1] Acoreus is a principal figure in Cleopatra's magnificent banquet, X 174 sqq. where, 194—331, in answer to a question of Caesar, he delivers himself of a dissertation upon the character and sources of the Nile. He is throughout treated with great respect, cf. 480, X 174, 176, 193.

and sacred office, gave his opinion first[1]—were for honouring
the obligations of gratitude and filial duty and for receiving
the fugitive. Others, with the fear of Caesar before them, were
for turning him away[2].

The Greek professor of rhetoric dissented from both. He
had been invited to this cabinet meeting as a special mark of
consideration—Plutarch says caustically 'in the absence of
better men[3]'—and he felt bound to justify the
compliment. In an oration which we can recon-
struct in all essentials from the report of Plutarch
and the speech that Lucan puts into the mouth of
Pothinus[4] Theodotus enlarged upon the dangers
that would follow on the adoption of either of the courses
proposed. If they received the stranger, they would have an
enemy in Caesar and a master in Pompey. If they turned him

On the
advice of
Theodotus it
is resolved to
kill Pompey.

[1] 'Consilii uox prima fuit,' Lucan 480.

[2] Plutarch c. 77 τῶν μὲν οὖν ἄλλων τοσοῦτον αἱ γνῶμαι διέστησαν ὅσον
οἱ μὲν ἀπελαύνειν ἐκέλευον οἱ δὲ καλεῖν καὶ δέχεσθαι τὸν ἄνδρα.

[3] Plutarch, *Brutus* c. 33 ἠξιωμένος τότε τοῦ συνεδρίου δι' ἐρημίαν
ἀνδρῶν βελτιόνων.

[4] There is no doubt that Lucan deliberately changed the name of
the speaker as to which we have the consensus of Livy, *periocha* l.c.
above, p. xliv n. 2; Plutarch in two places; Velleius 2. 53. 2 'consilio Theodoti et Achillae'; Seneca, *Dial.* 4. 2. 3 'quis non Theodoto
et Achillae et ipsi puero non puerile auso facinus infestus est?' That
metre had much to do with this we have already, p. xxxix n. 1, seen
to be improbable. Mr Duff, l.c. p. 132, suggests in addition that it
seemed to Lucan 'to deepen the horror of Pompey's end, that he owed
it to an unsexed monster like Pothinus.' It may be so. The motive is
an intelligible one; compare 552, though this is addressed to Ptolemy,
and Seneca, *Ep.* 4. 7 quoted above, p. lxiv n. 2. But it seems simpler
to suppose, as the last cited passage suggests, that the reason why
the speech is assigned to Pothinus is that it was the eunuch who was
responsible for the killing of Pompey. Pothinus, a person of considerable ability as it would appear, was at this time practically supreme in
the counsels of Egypt and Achillas little more than his instrument; and
if *he* had not assented to the proposal of Theodotus, all the Greek's
skilful pleading would have gone for nought.

away, he would be incensed by his rebuff and Caesar at his escape[1]. There was but one course open to prudence. He must be received and he must be killed. 'For,' the professor added with a smile, 'the dead do not bite!' The speech, as we know from Plutarch and as we could gather from what represents it in Lucan, was a brilliant exhibition of sophistical rhetoric. Its shameless cynicism, its callous disregard of everything but self-interest and material force must indeed revolt us. Yet we cannot but acknowledge the address with which it handles the essential facts and the power which it evinces to read a tyrant's heart[2]. It had the intended effect and it was

Achillas is despatched to perpetrate the deed.

agreed that Pompey must die[3]. The royal puppet, as etiquette enjoined, pronounced the sentence[4]; and ACHILLAS was appointed executioner[5]. But the envoys returned with an assurance that Pompey

---

[1] Plutarch, *Pomp.* l.c.   [2] *nosse tyrannos*, Lucan 482.

[3] Theodotus was naturally elated by this triumph, and he might be heard to boast that Pompey the Great had fallen to his skilful oratory. Plutarch, *Brut.* l.c. ἔκειτο Πομπήϊος Μάγνος, τῆς Θεοδότου ῥητορείας καὶ δεινότητος ἔργον, ὡς αὐτὸς ὁ σοφιστὴς ἔλεγε μεγαλαυχούμενος.

[4] The boyish delight of the king at being 'allowed to give such an important order' (Lucan 536 sqq.) is an excellent touch. It is natural under the circumstances that Ptolemy's responsibility should have been variously estimated. Dio (42. 3. 3) even implies that owing to his youth he had no part in the matter καὶ αὐτῷ (to Pompey) ὁ μὲν Πτολεμαῖος οὐδὲν (παῖς γὰρ ἔτι κομιδῇ ἦν) ἀπεκρίνατο and later on (4. 4) hints (not quite consistently) that, as the assassins feared, he might have spared Pompey's life. On the other hand Livy (*periocha*), Seneca and Florus ll. cc. above pp. xliv, lii, xxxviii notes represent the king as ordering the assassination.

[5] Caesar 104. 2 'ipsi clam consilio inito Achillam, praefectum regium, singulari hominem audacia et L. Septimium tribunum militum ad interficiendum Pompeium miserunt.' Lucan 538 'sceleri delectus Achillas,' agreeing closely with Livy, *periocha* above, p. xliv n. 2. Appian, c. 84, does not mention Achillas; and his words in 85 that the king did not come in person to meet Pompey nor send any persons of distinction (τῶν ἐπιφανῶν τινας) to do so shows that this was no accidental omission.

would be welcome in Egypt and with an invitation for him to come to the king[1].

Whether Pompey was contented with the answer, we cannot say. If Dio's account of his request[2] be correct, it was far from satisfactory, as it contained no specific promises or pledge of safe conduct. But in all these last scenes Pompey behaves like a man that is hypnotised. He flutters to his doom as the moth to the candle: an infatuation noted both by Plutarch and Lucan in more than one passage.

For the success of the Regents' scheme it was indispensable that the victim should be detached from his followers. Achillas accordingly had a two-oared boat made ready which would hold some dozen persons at the most, such a boat as still may be seen about the waters of the Nile[3]. Besides Achillas himself and three or four attendants, including the rowers, it had on board two Roman officers from the Egyptian army, these

---

[1] Caes. 104. 1 'iis qui erant ab eo missi palam liberaliter responderunt eumque ad regem uenire iusserunt.' ·

[2] Dio (42. 3. 2) describes the mission, ἔπεμψέ τινας τῆς τε πατρῴας αὐτὸν εὐεργεσίας ἀναμιμνήσκων καὶ δεόμενος ἐπὶ ῥητοῖς τέ τισι καὶ βεβαίοις καταχθῆναι· ἐκβῆναι γὰρ πρὶν ἀσφάλειάν τινα λαβεῖν οὐκ ἐθάρσησε.

[3] *nauicula paruula*, Caesar; *nauicula*, Livy *periocha*; ἁλιάς, 'a fishing boat,' Plutarch; σκάφος εὐτελές, 'a common boat,' Appian; ἀκατίων (plur.) ἐπιβάντες, ἐν πλοιαρίῳ Dio; *exigua—carina*, Lucan 541; *parua ratis*, id. 565; *non longa biremis*, in Lucan 562, which needs a word of comment. The usual meaning of *biremis* is 'a *two-banked* galley,' 'bireme,' such as was used in war. Here, however, and in Lucan x 56 *parua—biremi*, a phrase applied to the vessel in which Cleopatra escaped to Caesar, it must be used in the sense of a '*two-oared*' boat, *biremis scapha* in Hor. C. 3. 29. 62, which is what Cicero, *de Or.* 1. 174 calls '*duorum scalmorum* nauicula,' in Greek σκάφος δίκωπον. Lucan adds the epithets *non longa* (i.e. not a *longa nauis* or war-ship), *parua* to show that *biremis* is *not* to be understood as a 'bireme.' The double meaning of *biremis* (which perhaps was used in the account of Livy) may explain Velleius' mistake in calling the vessel a *nauis*, 2. 53. 2 'ut ex oneraria in eam *nauem* quae obuiam processerat transcenderet.'

purposely chosen to avert suspicion, SALUIUS a centurion and LUCIUS SEPTIMIUS a military tribune, the latter of whom had served, as a centurion, under Pompey in the war with the Pirates[1].

Meanwhile the Egyptian troops, it seemed in compliment to Pompey, had lined the shore, and the young Ptolemy in the purple robe of royalty was visible from the Roman galleys[2]. The boat was now nearing the trireme; and Septimius rose from his seat and greeted his old commander, who, with his wife and son and his principal friends gathered round him, was standing at the stern of the anchored trireme[3], with the highest title that the Roman soldier could employ, *Haue imperator*[4], while Achillas, addressing him in Greek[5], with all expressions of respect, invited him to step into the boat, for whose insignificance he offered the apology that landing from larger vessels was impossible in the shallow waters[6]. And he added that Ptolemy was impatient to see him.

[1] Caesar c. 104. 3 (infra); Dio c. 42. 3. 3 τῶν Αἰγυπτίων τινὲς καὶ Λούκιος Σεπτίμιος, ἀνὴρ Ῥωμαῖος, συνεστρατευκὼς μέν ποτε τῷ Πομπηίῳ συγγεγονὼς δὲ τῷ Γαβινίῳ καὶ πρὸς ἐκείνου τῷ Πτολεμαίῳ μετὰ στρατιωτῶν ἐς φυλακὴν αὐτοῦ καταλελειμμένος; Plutarch c. 78, who omits to mention that Septimius had now a higher rank than when he was with Pompey; Appian l.c., where his name is given as Σεμπρώνιος; Florus l.c. above, p. xxxviii n. 2, who in his rhetorical fashion calls Septimius a *desertor* of Pompey.

[2] Appian l.c. ἅμα δὲ ταῦτ' ἐγίγνετο καὶ ὁ στρατός, ὥσπερ ἐπὶ τιμῇ τοῦ Πομπηίου, παρὰ τὸν αἰγιαλὸν ἐξετάσσετο ἅπας καὶ ὁ βασιλεὺς ἐν μέσῳ τῇ φοινικίδι κατάδηλος ἦν περικειμένῃ. Cf. Plutarch τὸν αἰγιαλὸν ὁπλῖται κατεῖχον.

[3] Cf. Plutarch ἔτυχον δὲ πάντες εἰς αὐτὴν οἱ δοκιμώτατοι τῶν συμπλεόν-των ἐμβεβηκότες ὅπως εἰδεῖεν τὸ πραττόμενον.

[4] Plutarch l.c. Ῥωμαιστὶ τὸν Πομπήιον αὐτοκράτορα προσηγόρευσεν: cf. Lucan 596.

[5] There is nothing strange in this. Greek was then the international language of the East. But Mr John Masefield, in his *Tragedy of Pompey the Great*, absurdly puts into the mouth of the commander-in-chief of Egypt the broken English of a negro or a Chinaman.

[6] Plutarch l.c. ὁ δὲ Ἀχιλλᾶς, ἀσπασάμενος αὐτὸν Ἑλληνιστί, παρε-

This was not the royal reception that Pompey had expected
and the sanguine Theophanes prognosticated[1].

Pompey is induced to come ashore in a small boat.
And the explanation offered was not of a character
to reassure. His wife and friends had urged him,
while it was still possible, to take to the open sea[2].
Nor was he himself wholly free from misgivings.
But he was sick of the suspense, and, it may be, apprehensive
of what might happen if he were suspected of distrust. Retreat,
too, might no longer be possible; for he observed with uneasiness that some of the royal vessels were being got ready for sea[3].

He bade adieu then to his wife and son, and preceded by two
of his centurions, by Philippus his freedman and another servant
called Scythes[4], he passed down into the boat, where Egyptian
arms were ready to receive him[5]. As he did so, he turned to
his wife and son and repeated two lines of Sophocles which
have been thus translated:

> He that once enters at a tyrant's door
> Becomes a slave, though he were free before[6].

κάλει μετελθεῖν εἰς τὴν ἁλιάδα· τέναγος γὰρ εἶναι πολὺ καὶ βάθος οὐκ
ἔχειν πλόιμον τριήρει τὴν θάλατταν ὑπόψαμμον οὖσαν : cf. Lucan 565 sqq.

[1] Plutarch l.c. ταῖς Θεοφάνους ἐλπίσιν ὁμοίαν. The king should have
come himself as Lucan 572 sqq. and Appian l.c. say.

[2] Plutarch l.c. τῷ Πομπηίῳ παρῄνουν ἀνακρούεσθαι ἕως ἔξω βέλους
εἰσίν : cf. Lucan 571 sqq. and Dio 42. 4. 3.

[3] ἅμα δὲ καὶ ναῦς τινες ἑωρῶντο τῶν βασιλικῶν πληρούμεναι καὶ τὸν
αἰγιαλὸν ὁπλῖται κατεῖχον ὥστ' ἄφυκτα καὶ μεταβαλλομένοις ἐφαίνετο καὶ
προσῆν τὸ διδόναι τοῖς φονεῦσι τὴν ἀπιστίαν αὐτὴν τῆς ἀδικίας ἀπο-
λογίαν, Plutarch l.c.

[4] Plutarch l.c., whose account agrees with that in Caesar's more
summary narrative, c. 104. 3 'ab his (Achilla et Septimio) liberaliter
ipse appellatus et quadam notitia Septimii productus quod bello prae-
donum apud eum ordinem duxerat nauiculam paruulam conscendit cum
paucis suis.'

[5] δεξιουμένων, Plutarch; *ablatus*, Lucan ; see supra, p. xiv.

[6]   ὅστις γὰρ ὡς τύραννον ἐμπορεύεται
      κείνου 'στι δοῦλος κἂν ἐλεύθερος μόλῃ,

Soph. *Fragm.* 789 (Nauck). Lucan appears to glance at this in

Pompey took his seat in the boat; and it moved towards the shore. It was some distance to the land; but Achillas and his officers maintained a stony silence. Pompey's eyes fell upon Septimius who, as Roman military etiquette required, had remained standing in the presence of his former commander. 'Surely,' he said, 'I do not err in thinking you were once a comrade of mine[1]?' Septimius nodded; but added not a word. So Pompey turned to read the little speech which he had composed in Greek to deliver before the king[2].

They were now nearing the shore; and the anxious watchers

Pompey is killed before landing.

on the trireme's deck saw with a feeling of relief a great company crowding to the landing-place to receive them[3]. Pompey took the hand of Philippus to help him to rise, and on the instant Septimius stabbed him in the back; and Saluius next and then Achillas plunged their swords into his side[4]. A cry of horror burst from the trireme;

the words of 611 sq. '*Phariam*que (i.e. τυράννου) ablatus in alnum | *perdiderat* iam *iura sui* (i.e. δοῦλος ἦν),' as Ussani notes, p. 122.

[1] Plutarch l.c.; Appian, whose Greek is ἀρά σε γιγνώσκω, συστρατιῶτα; which may be a literal translation of Pompey's very words, 'num te noui, commilito?'

[2] Plutarch ἐν βιβλίῳ μικρῷ γεγραμμένον ὑπ' αὐτοῦ λόγον Ἑλληνικόν.

[3] Plutarch ὡς δὲ τῇ γῇ προσεπέλαζον, ἡ μὲν Κορνηλία μετὰ τῶν φίλων ἐκ τῆς τριήρους περιπαθὴς οὖσα τὸ μέλλον ἀπεσκοπεῖτο (cf. Lucan 590 sqq.) καὶ θαρρεῖν ἤρχετο, πολλοὺς ὁρῶσα πρὸς τὴν ἀπόβασιν τῶν βασιλικῶν οἷον ἐπὶ τιμῇ καὶ δεξιώσει συνερχομένους.

[4] Plutarch l.c. Caesar says more generally, 'ibi ab Achilla et Septimio interficitur,' and so practically Dio. Lucan agrees, though he goes his own way in describing the murder (606, 618). Florus l.c. mentions only Septimius. Appian 'Sempronius' and 'others.' Velleius says that he was killed by the sole order of an Egyptian slave, i.e. Pothinus, 'princeps Romani nominis imperio arbitrioque Aegyptii mancipii C. Caesare P. Seruilio consulibus iugulatus est.' Seneca's references are loose and hardly consistent, *Dial.* 6. 20. 4 'uidit *Aegyptium carnificem* et sacrosanctum uictoribus caput *satelliti* praestitit (Achillas),' 9. 16. 1 '(coguntur) Pompeius et Cicero *clientibus suis* praebere ceruicem (Ptolemy),' 10. 13. 7 'Alexandrina perfidia deceptus *ultimo mancipio*

and Cornelia shrieked and fainted away[1]. But Pompey fell with
hardly a groan[2], making no attempt at resistance and muffling
his face in his military cloak[3].

There follows in the narrative of Lucan a passage (622—635)
in which the vague unspoken thoughts of Pompey's dying
moments have been shaped to a soliloquy, the character and
aim of which are sometimes misunderstood. 'The thoughts of
one thus struck out of existence,' to quote what
I have said elsewhere[4], 'it is beyond man's power
to divine. We may believe only that their succession in the last few moments of consciousness is incredibly

Soliloquy
of Pompey
in Lucan.

(apparently Pothinus) transfodiendum se praebuit tum demum intellecta
inani iactatione cognominis sui.'

[1] Lucan 637, 661.

[2] Plutarch l.c. ὁ δὲ ταῖς χερσὶν ἀμφοτέραις τὴν τήβεννον ἐφελκυσά-
μενος κατὰ τοῦ προσώπου, μηδὲν εἰπὼν ἀνάξιον μηδὲ ποιήσας, ἀλλὰ
στενάξας μόνον, ἐνεκαρτέρησε ταῖς πληγαῖς. Lucan, 613—620, whose
nullo gemitu is a conscious improvement on his original. We may see
the truth escaping in the words that he puts into Pompey's mouth at
633 sq. 'tanto patientius, oro, | claude, dolor, gemitus.'

[3] The word that Plutarch uses of the garment which Pompey drew
with both hands over his face presents a difficulty. τήβεννος is the
recognised rendering of *toga* in Greek although it is sometimes used for
trabea. But why should Pompey have put on civil attire? He was
at the head of a military force; and accompanied by two military
officers he was going to an interview with the king of Egypt, himself in
name at least in command of an army. He had moreover been saluted
as *imperator* by Septimius, surely a strange and indecorous proceeding
if he were wearing the garb of peace. He must, I think, have been
wearing a general's dress. Then the τήβεννος would be an inaccuracy
of Plutarch's own; and the *uelamen* of Lucan would mean the *paludamentum*. Pompey may have put on a *white* paludamentum in order
not to challenge comparison with the royal purple of Ptolemy, just as
Metellus Scipio complied with the request of Iuba that he should not
wear his *sagulum* (=paludamentum) *purpureum* when that king had
come into the camp, *Bellum Africanum* 57. Or perhaps again Plutarch
was thinking of the end of Iulius Caesar, *Life of Caesar* c. 66.

[4] *Quarterly Review*, July, 1916, p. 54.

rapid and intense. But Lucan assuredly never intended his readers to take the utterance of the reflexions which he has ascribed to the dying Pompey as any real soliloquy. With the ancients a speech was a recognised literary form for conveying the import and lessons of a situation rather than for rendering with literal and psychological exactness what was actually thought or said. With every shape of violent and compulsory death, sudden or protracted, the Romans of the early Empire had become familiar. The illustrious victims who starved or bled themselves to death under the tyrannies of a Seianus, a Caligula or a Nero were careful so to order their last hours that they should furnish monition and example to posterity.' And so in these self-communings of Pompey we are not to seek a representation of his thoughts or feelings as his last breath departed; but rather a presentation of what he would have thought and said if Death had struck less swiftly. As such they seem no unworthy embodiment of the austere and self-respecting gravity of Rome.

Thus died the man who for many years had been the virtual master of the Roman world, on the eve of his fifty-ninth birthday and upon the anniversary of the day when he triumphed over the king of Pontus and the Pirates[1].

The butchers' work was not finished yet; a trophy had to be secured. The body appeared still to breathe; but **Mutilation of the corpse.** Septimius tore the covering from the face, hacked the head from the neck and flung the trunk naked on the shoals[2]. The head was placed on a pike and carried in triumph to the king. The Regents ordered it to be embalmed, to be preserved for a peace-offering to Caesar[3].

[1] Velleius 2. 53. 3; Appian 2. 86; Dio 42. 5. 5. Pompey was born on the 29th of September, Pliny *N. H.* 37. 13.

[2] τοῦ δὲ Πομπηίου τὴν μὲν κεφαλὴν ἀποτέμνουσι τὸ δὲ ἄλλο σῶμα γυμνὸν ἐκβαλόντες ἀπὸ τῆς ἁλιάδος τοῖς δεομένοις τοιούτου θεάματος ἀπέλιπον : so Plutarch briefly. Appian is briefer still, while Caesar omits the 'decapitation' altogether. But Lucan seizes his opportunity, and spares us not one of all the gruesome details, 667 sqq.

[3] Lucan 681 sqq., 689 sqq. Lucan's rhetoric finds capital in the

The tragedy of Pompey the Great was concluded ; and actors and spectators quitted the scene. His fleet had long ago plucked up its anchors and fled[1] ; and darkness was now falling on the deserted shore. The poet fitly chooses this moment for a strain of sombre and impressive reflexion.

circumstance that it was not Septimius himself but a *Pharius satelles*, 675, i.e. Achillas (see the note), who carried the head to the king. This may be the same 'satelles' who has displaced Theodotus at ix 1010, 1064 ; see below, p. lxv n. 2. The words of Lucan 'caesaries conprensa manust Pharioque ueruto...suffixum caput est' are illustrated by Suetonius *Galba* c. 20 of the decapitation of that emperor's corpse, 'gregarius miles a frumentatione rediens abiecto onere caput ei amputauit et, quoniam *capillo arripere* non poterat, in gremium abdidit, mox inserto per os pollice ad Othonem detulit. ille lixis calonibusque donauit qui *hasta suffixum* non sine ludibrio circum castra portarunt.'

[1] Cornelia and Sextus escaped to Tyre (n. on 662); and thence to Cyprus ; Livy, *periocha* 112 'Cypron refugerunt'; cf. Lucan ix 117 ; Dio 42. 5. 7. The rest were not all so fortunate in eluding the Egyptians. On this Dio says (l.c.) 'Of the companions of his expedition some were caught on the spot (αὐτίκα ἑάλωσαν) while others escaped, amongst them his wife and son.' The words of Appian c. 85 τὸ μὲν γύναιον τοῦ Πομπηίου καὶ οἱ φίλοι ταῦτα μακρόθεν ὁρῶντες ἀνῴμωξόν τε καὶ χεῖρας ἐς θεοὺς ἐκδίκους σπονδῶν ἀνίσχοντες ἀπέπλεον τάχιστα ὡς ἐκ πολεμίας refer only to those on board of Pompey's trireme, and these chiefly must be meant in the passage of Plutarch, which however is somewhat loosely expressed : 'When those on the ships saw the murder, they raised a cry of anguish which could be heard on land and fled, pulling up their anchors with all speed. A strong breeze assisted them as they ran out to sea, so that the Egyptians gave up their project of pursuit.' No mercy was shown to the captured : '(Pompeius) Aegyptum uenit ibique mox ut litus attigit iussu Ptolemaei adulescentis in gratiam Caesaris uictoris occisus est, Pompei uxor filiique ('filiusque' more correctly the schol. on Lucan VII 560) fugerunt. cetera Pompeiana classis direpta est, omnibus qui in ea erant crudelissime trucidatis, ibique Pompeius Bithynicus occisus est. Lentulus uero uir consularis aput Pelusium interfectus est,' Orosius 6. 15. 28 (in substance probably from Livy). Compare p. lxiii n. 1.

'With the same punctiliousness with which Fortune perfected the prosperity of Pompey did she strike him to death from the pinnacle of power; and in a single merciless day exact in payment all the miseries from which she had given him so many years exempt. Thus Pompey never had both joys and sorrows mingled in his cup—happy with no god to trouble him, wretched with none to pity him. Fortune long held her stroke and struck but once. He is tossed on the sands, torn by the rocks; the waves pour through his wounds; the sea makes him its sport and, as no shape is left him, the one sign that he is Pompey the Great is the neck from which the head has been torn' (700—711).

Lucan's reflexions on the tragedy.

The poor fragment of humanity was not to be utterly without friends. PHILIPPUS, the faithful freedman of Pompey, stayed by the trunk till the crowd of onlookers had satisfied their curiosity. When the last sightseer had departed, he washed the body in the sea water and wrapped it in an undergarment of his own[1]. Casting his eyes around he descried at a little distance the remains of a small fishing boat which would just suffice to make a pyre[2]. He was collecting and arranging these when he was accosted by an old Roman soldier who had served under Pompey in some of his first campaigns[3],

Pompey's freedman, Philippus, makes a fire to burn the trunk.

---

[1] These details and those of the following narrative are chiefly from Plutarch c. 80. Lucan's account differs a good deal, and its brilliance savours of romance. See notes 1, 2 on p. lxii infra. We are loth to surrender the touch of the moonlight struggling through the clouds (721 note). But astronomy is pitiless. The moon was then in its third quarter, only four days off new; and, as I learn from Sir F. W. Dyson, our Astronomer Royal, she would not rise more than three hours before dawn, that is not earlier than 2 a.m. and would be a thin crescent, whereas Lucan obviously makes her rise in the early evening.

[2] So Lucan 'lacerae fragmenta carinae,' 755; Manilius, quoted in the note ad loc. 'eiectae—fragmenta carinae'; Valerius Maximus 1. 8. 9 (infr. p. lxiii n. 1) 'concisae scaphae lignis.' The incident is historical without doubt and hardly less certainly from Livy.

[3] Like Septimius he had probably gone to Egypt with Gabinius. If

and whose name is given as Cordus[1]. The stranger inquired
who was he that was about to bury Pompey the
Great? Philippus answered, 'His freedman.' 'Then,'
replied the Roman, 'you must not keep this honour
to yourself. Let me, too, share in the treasure-
trove of duty that I may not have to deplore my
exile on every ground, but may find a recompense for many
distresses in touching and laying out with my own hands the
greatest of Roman imperators.'

He is aided by Cordus, a former officer of Pompey.

Presently the pile was lighted, by means of faggots taken, if
we may trust so far the narrative of Lucan[2], from a pyre at some

he was still serving in the army his fear of being detected burying
Pompey (717 and 780) is quite intelligible. It is not impossible that he
paid for his devotion and that this is hinted at in the obscure *infaustus*
of 717 for which see n. below and note ad loc.

[1] By Lucan. It is hard to say how much credit should be accorded
to Lucan here. He has suppressed Philippus just as he has suppressed
Theophanes and Theodotus. The reason is obvious. It was much
more dignified to be buried by a 'quaestor' than by a former slave ;
and the quaestorship of Cordus whom he calls a *iuuenis* may be a mere
invention for rhetorical propriety (compare note on 716). Another
problem is how did this quaestor get ashore when he followed his chief
from Cyprus. He was certainly not with Pompey in the boat. Had
he landed already from prevision that his services would be required?
Or did the Egyptian sea-captains spare him (above, p. lx, n.) to perform
the obsequies of their enemy? The writer of the suspicious passage in
the *De Viris Illustribus*, to which I have already referred, calls him
'*Seruius* Codrus.' '*Codrus*' is an unimportant corruption of '*Cordus*,'
but '*Seruius*' is less easy to explain and may possibly have been the
real praenomen. One thing is clear. Cordus himself is not an invention of the poet's. This the tense of *accepit* (not *accipiet*) in 782 proves,
as Ussani (p. 125) has acutely observed. It may be added that the
word *infaustus*, applied to Cordus in 717, shows by its very obscurity
that Lucan is condensing from some earlier account.

[2] In literary workmanship this portion of the book (712—822)
shows Lucan at his best, but if judged as a narrative of fact, it has
undoubted weaknesses. Burman in the part of his *praefatio* which he
devotes to castigating the delinquencies of Lucan has attacked the

distance which had been left to burn without the customary watch. All through the night Philippus and his solitary companion remained beside their charge, feeding at intervals the sluggish fire. The daylight saw it burning still; nor had it died away when Lucius Lentulus, who had left Cyprus after Pompey and was sailing along the coast to join his chief at Alexandria, sighted it from the sea. When he saw the pyre and the figure of Philippus standing near, he exclaimed, 'Who, I wonder, is this mortal that is gone to his rest, having paid the debt of fate?' and then after a while, with a sudden prescience, said, sighing, 'What if it be you, Great Pompey[1]?'

When the body was consumed, the ashes were collected and slaked with sea water. They were then reverently placed in a shallow grave, scooped out for them in the sand. The grave was filled up; and a block of sandstone placed above, to keep the earth in its place; and on it, by means of a burning stake, were scored the simple words HIC SITVS EST MAGNVS, '*Magnus lies here[2].*' An adequate inscription, the lack of which Lucan deplores at length, was for more than one reason impossible.

The ashes are buried in a humble grave.

credibility of this narrative on the ground that the burning of a Roman corpse is not intended and that of an Egyptian out of the question. This is not absolutely conclusive as the body might have been a Greek's. But there are other questionable features in the account. A sceptic may be pardoned for asking how the 'quaestor' carried burning logs in the sinus of his robes for some distance (743, 752) without setting himself on fire. And why he brought the wood to light the pyre before he gathered the wood to make it. Or is this a poetic licence—a 'hysteron proteron' of unusual enormity?

[1] Plutarch l.c.; Valerius Maximus i. 8. 9 'L. Lentulus litus praenauigans in quo Cn. Pompei Magni, perfidia Ptolemaei regis interempti, corpus concisae scaphae lignis comburebatur, ignarus casus eius, cum ipsi Fortunae erubescendum rogum uidisset, commilitonibus dixit "qui scimus an hac flamma Cn. Pompeius cremetur?"' (Lentulus was himself arrested as soon as he landed and put to death in prison by order of the king, Plutarch l.c.; Caesar c. 104. 3; Orosius l.c.) Did this suggest to Lucan the ridiculous fiction that *Sextus* saw the fire (IX 142)?

[2] Lucan 715.

The ashes of Pompey remained long in their solitary resting-place. For all we know it may hold them still. Many years after his wife and sons had passed away the geographer Strabo speaks of the Casian Mountain as the place 'where *lies the body of*

Pompey's Grave for long a place of resort.

Pompeius Magnus and where is the temple of Zeus Casius[1].' The grave was, as Lucan clearly implies, an object of interest to the Roman tourist in Egypt or the merchant on his way to the 'Red Sea[2].' It is given in the enumeration of Pliny and long after him in that of Solinus[3].

After a while it suffered from neglect. The bronze figures of the dead which kinsfolk had placed around it on

Afterwards neglected but restored by Hadrian.

Mount Casius were all defaced and removed to the inner chamber of the neighbouring temple of Iuppiter, and the gravestone itself was buried by the drifting of the sand.

Such was its condition when Hadrian during his visit to Egypt in 130 A.D. made a pilgrimage to the spot. When the emperor saw it, he is said to have exclaimed

τῷ ναοῖς βρίθοντι πόση σπάνις ἔπλετο τύμβου.
So many temples[4], and so scant a grave!

Hadrian offered sacrifice to the shade of Pompey and restored the grave with a sumptuousness befitting its associations[5]. The

---

[1] ὅπου τὸ Πομπηίου τοῦ Μάγνου σῶμα κεῖται καὶ Διός ἐστιν ἱερὸν Κασίου, Strabo 16. 2. 33 (p. 760).

[2] Lucan 851—858. The second of the routes mentioned by Pliny is meant 'alterum ultra Casium montem quod a LX p. redit in Pelusiacam uiam,' *N.H.* 6. 167.

[3] *N.H.* 5. 68 'A Pelusio Chabriae castra, Casius mons, delubrum Iouis Casii, tumulus Magni Pompei'; Solinus 34. 1, who places the tomb at Ostracine (perhaps through a misunderstanding of Pliny whose next sentence begins with this word), which is too far to the east.

[4] Compare Lucan's words 818 sqq. '*solitum*que legi super alta *deorum* | *culmina*...Pompei nomen.'

[5] Dio 69. 11. 1 διὰ δὲ τῆς Ἰουδαίας μετὰ ταῦτα ἐς Αἴγυπτον παριὼν καὶ ἐνήγισε Πομπηίῳ· πρὸς ὃν καὶ τουτὶ τὸ ἔπος ἀπορρῖψαι λέγεται τῷ ναοῖς—τύμβου καὶ τὸ μνῆμα αὐτοῦ διεφθαρμένον ἀνῳκοδόμησεν. Spartianus,

sand was cleared away, the abstracted images repaired and replaced, and over the renovated monument appeared the hexameter composed or adduced by the imperial *littérateur*[1].

The sand-swept promontory of Casius was not to be the sole possessor of a memorial of Pompey. At the time of his rival's murder Caesar appears to have been in Rhodes; but three days after he was off Alexandria. He had not yet landed when Theodotus[2] came on board with the Regents' peace-offering to the victor. The Greek professor now stood high in the councils of Egypt; and his present mission was the fit reward of his previous

Pompey's head brought to Caesar by Theodotus.

Hadr. 14. 4 'Pelusium uenit et *Pompei tumulum magnificentius extruxit.*' The fullest account is that in Appian 2. 86 Πομπηίου δὲ τὴν μὲν κεφαλὴν ἀποτεμόντες οἱ περὶ τὸν Ποθεινὸν ἐφύλασσον Καίσαρι ὡς ἐπὶ μεγίσταις ἀμοιβαῖς (ὁ δὲ αὐτοὺς ἠμύνατο ἀξίως τῆς ἀθεμιστίας) τὸ δὲ λοιπὸν σῶμά τις ἔθαψεν ἐπὶ τῆς ἠόνος καὶ τάφον ἤγειρεν εὐτελῆ καὶ ἐπίγραμμα ἄλλος ἐπέγραψε "τῷ—τύμβου." χρόνῳ δὲ τὸν τάφον τόνδε ἐπικρυφθέντα ὅλον ὑπὸ ψάμμου καὶ εἰκόνας ὅσας ἀπὸ χαλκοῦ τῷ Πομπηίῳ περὶ τὸ Κάσιον ὕστερον οἱ προσήκοντες ἀνέθηκαν, λελωβημένα πάντα καὶ ἐς τὸ ἄδυτον τοῦ ἱεροῦ κατενεχθέντα ἐξήτησε καὶ ηὗρεν ἐπ᾽ ἐμοῦ Ῥωμαίων βασιλεὺς Ἀδριανὸς ἐπιδημῶν, καὶ τὸν τάφον ἀνεκάθηρε γνώριμον αὖθις εἶναι καὶ τὰς εἰκόνας αὐτοῦ Πομπηίου διωρθώσατο. Appian appears to imply that the inscription, a most appropriate one, was there from the first; but this must be an error, compare supra, p. lxiii. Its authorship remains uncertain, as also the date, certainly after the death of Caesar, when the bronze figures of Pompey were set up near the grave.

[1] That the ashes of Pompey were believed to be still reposing in the grave when the Emperor Hadrian offered his sacrifice to the *manes* is a natural but not, as Ussani, op. cit. p. 128, appears to think, a necessary inference. Dr Warde Fowler cites the case of L. and C. Caesar, the two grandsons of Augustus, who were worshipped according to a regular ritual at their cenotaphs in Pisa (Dessau, *Inscr. Select.* 1. 140; *C.I.L.* XI 1421) although their bodies were not there but in the Mausoleum at Rome.

[2] Lucan has suppressed Theodotus here, as he has suppressed him at VIII 483 (above, p. lii) and Theophanes at 328, and put in his place an anonymous 'satelles,' IX 1010, 1064 (who is perhaps meant to be Achillas). But the speech of this 'satelles,' 1014—1032, if compared with

lxvi HISTORICAL INTRODUCTION

service⁶. Addressing Caesar in a short speech, which showed all the vanity and ingenuity of his kind, he produced his trophies, the embalmed head of his victim, now hardly recognisable, and his signet ring engraved with a figure of a lion grasping a sword. Caesar took the ring. But the sight of the head provoked him to tears; crocodile tears, as his enemies and Lucan were prompt to aver; and he turned his eyes away. He gave orders at once that it should be cremated, and with more than the customary tributes of respect[2,3].

VIII 484 sqq., at once bewrays him. The hands are the hands of Esau, but the voice is the voice of Jacob.

[1] The charge of hypocrisy which the partisan poet Lucan ('utque fidem uidit sceleris tutumque putauit | iam bonus esse socer, *lacrimas non sponte cadentis* | effudit,' IX 1037 sqq.; 'simulati fronte doloris,' ib. 1063) and the not over-acute historian Dio 42. 8. 3 ποθεῖν τε αὐτὸν ἐπλάττετο καὶ ἀγανακτεῖν τῷ ὀλέθρῳ αὐτοῦ ἐσκήπτετο bring against Caesar might just as well have been brought against Scipio for weeping over the fall of Carthage. It arises from a confusion of the emotion which Caesar not unnaturally betrayed with the regret which he assuredly did not feel. 'Tu l'as voulu, Georges Dandin.'

[2] Upon this Valerius Maximus quoted below says 'caput autem *plurimis et pretiosissimis odoribus* cremandum curauit'; the author of the *de Vir. Illustr.* 78. 6 '*honorifice* sepeliri fecit.' Lucan makes Caesar say, IX 1089 sqq., 'uos condite busto | tanti colla ducis sed non, ut crimina solum | uestra tegat tellus; iusto date *tura* sepulcro | et placate caput cineresque in litore fusos | colligite atque unam sparsis date manibus urnam.'

[3] On the whole incident compare Livy, *periocha* 112 'Caesar post tertium diem insecutus cum ei Theodotus caput Pompei et anulum obtulisset, †infensus (*usually corrected to* offensus, *perhaps* incensus *Nepos,* Eum. 10), est et inlacrimauit'; Valerius Maximus 5. 1. 10 (caput Pompei) 'abscisum a corpore, inops rogi, nefarium Aegyptiae perfidiae munus, portatum est ipsi uictori miserabile: ut enim id Caesar aspexit, oblitus hostis, soceri uoltum induit ac Pompeio cum proprias tum et filiae suae (i.e. Iuliae) lacrimas reddidit, caput autem plurimis et pretiosissimis odoribus cremandum curauit'; Plut. *Caes.* 48; Dio 42. 8. 1; Appian 2. 89, 90. As to Caesar's weeping, besides the passages already cited see Eutropius 6. 21. 3 'quo conspecto Caesar etiam lacrimas fudisse dicitur, tanti uiri intuens caput et generi quondam sui.'

Caesar was Caesar, and the 'peace-offering' had failed to propitiate. But Theodotus kept the influence he had acquired with the Egyptian court until the close of the Alexandrian War[1]. Before long however its price had to be paid.

After the defeat and death of his pupil and his associates he deemed it advisable to quit Egypt; and he wandered about Asia, destitute and execrated. Here he was found after the death of Caesar by the Liberators, Brutus and Cassius, and was executed by Brutus, or, according to Appian 2, c. 89, hanged by Cassius, after suffering every kind of indignity (Βροῦτος...αὐτὸν πᾶσαν αἰκίαν αἰκισάμενος ἀπέκτεινε, Plutarch, *Pomp*. c. 80 fin., cf. *Brut*. 33).

Fate of Theodotus.

From Ptolemy down everyone of those who had compassed the death of Pompey came to a violent end. But Appian, l. c., is wrong in supposing that this was the crime for which Pothinus and Achillas were put to death; though a Pompeian poet may be excused the fancy that the hand of Caesar wielded the sword of Nemesis: Lucan x 515 sq. 'nec poenas inde Pothini | distulit ulterius; sed non qua debuit ira, | non cruce, non flammis rapuit, non dente ferarum. | heu facinus! gladio ceruix male caesa pependit: | *Magni morte perit*,' 523 sq. 'terribilem iusto transegit Achillea ferro. | *altera*, Magne, *tuis* iam *uictima* mittitur *umbris*.' Florus 4. 2. 55 has the same idea, '*ultionem* clarissimi uiri *manibus* quaerente Fortuna.'

When the instructions of Caesar had been carried out and the head consumed, the ashes were placed in a mortuary chapel, or shrine, in the centre of a plot of ground a little way out of Alexandria which was named 'The "Sanctuary" of Nemesis' (Νεμέσεως τέμενος). This we learn from Appian, *B. C.* 2, c. 90 fin., who

The head is placed in the 'Sanctuary of Nemesis.'

---

[1] See Livy, *periocha* 112 'Caesar, dictator creatus, Cleopatram in regnum Aegypti reduxit et inferentem bellum Ptolemaeum *eisdem auctoribus quibus Pompeium interfecerat* cum magno suo discrimine uicit,' which is to be compared with the words of Florus, 4. 2. 60, who is here clearly drawing from Livy, 'Theodotus *magister auctorque* belli' (the Alexandrine war).

adds that the shrine was standing within his own time, but was pulled down during the revolt of the Jews in Egypt in the reign of Trajan (117 A.D.), these people (who had certainly no cause to reverence anything belonging to Pompey) using it for purposes of the war[1].

Curiously enough, the memory of Pompey is even now kept 'Pompey's Pillar' in Alexandria. alive in Alexandria. The granite column which stands on the highest part of the city is popularly known as POMPEY'S PILLAR. It has no right to the title, which does not seem to go further back than the fifteenth century of our era and to have been due to a legend, whose source is obscure, that it was connected in some way with a cinerary urn containing the head of Pompey[2].

In connexion with the burial-place of Pompey two other passages must be considered.

The first is an anonymous epigram, quoted by the scholiast on Hor. *A. P.* 301 and discussed by Madvig, *Opuscula Academica*, pp. 562 sqq.:

Variant Accounts.
The Epigram on Licinus.

> Marmoreo Licinus tumulo iacet; at Cato paruo,
>   Pompeius *nullo*. quis putet esse deos?

It appears to have been written on the wealthy freedman of Augustus who lived on into the reign of Tiberius. It cannot then be earlier than 14 A.D. and may well be later, since the splendour of the tomb of Licinus is mentioned by Martial (8. 3. 6). It would seem then that the *nullo* is to be explained

---

[1] καί τι αὐτῇ τέμενος βραχὺ πρὸ τῆς πόλεως περιτεθὲν Νεμέσεως τέμενος ἐκαλεῖτο· ὅπερ ἐπ' ἐμοῦ, κατὰ ʿΡωμαίων αὐτοκράτορα Τραιανὸν ἐξολλύντα τὸ ἐν Αἰγύπτῳ ʾΙουδαίων γένος, ὑπὸ τῶν ʾΙουδαίων ἐς τὰς πολέμου χρείας κατηρείφθη. τέμενος, like *templum* with which it is connected, is occasionally used, as by Herodotus in more than one passage, of the building erected on consecrated ground as well as the ground itself. This τέμενος would have the same sacred character as the *fanum* which Cicero proposed to put up to the memory of his daughter Tullia, *ad Att.* 12. 18 and 19. Dio 51. 20. 6, 7 uses τέμενος, τεμενίσαι of the temples erected by Augustus to Iulius Caesar in Rome and by the inhabitants of Asia to Augustus.

[2] See Botti, *Fouilles à la Colonne Théodosienne*, p. 14.

by the disappearance of the grave of Pompey under the sand, of which we have already spoken, and that the epigram, at first sight strange, falls into line with the other evidence.

The second passage is the concluding sentence of Plutarch's *Life of Pompey*, which states that Cornelia was allowed to take home the remains of Pompey, and that she buried them on his Alban estate: τὰ δὲ λείψανα τοῦ Πομπηίου Κορνηλία δεξαμένη κομισθέντα περὶ τὸν Ἀλβανὸν ἔθηκεν.

The Version of Plutarch.

This version of the facts, which considered by itself is not wholly impossible, inasmuch as Cornelia was amnestied by Caesar and permitted to return to Rome (Dio 42. 5. 7), has been hastily assumed to be true; and Lucan has in consequence been accused of very impudent fabrication. If the 'remains' of Pompey included, as we should expect, the ashes of both head and trunk, the statement of Plutarch is incompatible with the rest of the testimony; nor is there aught to confirm it elsewhere, unless we count as such the order which Lucan puts into Caesar's mouth (IX 1093 sq.; compare the hope expressed in VIII 772 sqq.) that head and trunk are to be reunited. Since in a matter of personality the head is of paramount importance[1] (as some commentators might have remembered at 434), Cornelia may, like the Isabella of Boccaccio and Keats, have rested content with recovering this[1]. Its ashes would, of course, have been collected into an urn, while those of the trunk were merely covered with the soil of a hastily dug grave.

Another difficulty meets us when we attempt to fix a date for the supposed removal of the remains. After Caesar's return to Rome from Alexandria, 47 B.C., the whole of Pompey's property was confiscated and sold by auction, as we learn from the second *Philippic* of Cicero[2] and elsewhere. Antony was the chief purchaser, but the Alban estate was acquired by Dolabella and was in his possession when Cicero delivered the thirteenth *Philippic*, 43 B.C.[3] How can these facts be reconciled with the

[1] It is worth observing in this connexion that Lucan says, l.c., IX 1092, 'et placate *caput*.'

[2] Cic. *Phil.* II 64.   [3] Cic. *Phil.* XIII 11, cited by Ussani.

story of Plutarch, if the incident it narrates is to be placed in
Caesar's or in Dolabella's lifetime? Again, does anyone imagine
that Cicero would have made no reference, neither in letters nor
in speeches, to so striking an occurrence? If he does, let him
read the sections of the second *Philippic* relating to Pompey
and reflect how much self-restraint he is imputing to the orator.
Nor can we place it anywhere in the next thirteen years. It is
true that there were negotiations and agreements for the restoration to Sextus Pompeius of his paternal estates. But they all
came to nothing. And after his defeat and death, was the time
auspicious for a petition on behalf of the ashes of the 'pirate's'
father[1]? When in 30 B.C. Octavian settled the affairs of Egypt
at Alexandria he may have given permission for the removal of
the head from the resting-place assigned to it by his venerated
'parent.' This shadowy possibility is the most that we are
warranted in conceding; and it leaves without explanation the
profound silence of antiquity upon an exhibition of magnanimity
hardly to be expected from one who was anything rather than
a 'Pompeian.'

In any case, whatever the origin, whatever the explanation
of the contradiction, we must abstain from using it to impugn
the credit of our poet, who has but adopted what was certainly
the current and probably the true account of his hero's sepulture.

---

[1] 'Siculus pirata,' VI 422.

EXCURSUS A

ON THE ROUTE AND CHRONOLOGY OF POMPEY'S FLIGHT

The beginning and the end of Pompey's flight may be determined with an approximation to certainty; but the data for the intervening portion, that is for his course from Mytilene to Cyprus, are very scanty, and the chronology is more uncertain than the route.

In the following reconstruction careful account is taken of the various considerations which may affect its conclusions. Its method is to strike a balance between contending possibilities; and its results claim at most to be reasonably probable. In drawing it up I have utilised the discussions of two predecessors, Baron Stoffel in his account of the closing scenes of Pompey's life, *Histoire de Jules César, Guerre Civile,* 2 pp. 32 sqq., and W. Judeich, *Caesar im Orient,* pp. 53 sqq. I have also had the advantage of liberal help and instructive criticism from Dr T. Rice Holmes, the accomplished historian of Caesar.

The determination of the earliest stage of Pompey's flight cannot be separated from that of Caesar's immediate pursuit. Caesar was not more than a day behind Pompey at Larisa, nor more than a day behind him at Amphipolis; and these coincidences must be strictly regarded. Stoffel and Judeich agree in the time to be allotted to Pompey's voyage to Amphipolis; but they differ widely in their estimates of the time required for the land march of Caesar. Assuming that Caesar took the direct road through Thessalonica, the total distance to be covered between Larisa and Amphipolis would be about

184 miles according to Stoffel, and not more than 160 according to Judeich. It would seem that Stoffel has over-estimated the distance. But even if we take the lower figure, Judeich's two days, or two days and a half, is completely out of the question. Such a march, even for cavalry, would be a physical impossibility. But Stoffel's estimate, seven days, is too high, and cannot be made to square with the arrival of Caesar at Amphipolis so soon after that of Pompey. It is to be observed, as Dr Holmes has pointed out to me, and as apparently Judeich also has seen, that the words 'cognito Caesaris aduentu' of *B. C.* 3. 102. 4 may just as well mean 'learning of the coming' or 'approach' as 'learning of the arrival' of Caesar. They would be satisfied if Caesar were then say 20 miles from the town. In this way, the distance to be accounted for could be brought down to some 140 miles, and Stoffel's estimate of seven days proportionally reduced. It would seem, furthermore, that Stoffel has not allowed sufficiently for the *celeritas* of Caesar[1], on which see Drumann *Geschichte Roms* (ed. Groebe) 3, pp. 671 and 723, where it is shown that in order to prevent the junction of the Haedui with Vercingetorix (*B. G.* 7. 40—41) Caesar marched his infantry, four legions, and the whole of his cavalry, over 20,000 men in all, some 46 miles in less than 20 hours, which is three times as fast as the average rate of German foot-soldiers; nor again for the urgency of this particular pursuit, unmistakable as it is in the emphatic language of the pursuer himself, as quoted above p. xxviii n. That the 140 to 145 miles *could* be covered in four days has been shown by experience. This was done in two instances during the Indian Mutiny, as I have learned from Dr Holmes. That the road taken was not unfavourable to the rapid movement of cavalry (from Larisa to Amphipolis through Thessalonica and Apollonia) may be seen from the contours in Murray's map of Northern Graecia; for the major part of the distance it passes over plains. If the rate of travelling laid a toll, even a heavy toll, on his horses, what was that to Caesar compared with the importance of fore-

[1] This *celeritas* would of course prevent the news of Caesar's coming reaching Pompey much in advance of his actual approach.

stalling Pompey in Macedonia? We can gather from what Caesar himself tells us about Pompey's proclamation in Amphipolis, and from the intimation in Lucan (14 sqq.) that volunteers from this quarter were still flocking to his camp, that there was still a considerable danger of a strong Pompeian force being raised in these regions. From the Larisaeans and from those among the following of Pompey who had been dismissed on the coast, supra p. xxvi, Caesar would hear of the escape of his opponent by sea. His destination might not be known, but it was not difficult to divine it. It was however known that he had at present no force at his disposal, and the actual or imminent arrival of even a small detachment of cavalry from the victorious army would be sufficient to prevent his collecting one.

There is another reason why the time allotted to Caesar's march by land must be a minimum. The normal duration of a voyage[1] from the mouth of the river Peneus to Amphipolis may be taken as two full days, and this is the estimate of both Judeich and Stoffel. Now it is perfectly possible that in Pompey's case this time was somewhat exceeded. In fact it is more than possible : it is probable. Had Pompey made a fair run to Amphipolis, he could have counted on being there two clear days in advance of Caesar, and there was no reason why he should not have brought his vessel into port. On the other hand, if he had lost several days on the voyage, our authorities might certainly have been expected to mention a delay of such moment; and to touch at Amphipolis at all would have been a useless and indeed dangerous proceeding.

To sum up results. Pompey reached the mouth of the Peneus[2] late in the night after the battle, and left by sea for Amphipolis late in the morning or early in the afternoon of the next day. Caesar did not arrive in Larisa before the following

---

[1] The word used by Plutarch *Pomp.* c. 76 init. is παραπλεύσας. But this can hardly mean that Pompey followed the coast line all the way.

[2] The statements of Valerius Maximus 4. 5. 5 and Appian 2. 81 that he was in Larisa on the morning after the battle are erroneous.

afternoon. Late that evening, or early the next morning, he left Larisa for Amphipolis, and on the evening of the fourth day (inclusive reckoning) he was at no great distance from that place. Pompey in the meantime had arrived in Amphipolis, and received the intelligence of his enemy's pursuit either on the evening of that day or more probably on the morning of the next, when he hastily weighed anchor for Lesbos.

For the length of the voyage from Amphipolis to Mytilene we have the statement of Caesar that it took a 'few' days. 'Few' is of course an elastic expression; but we may infer from Ovid *Tristia* 5. 4. 35 sq. 'te sibi cum paucis meminit mansisse fidelem | si *paucos* aliquis *tresue duosue* uocat,' that in its normal use it would not be applied to so small a number as three, which to three and a half is the number of days reckoned by Stoffel and Judeich for the voyage in question. Caesar's use of ' paucis diebus' on the whole does not discountenance this impression. Thus in *B. C.* 2. 21. 4 it is applied to the duration of the coasting voyage from Gades to Tarraco 'say 5 or 6 days' and in *B. G.* 6. 9. 4 it means 'about 10 days[1],' while in *B. C.* 3. 106. 1 'Caesar *paucos dies* in Asia *moratus*,' the few days of his stay in Asia must, as Judeich has seen, have extended to something like 3 weeks; compare the 'paucis ante annis' (= 22 years) of *B. G.* 3. 20. 1.

It should be noticed moreover that the phrase here is interposed between two specific indications of time, the duration of Pompey's stay off Amphipolis (*una nocte* c. 102), and that of his stay in Lesbos (*biduum* ib.). So that it may be supposed that Caesar either did not know the exact duration of the sea voyage, or thought this less important than the length of Pompey's stoppages on land. We shall probably be near the mark in giving 4 days, which would cover 3 days and a half, or possibly 5 days, as the most probable figure.

At Lesbos he stopped two days, as we know from Caesar (above). Leaving it in the forenoon, he passed after sunset between Chios and the Oenussae islets, as we may gather from

---

[1] These are the estimates of Dr Holmes who has examined the Caesarian usage with this very object in view.

Lucan (159 sqq.). The details of his subsequent course are largely matters of inference, based in fact on the indications, not always as clear or exact as we could wish, in the same poet's narrative. But on the next day (cf. ib. 202) he touched at Ephesus or at a point near it, where Deiotarus took the opportunity to leave him. Two days after this he should be at Rhodes, which refused to receive him, as Cnidos probably had done before. A day from Rhodes would bring him to Phaselis in Lycia, which was his first stopping-place, and another day to Attalia, which he would thus reach some six days after leaving Lesbos[1].

The next three weeks must have been spent on the Pamphylian and Cilician coasts in making the preparations of which Caesar has given us an account, l.c. above, p. xxxvii. The two last incidents in this period would be the council of war at Syhedra and the departure of the fleet from Selinus. These are best dated from the end of the expedition. A day may be allowed for the voyage from Selinus to Paphos, which was reached before nightfall, as the story preserved by Valerius Maximus, l.c. supra p. xli, shows. As some recruiting was done in Cyprus, three clear days at least must be allowed to Pompey here. The voyage from Paphos to the coast of Egypt should not have taken more than three days. Theophanes, in his speech at the council of war, as reported by Plutarch *Pomp.* 76, says that 'Egypt is only three days' sail away.' This may well be an orator's under-statement; particularly as the distance is probably, though not certainly, to be reckoned from the Cilician sea-board[2]. Caesar, it is true, took only three days for the longer voyage from Rhodes to Alexandria; but, as we learn from Lucan IX 1000 sqq., he was helped by a strong breeze behind, whereas Pompey had the wind against him. All things considered, we must allow at least three full days, and perhaps nearer four days, for this portion of Pompey's flight. What was left of the day of his arrival in Pelusium would suffice for the continuation of the voyage to Mount Casius, for which the wind

---

[1] Five to six days is Judeich's estimate for the voyage.

[2] See above, pp. xxxviii n. 2, xlii n. 1.

was now favourable, while all the subsequent events, as set forth in pp. xlviii sqq. above, may, without crowding, be assigned to the following morning and afternoon.

In the subjoined chronological table the dates are given both according to the unreformed pre-Julian calendar and also according to the true or Julian reckoning. The double dating is necessary, as confusion of the reputed and the actual calendar has betrayed Lucan into bringing Pompey to Pelusium at the autumnal equinox, instead of in the middle of the summer; and M. Pichon, in a passage devoted to showing that Lucan's 'astronomical periphrases enable us to discover the date of such or such an event,' repeats the poet's statement with an error of his own, ' Pompée est parti de Paphos pour l'Égypte lors de l'équinoxe d'automne,' op. cit. p. 158.

CHRONOLOGICAL TABLE

The synchronisms of the dates of the reformed and the unreformed reckoning are given according to the Appendix in vol. 3 of Drumann's *Geschichte Roms*, ed. P. Groebe, pp. 753 sqq.

48 B.C.

June 7 (=*August* 9).			BATTLE OF PHARSALIA decided about midday. Pompey flies past *Larisa* through Vale of Tempe. Late at night reaches the *Mouth of the Peneus*.
,, 8 (	,,	10).	Midday or afternoon. Leaves by sea for *Amphipolis*.
			Afternoon or evening. Caesar arrives at Larisa.
,, 9 (	,,	11).	Morning (at latest). Caesar leaves Larisa.
,, 12 (	,,	14).	Pompey arrives off Amphipolis.
			Caesar approaching Amphipolis.
,, 13 (	,,	15).	Morning. Pompey hears of Caesar's coming and leaves Amphipolis for Lesbos.
			Evening. Caesar arrives in Amphipolis.
,, 16 (	,,	18).	Pompey arrives in *Lesbos*.
,, 19 (	,,	21).	Forenoon. Leaves Lesbos.
			Evening. Passes *Chios* and the *Oenussae* islets.
,, 20 (	,,	22).	Evening. Touches at (or near) *Ephesus*.
,, 21 (	,,	23).	Leaves Ephesus.
,, 23 (	,,	25).	Arrives at *Rhodes* but is not received.
,, 24 (	,,	26).	Arrives at *Phaselis*.
,, 25 (	,,	27).	Leaves Phaselis.
			Arrives at *Attalia*.

June 26 (*August* 28) to July 16 (*September* 19).

        Pompey on the *Pamphylian* and *Cilician* coasts.

        War Council at *Syhedra*.

                Towards the end of June (*August*) Caesar arrives in Asia.

July 16 (*September* 19).			Pompey leaves *Cilicia* (*Selinus*).
,, 17 (	,,	20).	Arrives at *Paphos*.
,, 21 (	,,	24).	Early morning. Leaves Paphos.
,, 24 (	,,	27).	Arrives at *Pelusium*, early afternoon.
			Arrives at *Mt Casius* (night, before dawn).
July 25 (*September* 28).			MURDER OF POMPEY.

EXCURSUS B

ETHNOGRAPHICAL AND GEOGRAPHICAL

I. General Considerations

When considering the inaccuracies which the Roman poets permitted or excused themselves in the employment of Proper Names, there are two habits for which we have first to make a liberal allowance—the use of the name of a Part instead of the name of the Whole; and the use of Typical epithets in lieu of Descriptive ones. Both these are 'learned' uses. The first supposes, for example, that the reader has sufficient geographical knowledge to perceive that '*Nile*, tuus tibicen erat' (Propertius 4. 8. 39) means simply that the flute-player came from Egypt. And the second that, when he finds the nomad herdsman of Libya moving his 'armaque *Amyclaeum*que canem *Cressam*que pharetram' in Vergil *Georg.* 3. 345, he will understand this to mean that the herdsman takes with him his good dog (let us call it 'Spartan') and his trusty quiver (let us call it 'Cretan'). Of these inaccuracies, as well as of others, such as the usage of *Medus* and *Persa* for *Parthus*, for which Lucan might plead the example of his predecessors, we take no account in what follows; and we leave out of the reckoning also anything that may be regarded as merely verbal extravagance.

II. Parthians and the Parthian Empire

The remoteness and the loose and fluctuating composition of the great Parthian Empire—a central government commanding a comparatively small area with a large environment of dependent or semi-dependent kingdoms—opened a wide door to misconception and exaggeration. And in judging the expressions of Lucan we should allow for this the greatest possible amplitude.

Susa then, and *Babylon* (425 sq.), may pass for Parthian cities, though they could hardly either of them be pulled down on the graves of Romans who fell at Carrhae, any more than the Euphrates, and still less the Tigris, could carry away the bodies of the slain (437 sqq.). But *Bactra* (423, cf. 299) never belonged to the Parthian Empire. nor is it easy to see why it should be called *Medorum sedes*. *Persis* (229 n.) was one of the kingdoms within the Parthian zone. The same cannot be said of *Armenia*, so often the cause of strife betwixt Parthia and Rome; but the many common features of the Armenian and the Parthian civilisation[1], and the fact that, when Lucan wrote, a Parthian prince was on the throne of Armenia, sufficiently explain the use of *Armenius* for *Parthicus* (221 n.), and the mention of the Armenian river *Araxes* in 431. On the North and North East the Parthian empire reached to the Caspian and the nomad tribes of 'Scythia.' But this does not justify Lucan's making Pompey boast that the Parthians had seen him on the Don and beyond the Sea of Azof (318 sq.). Neither he nor they were ever there. Nor again were they '*Sarmaticos* inter *campos*' (369) if these are τὰ τῶν Σαρματῶν πεδία, to the north of the Caucasus, Strabo 11. 2. 15 (p. 497). *Scythicus* for *Parthicus* (302 n.) is to be differently explained. The Parthian invaders of Irān were originally a Scythian tribe, Justin 41. 1. 1, Ammianus Marcellinus 31. 2. 20 quoted on 294.

Lucan's equation, *Geticus = Scythicus = Parthicus* (221), is more arbitrary. The excuse has to be that in the land of the Getae west of the Euxine there was a considerable admixture of the 'Scythian' or 'Sarmatian' element; cf. Minns, *Scythians and Greeks*, p. 122 sq., Müllenhoff, *Deutsche Altertümer* 3, pp. 159 sqq. where a number of references from Ovid's *Tristia* and *Ex Ponto* are given.

---

[1] Mommsen, *Provinces of the Roman Empire* (Eng. Tr.) 2 p. 20.

Pompey's boasting in 226 sqq. cannot be squared with fact; but the falsification is as much historical as geographical; cf. 342 sq. On the extravagant claims put forward by Pompey and on his behalf see T. Reinach's *Mithridate Eupator*, Appendix p. 419.

In regard to the extent of the empire there is no doubt that it reached as far as the Persian Gulf and the Arabian Sea, that is the northern portion of the Indian Ocean, so that 293 sq. are strictly accurate. But though its most southerly portion fell within the Tropic of Cancer, to place any part of it in the Southern Hemisphere, as appears to be done in 292, is a gross perversion of fact.

III. THE ALANI[1]

In VIII 223 Lucan makes Pompey say that he drove before him the hardy Alani, who are always fighting. The scene of this pursuit, as is shown by the mention of the Caspian Gates (222 note) and the 'Achaemenian plains' (224) etc., is laid in the interior of Asia. The only other mention of the *Alani* is at X 454, where they are coupled with the *Scythae* 'quem non uiolasset *Alanus*, | non Scytha, non fixo qui ludit in hospite Maurus.'

Now history knows nothing of any defeat of Alani by Pompey. In fact, in his time and for long after, the Romans were ignorant of their existence. Strabo does not name them, and the first mention of them, in Josephus *Ant.* 18. § 97 (Niese), is supposed to be derived from a Parthian source. On the other hand, one of the most noticeable features of Pompey's Mithridatic campaigns was his routing of the *Albani*, a powerful tribe who lived near the 'Albanian Gates,' sometimes called the 'Caspian Gates,' on the southern spurs of the Caucasus and adjoining the Caspian Sea.

The confusion must be held to be established[2]. Is there

---

[1] On the Alani in general see E. Täubler's instructive discussion in *Klio*, vol. 9, pp. 14 sqq.

[2] The converse mistake occurs in Tac. *H.* 1. 6.

any reason or excuse for it beyond the similarity of the names[1]? It would seem that there is.

Täubler has pointed out that the first three books of Lucan were probably composed and published in the year 63 A.D.; and that in the long list of nations in III 266 sqq. there is no mention of the Alani, who first began to be troublesome in 63—64, and against whom Nero made preparations for an expedition; which however was dropped and the troops recalled, owing to the rebellion of Vindex.

Furthermore, the Alani, a branch of whom have been identified with the Ossetes of Georgia, now confined to the valleys on the north side of the Caucasus[2], are referred to as 'Scythians' as in Ptolemy 6. 14 (p. 426 Wilberg) οἱ κοινῶς καλούμενοι Ἀλανοὶ Σκύθαι; cf. Pliny *N.H.* 4. 80. And Pompey in the vainglorious *praefatio* of his triumph, preserved by Pliny *N.H.* 7. 98, claimed, we do not know on what grounds, to have triumphed over Scythians, 'ex Asia Ponto Armenia Paphlagonia Cappadocia Cilicia Syria *Scythis* Iudaeis Albanis Hiberia insula Creta Bastarnis et super haec de rege Mithridate atque Tigrane triumphauit.' And long after Lucan Ammianus Marcellinus, in the speech he attributes to Julian when he addressed his troops in Mesopotamia on his march against the Parthians, makes the Emperor say in refutation of the calumny that his was the first invasion of Parthia by the Romans, 'non nunc primitus, ut maledici mussitant, Romanos penetrasse regna Persidis. namque, ut Lucullum transeam uel Pompeium qui per *Albanos* et *Massagetas* quos *Alanos* nunc appellamus, hac quoque natione perrupta, adiuit Caspios lacus, Ventidium nouimus Antoni legatum strages per hos tractus innumeras edidisse,' 23. 5. 16.

Lucan's misplacement of the Alani may be due to some

---

[1] What Lucan is capable of in this respect may be seen from x 449 '*Thessalici*...rupe sub *Haemi*' (of Pharsalia), *Haemus* and *Haemonius* both beginning with *Haem*. A similar confusion has betrayed Silius Italicus (10. 11) into calling '*Boreas*' *Haemonian* instead of *Thracian*.

[2] Minns, *Scythians and Greeks*, pp. 35 sqq.

vague knowledge of the other branch on the south of the
Caspian in what is now Turkestan (cf. Ptolemy l. c.), but more
probably to what Pliny *N. H.* 6. 30 calls the serious confusion
(*magnus error*) of the Caspian and the Caucasian Gates. See
note on 222.

IV. Mount Taurus and the Fall of the Dipsus

A consideration of VIII 254 sq.,

> tendens hinc carbasa rursus,
> iam Taurum Tauroque uidet Dipsunta cadentem,

raises interesting questions.

After setting sail from Phaselis, as Lucan tells us, Pompey
'comes in view of Taurus and Dipsus that falls from Taurus.'

The first part of the statement presents little difficulty.
Strabo, 14. 3. 8, p. 666, says that it was the common view, from
which however he dissents himself, that the range of Taurus
started from the Sacred Promontory and the Chelidonian islets,
ἐντεῦθεν νομίζουσιν οἱ πολλοὶ ἀρχὴν λαμβάνειν τὸν Ταῦρον,
e.q.s., the equivalent in sense of the *iam* of Lucan. And Leake,
Journal of a Tour in Asia Minor (1824), p. 190, says 'The
whole coast from the ruins of Phaselis to the western corner of
the plain of Attaleia consists of a lofty mountain rising abruptly
from the shore.' Mr H. A. Ormerod, who has visited the neighbourhood in recent years[1], in a private letter to me, says 'the
Taurus range starts in the Pamphylian plain to the N., the
mountains rising sharply from the plain only a few hours from
the coast. (West of Adalia the line of the mountains changes
from E.-W. to a N. and S. direction.) Just west of Olbia they
come down close to the coast, hence the difficulty of Alexander's
march by the Climax.'

But what of the following words? A torrent or waterfall of
a *Dipsus* is otherwise unknown. But Burman long ago ad loc.

[1] 'Notes and Inscriptions from Pamphylia,' H. A. Ormerod and
E. S. G. Robinson. *Proceedings of the British School at Athens*,
vol. 17, pp. 215 sqq.

identified it with a river mentioned in Strabo l. c. 4. 1. In 3. 8 sq. the geographer says that 'from the Sacred Promontory to Olbia is a distance of 367 stades, that in this space is Crambusa and Olympus, a large town with a mountain of the same name, also called Phoenicūs, and then the beach called Corycus. After this comes Phaselis, a considerable town with three harbours and a lake. Above it is the mountain called Solyma, which commands the defile by which we pass into Milyas' (in S. W. Pisidia)....'Near Phaselis is the defile on the sea coast through which Alexander led his army. The mountain is called Climax....After this Phaselis comes Olbia, where Pamphylia begins, a great fortress. And after this the so-called *Cataractes*, a copious and torrent-like river, which precipitates itself from a lofty rock with a noise audible at a great distance (μετὰ ταύτην ὁ Καταράκτης λεγόμενος ἀφ' ὑψηλῆς πέτρας καταράττων ποταμὸς πολὺς καὶ χειμαρρώδης ὥστε πόρρωθεν ἀκούεσθαι τὸν ψόφον). Then the city of Attalia,' e. q. s.

That the *Cataractes* of Strabo and Mela, 1. 79, 'deinde alii duo ualidissimi (fluuii) Cestros et Cataractes : Cestros nauigari facilis, hic quia se praecipitat ita dictus' is the modern *Duden* authorities are generally agreed[1]; cf. G. Long in Smith's *Dict. of Classical Geography* under *Attaleia* and *Catarrhactes*. This is the opinion of Sir F. Beaufort, *Karamania* (1817), p. 127, Col. Leake, op. cit. p. 191, Mannert, *Geographie* VI ii pp. 128 sq., Spratt and Forbes, *Travels in Lycia etc.* (1847) I, 218 sqq., Count Lanckoroński, *Städte Pamphyliens und Pisidiens* I, p. xi ; and Mr Ormerod agrees. The only difficulty is that Strabo, whose description of the coast travels from E. to W., places it to the West of *Attaleia*, whereas other authorities, Ptolemy and the *Stadiasmus Maris Magni*, put it on the East, and the Duden is to the E. of Adalia.

To fix the place of the waterfall is not so easy. The words of Strabo do not tell us into what the river fell from the rock, and it is therefore natural to suppose that it fell into a basin of its own. Accordingly Mannert l.c. pp. 148 sq. places the water-fall in the interior, not far from the site of the ancient Termessos,

---

[1] On Schönborn's and Ritter's view see below.

where he says the little river Duden plunges over an enormous rock and disappears twice under the earth, until in the neighbourhood of Satalia [*Adalia*] it reaches the sea. I have been unable to discover any confirmation of this. Mr Ormerod, who has examined the lower course of the Duden and the two points where it emerges from beneath the ground, can only say: 'In these places there are great holes or cañons in the plain, and a large volume of water, in each case flowing at great speed, comes out and disappears after 100 yards or so.'

The prevalent view is that the waterfall was over the cliff where the Duden fell into the sea, and that the natural configuration of the place has changed since the time of Strabo. Leake, op. cit., p. 191, says:

> The river on approaching the coast divides itself into several branches which falling over the cliffs that border the coast from Laara to Adália form upon their upper part a mass of calcareous deposition, projecting considerably beyond the perpendicular line of the cliffs. Through the calcareous crust, the water makes its way to the sea and being thus separated into several streams by a natural process, which has been rapidly increasing in its operation in course of time, the river has no determinate mouth (as it may perhaps have had in former ages) unless it be after heavy rains, when, *as I saw it in passing along the coast, it precipitates itself copiously over the cliffs*[1] near the most projecting part of the coast a little to the W. of Laara.

Beaufort, op. cit. p. 128, says:

> A number of small rivulets which fertilise the gardens, and turn the mills near the town, rush directly over the cliff into the sea; and if these rivulets had ever been united they must have formed a considerable body of water...Now the broad and high plain which stretches to the eastward of the city terminates in *abrupt cliffs* along the shore. *The cliffs are above 100 feet* high and considerably overhang the sea; not in consequence of their base having crumbled away but from the summit projecting in a lip which consists of parallel laminae, each jutting out beyond its inferior layer as if water had been continually flowing over them

---

[1] Italics are mine. Laara is E. of Adália.

and continually forming fresh accretions. It is therefore not impossible that this accumulation may have gradually impeded the course of that body of water which had once formed a magnificent cataract and may also have forced it to divide into various channels.

Spratt and Forbes, op. cit. p. 220, assenting to Beaufort's view, add that the present appearance of the Catarrhactes 'depends on the geological structure of this part of Pamphylia,'

> the rivers of which charged with calcareous matter are continually depositing calc-tufa and changing their beds; so that, two or three centuries hence, their courses will, in all probability, be as different from those they now run as their present beds from their ancient: even the present disposition of the streams differs from that described by Captain Beaufort, doubtless having altered since his visit.

It may be added that the *Stadiasmus Maris Magni* (221), as Leake observes, speaks of τοὺς καταράκτας, which may indicate that the division of the waterfall had begun in ancient times.

For the identification of Lucan's *Dipsus* with Strabo's *Cataractes* the exact place of the waterfall is of but minor importance. But the discrepancy in the names requires consideration. If 'Cataractes' was the proper or the only name of the river, there is no reason why Lucan should not have used it; he has *cataractae* of the Nile cataracts at x 318. Is it possible that he has preserved a local name that we should otherwise have lost? It would seem that it is.

Dipsunta is obviously a Greek accusative, Διψοῦντα from Διψοῦς. This formation occurs in names of rivers elsewhere. Examples are Οἰνοῦς, Σελινοῦς, Σχοινοῦς. If it is the proper name of the river, it should express some characteristic feature of the stream. One of its peculiarities was its *fall*, which was expressed in Strabo's name for it, *Cataractes*. This name Lucan does not use, but hints at in his *cadentem*. Another peculiarity is the *quality of its waters*. On this I quote from the traveller Beaufort, who l.c. says of the rivulets of the *Duden*:

> It is remarkable that the water of these streams is so highly impregnated with calcareous particles that it is reckoned unfit for man or beast,

and again, p. 135 :

> An old fisherman cautioned us *not to drink* the water of any of the streams as it was highly deleterious.

Διψοῦς can only be a derivative from δίψα or δίψος, and mean a stream which leaves you thirsty, from which you cannot quench your thirst. This seems possible in view of the use of δίψιος with κόνις, of διψάς as the name of the 'thirsty' serpent whose venomous bite 'ebibit umorem circum uitalia fusum' Lucan IX 743 (see the whole passage) and especially of δίψιος as applied to *water* by Hermippus in his life of Pythagoras quoted by Josephus *contra Apionem* I, c. 22 (§ 164) τῶν διψίων ὑδάτων ἀπέχεσθαι, which the Latin version renders by *feculenta*. And not very dissimilar is 'pocula sicca' Lygdamus (Tib. 3.) 6. 18, which means 'draughts that do not quench the thirst' of the wine-bibber[1].

If however this explanation of *Dipsunta* should be thought too artificial, we might perhaps without violence suppose that the word is a corruption of *Gypsunta*, which would involve little more than the change of a single letter ; for $i = y$ is a perpetual misspelling in our MSS. This would be a direct reference to the calcareous quality of the water, as γύψος 'gypsum' and τίτανος 'chalk' do not seem to have kept quite distinct in usage. In Hesiod *Scut. Herc.* 141 τίτανος is generally taken to be 'gypsum' and *cretatus* (from *creta* 'white chalk') is used by Propertius 4. 5. 52 of the whitened feet of slaves for sale, for which Tibullus 2. 3. 60 uses *gypsatus*. Cf. Pliny *N.H.* 36. 182 'cognata *calci* res *gypsum* est.'

Before leaving the subject, we must mention the view of the German traveller A. Schönborn (1842) which is given in C. Ritter's *Erdkunde*, part 19, p. 639. He identifies the *Cataractes* torrent with one called *Karamani* or *Karaman*, whose beautiful falls, of which he gives a glowing description,

---

[1] A scholiast on the present passage has DIPSANTA C. 'nomen est fluuii ueluti ab *undis sitientibus* appellatum,' but what follows shows this is a guess, 'hic autem de Tauro monte profluit aut in fluuium Taurum decurrit.'

form a noticeable feature at the entrance to the lower Tschandyr valley, which lies to the west of Adalia. So far as I know, this view has not been taken by any subsequent traveller. Lanckoroński does not mention Schönborn's theory, though he marks the *Karaman Tschai* in his excellent map of the country. It comes down from the mountain heights on which the ancient Termessus stood and, so far as we can tell from the map, such a fall as Schönborn reports might well have been visible from the coast.

V. MISCELLANEOUS. 'LITTLE SAMOS'

We have not yet exhausted the list of geographical difficulties in the text of Lucan VIII.

Asinae cautes (195, Crit. App. note) and the relations of *Syhedra* and *Selinus* (259 sq.) present problems still unsolved.

'Little' (245 sq.) is an unexpected epithet for *Samos*, of which Scylax *Peripl.* 98 says αὕτη ἡ νῆσος οὐκ ἐλάσσων ἐστὶ Χίου. Apuleius *Florida* 15, § 49 says, without overstepping the facts, '*Samos* Icario in mari *modica* insula est.' Professor J. B. Bury has suggested to me that *parua* may be used to distinguish Samos from Cephallenia, an old name for which was Σάμος or Σάμη, Strabo 10. 2. 10 (p. 453)[1]. Scylax however, 114, puts Samos 10th in the list of islands after Lesbos, Rhodes and Chios, and Cephallenia 13th. Possibly Lucan was thinking of the town, and mentally contrasting it with *Ephesus*. Apuleius, l.c., says of this '*oppidum* habet *nequaquam pro gloria* sed quod *fuisse amplum* semiruta moenium multifariam indicant.'

The coast from Paphos to Cape Curias (460 sq.) does not seem to be the best route for Alexandria, *Introd.* supra p. xlii and n. 4[2]. The impression left on us by 244, 246 is certainly

---

[1] The name, taken from the Odyssey, is found in Latin also, Ovid *Met.* 13. 711, *Trist.* 1. 5. 67 'nec mihi Dulichium domus est Ithaceue Samosue.'

[2] Lucan's precision of statement '*totos* | emensus Cypri scopulos quibus exit in Austrum, | *inde* maris uasti transuerso uertitur aestu' suggests that it is deliberate and possibly a contradiction of a predecessor; compare p. xxxvi n. 4.

that Icaria is nearer to Samos than it should be[1]. But editors have agreed to desert the MSS when (at 716) they make Lucan speak of the 'Icarian' shore of Cyprus.

'Pelusian Canopus' (543) is a strange expression, but not necessarily an error; see ad loc. The Pelusian mouth of the Nile (825) needs no defence. The 'infima Aegypti litora' (464), if taken literally, happens to be correct: and so is the sailing direction for the Syrtes in 184. On the other hand, their location as regards Mt Casius (540 n., cf. 444) is very wide of the mark. This however is nothing to the outrageous falsity of the Indian geography in 228, where see the note.

For the confounding of Pharsalia and Philippi, with its attendant confusions, see VII 872 n. The predecessors of Lucan are primarily responsible.

[1] See Note on the Map, p. 146.

EXCURSUS C

THESSALIA, PHARSALIA AND PHARSALVS[1]

Thessalia has three meanings in Lucan.

(1) The whole country of *Thessaly*; e.g. at VI 333.

(2) The part of Thessaly in which the great battle was fought. It is difficult to produce an example in which this sense is beyond dispute, inasmuch as the wider signification of (1) might be fitted to most passages; but VII 164 'usque *ad Thessaliam* Romana et publica signa' is most reasonably thus understood. For the sense is not that the standards remained Roman and national till Pompey reached Thessaly,

Lucan's use of Thessalia and of Pharsalia,

which he did at VI 332, 'contigit *Emathiam* bello quam fata parabant. | *Thessaliam*,' e.q.s.; but that they remained so till he reached the place of battle.

(3) The great battle itself, e.g. at VIII 45.

Pharsalia, which occurs 15 times in the poem, has two meanings.

(1) The district round about Pharsalus, where the battle was fought; its normal signification both in Greek (Polyb. 18. 3. 6 περὶ τὸ Θετίδειον τῆς Φαρσαλίας al.), and Latin (Pliny, *N.H.* 6. 216, Ov. *M.* 15. 823 infra, Tac. *H.* 2. 38 'in Pharsalia ac Philippis,' VII 175, 535).

(2) The battle itself, in VIII 273 and 11 other places.

---

[1] In this excursus I have drawn freely from my paper entitled *Pharsalia nostra* and published in the *Classical Review*, vol. 19 (1905), pp. 257—260.

It has also been thought, in IX 985, to have a third sense, the poem of Lucan or a portion thereof. But a close examination of the passage (a remarkable one) shows this to be inexact. The words are these:

> o sacer et magnus uatum labor, omnia fato   980
> eripis et populis donas mortalibus aeuum.
> inuidia sacrae, Caesar, ne tangere famae;
> nam si quid Latiis fas est promittere Musis,
> quantum Zmyrnaei durabunt uatis honores,
> uenturi *me teque* legent; *Pharsalia nostra*   985
> uiuet et a nullo tenebris damnabimur aeuo.

Pharsalia nostra here does not mean 'my tale of Pharsalia shall live.' It means 'the memory of Pharsalia in which you and I, Caesar, have a share, shall never die'; and the same two persons are meant in the 'we' of *damnabimur*. The passage gains much in force when thus interpreted. *V.* 982 is addressed to Iulius Caesar, but its phrasing seems to glance at another Caesar whose 'envy' of Lucan's 'divine fame' (as a *sacer uates*) had forced the poet into ignominious silence[1].

In Lucan then Thessalia is practically a synonym for Pharsalia, and the usage of the nouns is followed by the corresponding adjectives **Thessalicus** and **Pharsalicus**[2].

---

[1] The claim in 984 is worth attention. Lucan directly challenged the title of Vergil to be the Homer of Latin epic. Compare the epigram quoted on p. xci n. 1 (in which *Simoenta* typifies the *Iliad*, cf. e.g. Prop. 3. 1. 27 sqq.), Lucan's own phrase 'et quantum mihi restat ad *Culicem*?' and in his behoof Statius *Silu.* 2. 7. 79 sq. 'quin maius loquar. ipsa te Latinis | Aeneis uenerabitur canentem,' much more than he hoped for his own Thebaid *Theb.* 12. 816 sq. 'nec tu diuinam Aeneida tempta, | sed *longe sequere* et *uestigia* semper *adora.*' It is curious, in fact surprising, that Shelley in a letter to T. J. Hogg, of Sept. 1815 (no. vii in Garnett's *Select Letters of Percy Bysshe Shelley*), takes the same view as Lucan, 'I have also read the four first books of Lucan's " Pharsalia " a poem, as it appears to me, of wonderful genius and transcending Vergil.'

[2] The need for a synonym for the battle does not appear to have been felt before the Seventh Book was reached. Up till then *Pharsalia*

To give some examples: VII 164 'Thessaliam' (already quoted), 175 'Pharsalia,' 454 'Thessaliae,' 591 sq. addressed to Brutus 'nec tibi fatales admoueris ante *Philippos*, | *Thessalia* periture tua*'; IX 232 sq. 'nam quis erit finis si nec *Pharsalia* pugnae | nec Pompeius erit?' 849 'reddite *Thessaliam*,' 1084 '*Thessaliae* fortuna'; VII 787 '*Pharsalica* damna,' 448 '*Thessalicas*—caedes,' 302 '*Thessalicae*—orae,' 823 '*Pharsalica* rura'; IX 1073 'in *Thessalicis*—aruis.' For book VIII it is enough to cite the numbers of the lines: 'Thessali*am -ae, -ā*,' 45, 108, 428, 441, 510, 602; 'Pharsali*ă*,' 273; 'Thessalic-*ae, -ās, -ōs*,' 331, 507, 530; 'Pharsalic*ă*,' 14, 516[1].

Besides these two names and the adjectives associated with them, Lucan has in one place, in a paragraph of borrowed geographical and ethnographical learning, the name **Pharsalos,** of Pharsalus.

>   melius mansura sub undis
> Emathis aequorei regnum Pharsalos Achillis
> eminet, et prima Rhoeteia litora pinu
> quae tetigit Phylace Pteleosque et Dorion ira
> flebile Pieridum e.q.s.   VI 349 sqq.

where, as the context, of which I have quoted only a part, with

---

and *Pharsalicus* are alone employed in this connexion, I 38, III 297, IV 803, VI 313, V 391.

[1] This use of *Thessalia* seems to have attracted attention in ancient times. For an epigram in verse with the superscription *Caesaris*, Anthol. Lat. 233 (Riese), runs as follows, 'Mantua, da ueniam, fama sacrata perenni; | sit fas *Thessaliam* post Simoenta legi,' where one MS Par. 8209 has *Pharsalia* just as at Statius *Ach.* I. 152 the best MS corrupts *Thessaliae* into *Pharsaliae*.

If M. Pichon had fully realised that to Lucan the words were absolute synonyms as names for the battle, he would hardly have offered as a defence for the poet's use of *Philippi* the incompatibility of *Pharsāliam* and *Pharsāliā* with his metre, p. 111 n. 1, 'Sur six passages cités plus haut, *Philippi* est cinq fois à l'accusatif et une fois à l'ablatif, c'est-à-dire toujours à des cas où la forme correspondante de *Pharsalia* ne pourrait entrer dans un hexamètre.'

its series of proper names sufficiently indicates, both a town and a district are included under the title of *Pharsalos*.

At the time of the Civil Wars there were two places of this name, distinguished as Old and New Pharsalus respectively (Strabo 9. 5. 6, p. 431). And it was near the former, or *Palaepharsalus*, that the battle was fought (*Bellum Alexandrinum* 48, Strabo 17. 1. 11, p. 796, Frontinus *Strat.* 2. 3. 22, Orosius 6. 15. 27, Eutropius 6. 16). It was from the more ancient town of course that the district received its name. And Lucan is no doubt correct, whether by design or not is immaterial, when he connects the name *Pharsalus* both with the famous hero and the no less famous conflict, just as the author of the *Bellum Alexandrinum* (c. 42) is correct in calling the battle 'proelium *Pharsalicum*' instead of inventing pedantically the appellation 'proelium *Palaepharsalicum.*' The foundation of New Pharsalus, whenever this happened, could obviously make no difference to the appellation of the district; but, as in other instances, for example with our own towns *Salisbury* and *Old Sarum* (an abbreviation of Sar*isberia*) the more ancient place sank into insignificance; and then it was the New town with which the district was associated.

Pharsalia the district of Palaephar-salus and (New) Pharsalus.

This is the explanation of what at first sight seems very strange, that contemporary writers for the most part do not tell us where the great battle was fought. Caesar in each of the three places of his *Civil War* where the battle is mentioned calls it 'proelium *in Thessalia* factum' (3. 100. 3, 101. 7, 111. 3). For Cicero it is the *Pharsalicum proelium*, the *Pharsalica acies*, the *Pharsalia pugna*, the *Pharsalia fuga*, and so on.

Cicero's expressions do not surprise us. But we must confess to some astonishment that Caesar should have thought 'the battle fought in Thessaly' an adequate designation. Perhaps the mystery may be unravelled.

When the area covered by the name of a region or of a people is shifted or enlarged, its old and limited application does not necessarily disappear. It often lives on to inform or puzzle the antiquary: cf. note on 'Haemoniae' VIII 1.

Now an unchallenged tradition declares that the Thessali were immigrant Thesprotians; and the district which they would seize and settle first is that region of Thessaly which as early as Herodotus was called *Thessalietis* or *Thessaliotis*. Θεσσαλιῆτις (-ῶτις) is a derivative from Θεσσαλία *Thessalia*: and this derivative was called into being by the inconvenience of giving a whole country and a quarter of it one and the same name. That the name 'Thessalian' continued in use for the region of Thessaly that was nearest to Thesprotia, we may learn from the words of Strabo 9. 5. 3, p. 430, '(Of the four divisions of Thessaly) Phthiotis comprises the southern portions extending along Oeta from the gulf of Malis or Thermopylae and spreading out till they reach Pharsalus and the Thessalian plains (πλατυνόμενα δὲ μέχρι Φαρσάλου καὶ τῶν πεδίων τῶν Θετ-ταλικῶν).' These 'Thessalian plains' of Strabo are the 'Pharsalian plains' ('*Pharsalii* campi') of Pliny *N.H.* 4. 29, 8. 55.

'Thessalia' of Pharsalia and Thessaliotis.

When therefore Caesar speaks of the 'proelium *in Thessalia* factum,' we are not to thrust upon his words the meaning 'the battle fought *in Thessaly*': with hardly less unreason should we make Field-Marshal French talk, not of the battle of Ypres, but of the battle 'fought in Flanders' (and Flanders has a smaller area than Thessaly). But we are to understand that he is adopting the ancient local appellation, still applied to the district in which lay the two Pharsaluses, Old and New. If it be asked why did he not give the more specific designation 'at Palaepharsalus,' the answer has already been suggested. Pharsalus the New, the modern *Férsala*, was an important place with a considerable rôle in history. Pharsalus the Old has escaped oblivion solely through its connexion with our battle. At the time of the engagement it can hardly have been more than 'an insignificant hamlet' (*C. R.* l. c. p. 260*a*); and, for all the difference it made, the armies might have fought in the open fields.

A short excursion into the realm of mythology may be excused us. The appearance of the cult of a goddess, whose connexion with the sea is, so to speak, always being underlined

Thetis a goddess of the invading Thessali. by our authorities, in the interior of a country which is ramparted by mountains from every point of the compass (compare Herodotus 7. 129), is. at first sight astonishing; and the resemblance of Θέτι-s to Θεσσαλοί, easily derivable by a common phonetic law of Greek from Θετιαλοί, hardly less striking. An obvious explanation is that this immigrant tribe of the maritime Thesprotians brought their goddess with them and established her in the fertile fields of 'Thessalia,' at *Thetideum* (so named after the stranger), whose importance as the chief seat of her worship is clear from Euripides (infr.) and Strabo 9. 5. 6, p. 431.

Myths, it is now well understood, are often pre-historic history; and the legends preserved or indicated in Pindar and **Meaning of the Thetis and Peleus myth.** Euripides shed and receive new light when connected with this 'Thessalian' invasion. In the well-known legend of the struggle between Thetis, the stranger from the West, and Peleus, whose associations are with Pelion and Aegina in the East, and its termination in a marriage alliance, it is not difficult to trace the outlines of a settlement of the affairs of Thessaly after their disturbance by the inroad. Other significant features in the story, which we only want more details to interpret with precision, are the reappearance of the grandson of Thetis and Peleus in Epirus, the native land of the former, and the capture of Iolcus by Peleus and his surrender of it to the Haemonians. It is worth while transcribing the passages from Pindar and Euripides in full. *Nem.* 4. 50 sqq. Θέτις δὲ κρατεῖ | Φθίᾳ· Νεοπτόλεμος δ' Ἀπείρῳ διαπρυσίᾳ, | βουβόται τόθι πρῶνες ἔξοχοι κατάκεινται | Δωδώναθεν (the close connexion of Thetis and Zeus in the myth will at once occur to the reader) ἀρχόμενοι πρὸς Ἰόνιον πόρον. | Παλίου δὲ πὰρ ποδὶ λατρίαν Ἰαωλκὸν | πολεμίᾳ χερὶ προστραπὼν | Πηλεὺς παρέδωκεν Αἱμόνεσσιν, | δάμαρτος Ἱππολύτας Ἀκάστου δολίαις | τέχναισι χρησάμενος. On Thetis a Pindar scholiast quotes Pherecydes (fragm. 16· ed. Muell.) ἔοικε δὲ ὁ Πίνδαρος μνημονεύειν τοῦ Θετιδείου περὶ οὗ ἐν πρώτῳ Φερεκύδης οὕτω γράφει· ἔπειτα Πηλεὺς ᾤχετο εἰς Φθίαν, καὶ Θέτιν ἐπὶ τῶν ἵππων τούτων ἄγων οἰκεῖ ἐν Φαρσάλῳ καὶ ἐν Θετιδείῳ ὃ καλεῖται ἀπὸ τῆς Θέτιδος ἡ πόλις. Another scholiast quotes a long passage from Phylarchus giving an account of an incident affecting Thetis and Hephaestos, which thus concludes : τὴν δὲ κακῶς διατεθεῖσαν ἐλθεῖν εἰς Θετταλίαν καὶ ἰαθῆναι ἐν τῇ πόλει τῇ ἀπ' αὐτῆς Θετιδείῳ καλουμένῃ. Euripides *Andromache* 16 sqq. Φθίας δὲ τῆσδε καὶ πόλεως Φαρσαλίας | σύγχορτα ναίω πεδί' ἵν' ἡ θαλασσία | Πηλεῖ ξυνῴκει χωρὶς ἀνθρώπων Θέτις | φεύγουσ' ὅμιλον· Θεσσαλὸς δέ νιν (the πεδία) λεὼς | Θετίδειον αὐδᾷ θεᾶς χάριν νυμφευμάτων· | ἔνθ' οἶκον ἔσχε τόνδε παῖς Ἀχιλλέως, | ζῶντος γέροντος σκῆπτρον οὐ θέλων λαβεῖν. For the connexion of Peleus, Pelios and Iolcus see 1277 sq., and ib. 1265 sq. ἐλθὼν παλαιᾶς χοιράδος κοῖλον μυχὸν | Σηπιάδος ἵζου, and for the establishment of the descendants of Neoptolemus in Epirus ib. 1246 sqq., which agrees with Pindar *Nem.* 7. 38 sqq.

The passage of Euripides just quoted raises an interesting question of ancient topography. Where and what was the PHTHIA of Homer, whether it was not both a town and a territory, as it may well have been, has been from ancient times

Palae-pharsalus the ancient PHTHIA, home of Achilles.

obscure. See e.g. Ebeling's *Lexicon Homericum* s.u. Φθίη and the authorities there cited. Strabo, 9. 5. 6, p. 431, speaking of Ἑλλάς and Φθίη, puts the matter in a nutshell ὁ μὲν οὖν ποιητὴς (Homer) δύο ποιεῖ, πότερον δὲ πόλεις ἢ χώρας οὐ δηλοῖ.

In the quotation from the *Nemeans* of Pindar the correspondence of Φθία to Ἀπείρῳ suggests that it is the district where Thetis and her cult were established that the poet has in view.

But that in the *Andromache* it is primarily the name of a town is an obvious conclusion from the way it is used in the extract first quoted (16 sqq.). The correspondence of the names is strikingly illustrated by another passage of Euripides where σύγχορτος occurs, *Fr. Antiope* (179 Nauck) Οἰνόη | σύγχορτα ναίω πεδία ταῖς τ' Ἐλευθέραις, and enables us at once to draw the proportion that Φθία is to the πόλις Φαρσαλία as Oenoe is to Eleutherae; cf. also l. 1176 (infr.).

Leake in his *Travels in Northern Greece* identifies Phthia with (New) Pharsalus. He says, vol. 4, p. 484, 'It is generally believed among the Greeks of Thessaly, having any pretence to erudition, that Férsala is the site of an ancient city Phthia, capital of the homonymous district, Pharsalus not being acknowledged by them as an ancient name. That the city as well as the district was named Phthia at a remote period is not an absurd supposition, as Pharsalus is not mentioned by Homer, though it was probably the capital of Phthiotis,' e.q.s. Weight undoubtedly attaches to what is urged by Leake; but a consideration of all the facts points to another conclusion. The words of Euripides mean that a place called *Thetideum* lies between *Phthia* and a 'city of Pharsalus,' which city to Euripides would be New Pharsalus. Now Strabo (p. 431) says that Thetideum lies between Old and New Pharsalus. 'In this district is also Thetideum which is near to both the Pharsaluses, the Old and the New' (ἐν δὲ τῇ χώρᾳ ταύτῃ καὶ τὸ Θετίδειον ἔστι πλησίον[1] τῶν Φαρσάλων ἀμφοῖν τῆς τε παλαιᾶς καὶ τῆς νέας). The inference seems inevitable. *Phthia* is *Palaepharsalus*. And the usage of 'Thessalian' as set out in what precedes enables us to see why in *v.* 1176 *Phthia* is apostrophised as ὦ πόλι Θεσσαλία.

The statements of ancient writers that Achilles reigned in Pharsalus or came from Pharsalus (Lucan l.c., Schol. *Il.* 23. 142) are no longer mysterious. We have only to bear in mind that 'Pharsalus' means *Palaepharsalus*, and that this is the ancient town of *Phthia*.

To return to Lucan. His choice of nomenclature for the battle we are now in a position to understand. *Palaepharsalus*, the most exact of all the appellations, he would reject as bizarre and unwieldy. But he did not choose to cut it down until it was indistinguishable from a well-known town which had no connexion with the battle. Perhaps, unlike Drumann and

Ancient nomenclature of the battlefield: (1) 'Palaepharsalus.'

---

[1] This does not necessarily mean that Old and New Pharsalus were themselves very near together, as I pointed out in *Classical Review*,

Mommsen and their long tail of adherents, he felt that to name it Pharsalus would be a needless obscuration of historical truth ; or perhaps, again unlike these votaries of historical science, the rhetorical poet was merely proof against the temptation to displace the designation of contemporary witnesses for an invention of his own[1].

In any case he had before him two names of almost identical signification applied by accredited predecessors to the scene of the event he would describe, *Thessalia* and *Pharsalia*, with their related adjectives *Thessalicus* and *Pharsalicus*. It was true that neither of these names had, so far as we know, been as yet applied to the engagement. For in Ovid *Met.* 15. 822 sqq. 'illius auspiciis obsessae moenia pacem | uicta petent *Mutinae : Pharsalia* sentiet illum | Emathiaque iterum madefient caede *Philippi*' the *sentiet* which follows *Pharsalia* as well as the *Mutinae* and *Philippi* which correspond to it, show that it is the battlefield, and not the battle, that Ovid has in mind. But this extension of their meaning was a common and a legitimate one ; and the two words together afforded him all the facilities that a versifier could demand. Accordingly, as we have already observed, he employs both the nouns and both the derivatives without distinction, just as fancy or convenience may suggest ; and hence, as I wrote in the *Classical Review*, l.c. p. 258 *b*, 'In Lucan's metrical declension, as we may call it, of *Pharsalia* the cases are N.V. *Pharsalia*, G.D. *Thessaliae*, Acc. *Thessaliam*, Abl. *Thessalia*.'

(2) 'Pharsalia' ('Thessalia').

What is true of Lucan's naming of the battlefield is true of the rest of the ancient Roman authorities[2]. With various

l.c. 258 *a*, unless we adopt the novel geometrical axiom that 'things which are near to the same thing are near to one another.'

[1] As I asked in the *Classical Review*, l.c. p. 258 *b*, 'Does he who uses *Utica*, *Munda* and *Cannae* for the battles summon to his aid the obvious and convenient *Pharsalus*? He does not dream of it.'

[2] The Greek writers after Strabo and Plutarch do not count. *Classical Review*, l.c. p. 259 *b* q.u.

degrees of precision, but all of them with substantial accuracy, they place the battle 'at Old Pharsalus' (*Palaepharsali* ll. cc. supra, p. xcii), 'in Pharsalia' ('apud Pharsaliam' Pliny *N.H.* 7. 94, 'ad Pharsaliam' id. 26. 19, 'in Pharsalia,' Tacitus *Hist.* 2. 38), 'in the Pharsalian plain' (Pliny *N.H.* 8. 55 supra, p. xciii), or 'in Thessalia' (Caesar ll. cc. p. xcii). If they use a single word, that word is PHARSALIA, Lucan *passim* and Tacitus *Hist.* 1. 50 '*Pharsaliam* Philippos et Perusiam ac Mutinam nota publicarum cladium *nomina.*'

Pharsalus, the modern title for the battlefield, is not merely in itself an error both gross and gratuitous; it is implicated (3) 'Pharsalus' with another that is more serious still. In 1896 an error of (*Hist. Introd.* pp. xxxvi sqq.) I protested against the moderns. the theory, then currently associated with the name of Baron Stoffel, the Napoleonic chronicler of Caesar's Civil Wars, that the engagement took place to *the south of the river Enipeus*[1]. The exact site of the battlefield is still unknown, as the position of Old Pharsalus has not been determined. But anyone who will review the serried arguments of Dr Rice Holmes in his learned article on 'The Battlefield of Old Pharsalus,' *Classical Quarterly* 2. (1908) p. 291, or even cast a seeing eye over the excellent map which accompanies that article, will wonder how such a theory could ever have been proposed or maintained. It will lessen his astonishment to reflect that it is through the same tendency to error which has deflected the name of the battle from Pharsalia to Pharsalus that the field has drifted towards the town.

[1] The contrary view that it was fought on the north of the river is also that of Von Göler, G. Long, Sir W. Napier and Mr B. Perrin in a valuable paper in the *American Journal of Philology*, 6. 170 sqq. (1885).

CRITICAL APPARATUS

The following notes are intended in the first instance to give the reader the means of estimating the foundations of the text of Lucan VIII as presented in this edition, and in the second place to lighten the commentary by removing from it the discussion of rejected readings and punctuations.

The readings of the MANUSCRIPTS there given are extracted from the third edition of Dr C. Hosius' critical text, supplemented in respect of the readings of the two 'Vossian' MSS U and V by information kindly furnished by Dr P. J. Enk of Leyden.

The following in the alphabetical order of their abbreviations[1] are the principal MSS cited by Dr Hosius for book VIII with their approximate dates:

G   Gemblacensis, now Bruxellensis 5330 bibliothecae Burgundicae; 10th or 11th cent.   [Brussels.]

M   Montepessulanus H 113; 9th or 10th cent.   [Montpellier.]

P   Parisinus bibl. publ. Lat. 7502; 10th cent.   [Paris.]

Q   Parisini fragmentum bibl. publ. Lat. 10403; 9th cent.   [Paris.]

U   Vossianus XIX f 63; 10th cent.   [Leyden.]

V   Vossianus XIX q 51; 10th cent.   [Leyden.]

Z   Parisinus bibl. publ. Lat. 10314; 9th cent.   [Paris.]

In addition to these we have

C   Commentum Bernense (no. 370) which consists of extracts (lemmata) from Lucan with comments (scholia) upon them; 10th cent. [Berne]

and

a   'Adnotationes super Lucanum,' a collection of scholia included in the same MS as C and appearing as adscripts in other MSS. [Berne.]

---

[1] M_1 and the like symbols mean the original reading of the MS in question where that has been altered subsequently by correction.

Amongst the MSS occasionally cited are:

A Ashburnhamensis, Parisinus bibl. publ. Lat. 1626; 9th cent. [Paris.]

B Bernensis 45; 10th cent. [Berne.]

The relations and consequently the genealogy of the different MSS are very difficult to determine. As to their authority it may be briefly said that none of them is entitled to a distinct preference over the rest, and that each reading that they offer is to be judged on its intrinsic merits.

In reconstituting the text regard must be had to the clues furnished by the SCHOLIASTS in respect both of reading and interpretation. The collections which have been used for this edition are Usener, *Scholia in Lucanum* 1, 1869, and L. Endt, *Adnotationes super Lucanum*, 1909, supplemented by C. F. Weber, *Lucanus*, vol. 3, *Scholiastae*, 1831.

It is certain that the *de Bello Ciuili* of Lucan is u n f i n i s h e d; and it is more than probable that the later books never received his final revision. We must therefore exercise caution in the removal by conjecture of *maculae* 'quas aut incuria fudit | aut humana parum cauit natura,' Hor. *A. P.* 352 sq. Bentley went too far in this direction, and this is in main the reason why some convincing corrections of his have been neglected by the editors. A notable instance is his *illis* in 817. Speaking generally I have only cited c o n j e c t u r e s other than those adopted in the text if they remove a real difficulty.

Lucan's s p e l l i n g may be restored, at least in great part, from the indications furnished by the variants in the MSS, with respect to which the apparatus criticus and the grammatical index of Dr Hosius's 3rd edition, 1913, give valuable help. I have proceeded on the principles that the preservation of an ancient spelling by even one of our authorities outweighs the contrary testimony of the rest, and that inconsistency in such matters should not be lightly ascribed to the author. For example, I have printed *Ptolemaeus* rather than *Ptolomaeus*, though the evidence for the *e* is not very strong, and I have not left *semustus* to stand by *semianimis*. For metrical considerations I have consistently given *st*, not *est*, where a vowel precedes.

In p u n c t u a t i o n my sole aim has been to give as much help as I could to the reader who desires to arrive at the meaning of Lucan, and thus abbreviate the commentary.

BOOK VIII

16 *occursu* UV (Enk).

18 *laborum* V.

20 *per orbem* PU.

23 *factisque* VC.

27 *pudet* V and correctors in M and other MSS.

32 *tradere*] *credere* Heinsius a slight improvement.

36—39 Several editors punctuate 'altum, cuius—Leucadii. Cilicum dominus,' e.q.s.   But the older punctuation gives better balanced antitheses.

40 *secretae* P Bentley, *secreta* the majority of MSS and editors for which v 376 'secretaque litora Leucae' is compared; but there *secreta* is metrically preferable.   For the form of the verse-ending here cf. 74.

50 Hosius places a full stop after *portus* which gives an unnatural prominence to a mere detail.   A ship making for Lesbos was nothing remarkable.

51 *et* MZG, *sed* VPU, *en* C.

54 *tum* VG.   *times?* W. E. Weber, *times.* uulg.

57 *canitie* VG which is defensible.

59 *clausit* VG, *clusit* MPUZ.   In this and six other passages of Lucan (634, 789 below, IV 237, 370, VII 157, X 459) the MSS are divided between the two spellings, whereas there are some 34 where no variant is recorded.   I see no sufficient reason for adopting the latter spelling (which has come from the compounds) in a small minority of places.   *animam* G, *animum* the rest.

75 *legum cura* Markland.

85 *amasti?* ed. *Classical Quarterly*, vol. I (1907) 75. *amasti.* vulg. The difference between the two punctuations is this.   The first suggests that it is not consistent with Cornelia's affection for her husband to grieve so much for his vanished fortune, while the second is a brutal assertion that what she really loved was his prosperity.

102 Beroaldus and others punctuate *. tuas, ub. iaces. ciuilibus* with the interpretation of a W(eber) scholiast ' *ubicunque* illi iacent qui erant sustentamen tuum sicut senatores, ibi tu *iaces* quasi mortuus'; cf. VII 652 sq. n.

104 *Iulia, crudelis,* ed. *Classical Quarterly* 9. (1915) 99. *Iulia crudelis,* vulg.   *crudeles* V Burman.

108 *Thessaliae.* V has *thessalia.* This lection and the variants at 428 raise an interesting syntactical question. The disappearance of the old locative case and its apparent division between the genitive (singular of -*a*- and -*o*- stems) and ablative (singular of other stems and all plurals) confused the Romans' feeling for idiom. So when names of countries, e.g. *Italia*, were used on the analogy of names of towns *without a preposition*, the user ᴡas in doubt whether the case should be the genitive (*Italiae*) or the ablative (*Italia*). The GENITIVE appears in *Aegypti* (Varro, *L. L.* 5. 79, Val. Max. 4. 1. 15), *Graeciae,* apparently in Cicero, *Rep.* 3. 14 'deinde *Graeciae,* sicut *apud nos,* delubra magnifica humanis conservata simulacris quae Persae nefaria putauerunt' (unless *Graeciae* is to be taken as a dat. or true gen.), Sallust, *Iug.* 33. 4 ' Romae *Numidiae*que facinora eius' (Iugurthae) 'memorat' (where the possibility of dependence on *facinora* helps out the construction). Pliny (a lax writer) appears to use gen. and abl. side by side, *Nat. Hist.* 32. 60 (ostrea) 'uariantur coloribus, rufa *Hispaniae,* fusca Illyrico, nigra et carne et testa Circeis' (though perhaps *Hispaniae* is a possessive genitive and *Illyrico, Circeis* ablatives of place of origin). Florus has *Lucaniae* 1. 18. 11 and 'iam *Africae,* iam Balearibus insulis fortunam expertus' in 3. 22. 2; and the same case is found in later writers.

The ABLATIVE is common in Vitruuius. Vergil has it in *Latio* (several times), *Ponto Eclog.* 8. 96, *Lycia Aen.* 12. 344. So Lucan in v 266 'pars iacet *Hesperia,*' and VII 592 '*Thessalia* periture *tua*' (though *Thessaliae—tuae* would have been very strange).

Lucan probably followed Vergil's use, and so *Thessaliae* in a *local* sense is not likely either here or at 428 (below), which see. If right, it must be understood as a dative 'dry for Thessalia,' meaning ' facing Thessalia (Pharsalia) without shedding a tear.' The same sense might be expressed by *Thessalia,* an abl. of 'place and cause mixed,' i.e. 'left dry by Thessalia.' And V may be right, as the two terminations are frequently confused in the MSS of Lucan. See the variants at 157, 239, 387, 428, 564.

109 *iam pleno* V.

113 *dignere* VZG, *dignare* the rest; *a* M over an erasure.

114 *reuissent* U, *a* superscribed.

118 sq. *quid—ratibus?* I have adopted the punctuation of Burman and Bentley instead of the *quid—ponto? Caesar eget ratibus.* of the edd. The sense is clearly ' Then there is the consideration that Lesbos is an island *and* Caesar has no fleet.'

119 *eges* M₁Z₁.

124 As Francken has pointed out, the author of this line intended it to follow on 121. Its appearance after 123 is due to its having been omitted by homoeographon, the eye skipping over one of the *Accipe*'s. It is weakly attested; but it may possibly be genuine. So I have printed it in the text but in spaced type.

133 *puppim* UG, *-i* P, *-em* the rest.

137 *materiem* V$_1$. *nocentes.* A full stop is generally placed after this word; but this obscures the antithesis between this and the following line. See comm.

141 *certum est* VUPGC, *certum* the rest. But Lucan usually adds *est* at the end of a line. See 281, 285 n., 305, 308, 326, 370, 385 n., 388, 395, 428, 429, 691, 742, 749 n.

143 *es* VPU, *est* the rest, grammatically just possible but a natural corruption of *es.* Cf. *at est* M$_1$Z$_1$ for *ades* 103, *potest* M$_1$Z$_1$ for *potes* 441, 766, and 455 n.

155 *iam* MPZU, *non* VG.

156 *cultus* Markland.

157 *summissa animis* Heinsius editors, a useless conjecture. See *Classical Quarterly* 1. (1907) 75 sq. *turba* A$_1$B$_1$, *turbae* the rest.

158 *fatis* M$_1$Z$_1$.

160 *si*] *se* a corrector of A, and (according to Burman) Heinsius, taking *orbe*, which he read for *orbem*, with *totus.*

173 *miseros.* *tacitos* M$_1$Z$_1$ which has come from *tacito* in 171.

181 *tendit* MVP$_1$G, *-at* Z$_1$, *-et* the rest.

191 *tum* G, *cum* V (*tum* corr.), *tunc* (*nunc*) the rest. G, as may be observed from these notes, preserves some excellent spellings.

195 *asin*(a)*e* MUVZ(C)a Priscian, *sasin*(a)*e* PG$_1$. I have discussed this passage in *Classical Quarterly* 1. (1907) 76 sq. and given reasons for rejecting the conjectures *Asiae, Psyriae, Samiae.* The MS tradition *Asinae* (*sasinae* appears to be only *asinae*, with the *s* of *quas* repeated) may be defended with either of two assumptions: (1) That Lucan has committed a gross geographical error, the only *Asine*'s known to us being towns in the Peloponnese, Cyprus and Cilicia. This must be admitted to be possible but hardly probable, as Lucan in the rest of this narrative appears to be following closely an exact authority. (2) It is not absolutely impossible that the name *Asine* was attached to one of the Oenussae islets to the E. of Chios, and in that case Lucan will have preserved a name which elsewhere has perished; cf. p. lxxxv. The question is complicated by the fact that there was an *Asine* adjoining the Oenussae islands to the S. of Messenia, Pliny *N. H.* 4. 55. There is

no doubt as to Pompey's route, and I have (l.c. p. 77) suggested and defended the conjecture ' *Oenusae cautes*': that is ' quas undas Oenusae cautes et Chios asperat.' *cautis* $M_1Z_1U_1$.

217 *totum*] *notum* Heinsius.

222—235 This passage which forms one single long sentence is mispunctuated by all the editors, except that Francken rightly makes 235—7 the apodosis of the conditional clause. See *Classical Quarterly* 1. pp. 216 sq. where I have cited other examples from Latin poets (Horace, *Ep.* 1. 15. 1—25, *S.* 1. 8. 3—20, Propertius 3. 22. 5—17, 3. 15. 1, 2, 43, 44, 3—10; Tibullus 2. 5. 19 sqq., Catullus 68. 51 sqq.) where the thought is held in suspension in ways that are to us impossible.

223 *Alanos.* At X 454 the first hand of M has *alannus* which would agree better with the *A-lan-na* of the Chinese Annals.

224 *discurrere* P_1 perhaps rightly. There is a similar disagreement at IV 733 ' ignotisque equitem late *decurrere* campis.'

237 *Zeumaque* MZUC, with the vulgar pronunciation of the word.

239 *aula* MZ_1.

240 *famuli* VG, *famulo* PU, *famulos* Z(? M).

244 *ephesumque* VU (Enk).

247 *cnidon* P, *nidon* M_1Z, *gnidon* the rest.

251 *phaseli* V_1, *faselo* C (but *O faseri*, i.e. *o Phaseli*, on 254), *phaselis* the rest. A good example of the merit of V, which has preserved the vocative *Phaseli* that all our other witnesses have corrupted through thinking it a common noun.

Augustan poets used -*ĭ*, and not the -*ĭs* of ordinary Latin, for the vocative of Greek nouns in -*ĭs*; cf. Neue-Wagener, *Formenlehre* 1. 443 sq., and my note in *Classical Review* 23. (1909) p. 187.

254 *hinc* VU, *hic* the rest. *rusus* M_1Z.

255 *dipsunta* VU(C), (-*umpta* MZ), *dipsanta* G, -*ampta* M, *adipsūta* P. These lections indicate an early variation between *Dipsunta* and *Dipsanta*. Possibly *Gypsunta*; see Excursus B pp. lxxxii sqq.

256 *cum pacem* U.

259 *Syhedris* Usener, *synedris* the MSS.

265 *nouis* U, *nobis* P, *meis* the rest, a corruption found elsewhere, e.g. at Tibullus (Lygdamus) 3. 1. 8.

274 *tueri* MVZ, *iuuare* PUG.

278 *quemnam*] *qu(a)enam* VUG which is due to *regna*.

285 *uano est* VPZUGC and a corrector of M, *uano* M₁; see on 141.

290 *ingenti* Grotius.

293 *est nostro* all our authorities except MC which omit *est*. The choice is not easy. For the omission of *est* with a number of nouns cf. 51, 380.

294 *pugnandi* Schrader, *regnandi* the MSS (and all editors !). For the corruption compare VII 525, where the Palatine palimpsest (Π) has REGNAE for *pugnae*.

295 *in*] *it* Heinsius.   *campis* VG, possibly right, though *campo* receives some support from II 501 'leuis totas accepit habenas | in *campum sonipes.*'

306 *tota* ed. *Classical Quarterly* 1. (1907) 78, *tanta* the MSS illogically which Prof. W. B. Anderson, *Classical Quarterly* 8. 106, seeks to defend by interpreting 'I could wish that my confidence in their might were not so great as to make me prefer their alliance.' But this cannot be extracted from the Latin.

309, 310 placed by ed. before 289, *Classical Quarterly* 1. 79. If they follow 308, *alia tellure* must mean a different land *from Parthia*, which contradicts both the preceding and the following context, which both assume that he *is* going to Parthia, and in addition is incompatible with the *ortus* of 307.

311 *fallent* MZ, *-unt* the rest.

318—19 So punctuated by ed. *fui; quantus—ortu?* Hosius. But the omission of *sum* is a needless harshness: 647 sq. is different.

327 *sensit* VUG, *sentit* the rest. Choice is not easy.

336 *totos* the MSS, tolerable as a laxity, but *notos* Guietus is attractive.

343 The rare hyperbaton in this line, which it has been vainly attempted to remove by conjecture, has been discussed in *Classical Review* 30. (1916) pp. 142 sqq. and Ov. *M.* 8. 9 'inter *honoratos* medioque in uertice *canos*,' Manilius 1. 429 '*discordes* uultu permixtaque corpora *partus*,' Luc. v. 800 'fertur ad *aequoreas* et se prosternit *harenas*' cited as showing that this dislocation conforms to no. *vii* of the limitations of hyperbaton there laid down, to wit that 'Words which are obviously in close syntactical connexion may be moved a considerable distance if they occupy *corresponding positions in the verse.*'

353 *clades* has caused great trouble through its apparent correspondence to *populos* and Guietus, Burman (reading *ad Parthos*) and Cortius wished to take it with the next line. It has probably intruded

from 350 (cf. critical notes on 173, 770) and has replaced another substantive, perhaps *sedes* or *oras*: cf. Hor. *C.* 1. 37. 23 sq. 'nec *latentis* | classe cita penetrauit (*Bentl.*) oras.' The suggestion that Pompey wants to do what even the beaten Cleopatra did not do has a bitter appropriateness.

356   *suo?* I have taken this from Mr Heitland's text in the *Corpus Poetarum Latinorum. suo.* editors.

366   *labitur* VG, 'sinks down,' a possible reading, inasmuch as the subject can be taken from the next line, *clementia caeli* being practically the same as *caelum clemens* (compare also explanatory notes on 366, 568), and it is of course customary to speak of the South as lower than the North.

378   *sequente* G, *-tè* U₁.

384   *uolent* V. I have removed the commas before *quo* and *per-mittere*, upon which latter word *ferre* depends, as well as upon *uelint, Classical Quarterly* 9. (1915) 99.

385   *uirorum est* VPUG, the rest *uirorum.* See on 141. Here also emphasis seems to make *est* preferable.

387   *uacuaeque—pharetrae* V.

390   *uenisse p. est* PU₁, *quis—uenisse* Heinsius.

395   *leuior* PUG, *melior* MVZ.

397   *nobis* V and most MSS, *uobis* VP₁G, but Lentulus does not elsewhere address the audience, but Pompey only; *uobis* in 421 is different.

400   *latent* Schrader, *patent* the MSS by a common mistake, which involves a very awkward coupling of a question and statement by *que.* Some editors for no apparent reason stop the sentence after *nurus* instead of after *nefandi.*

402   *audet*] *horret* V, a bad conjecture.

413   *stimulante* V.

427   *pacis* MZ₁, *paci* the rest.

428   *thessaliae* PU, *-iam* Z, *-icam* (?)M, *-ia* V with the rest. The weight of MS authority is then for *Thessalia*; and it has been shown above on 108 that it is not probable that Lucan used *Thessaliae* of the 'place where.' Hence, if *Thessaliae* is right, it must be understood as a dat. of the agent = ' if Pharsalia has ended the civil war.'

431   *araxe* MZ, *-em* G, *araxen* VU.

435   *tum* PUG, *tunc* the rest.

444   *aegiptus* VUG, *-os* the rest.

448   *ptoloma(e)us* the MSS ; see on 696.

450   *ne*] *nec* V, adopted by Weise and Prof. Elmer *American Journal of Philology* 21. (1900) p. 82 and giving a satisfactory construction and sense ('accedit ait quod novissimus quisque rex mitissimus ; contra assuetos sceptris nihil pudet' Weise). For *ne* however see Prof. Clement's collections in the same volume pp. 156, 157.

451   *ueteris—aulae* V ('*ae* in ras.' Enk) PGC, *ueter*i—*aul*a U, the rest Madvig and most recent editors, a local abl. Perhaps *ueter*i—*aul*ae (dat.) which would explain both readings.

455   *habes* MPZ, *habet* the rest, an easier reading; compare the corruption *potest* in 766 and 143 n.

456   *tunc* V.

463   *gratum*] *casium* PU (*si* in ras.), *carsum* G.

475   *achoreus* V and similarly VG at X 175, 193, perhaps correctly if the name is to be identified with those cited in *Introd.* p. l.

479   *uexerat* V.

483   *ausus :* editors. I have taken the punctuation of the *Corpus* text, as it is more likely that *inquit* should be the main verb and *ausus* the participle; cf. II 67, III 135, V 577, 739, VII 342.

490   *incipis* Heinsius.

498   *nos* PU (*nas* Z, ? M), *te* VG.

499   *pharonque* VPUG, *-umque* to rest. *Pharon* is the only well attested form in Lucan and is required by metre at VIII 184, 443, 514. *nilonque* PG, *-umque* the rest. If Lucan has ventured on the Greek acc. in this common substantive, it was for the mocking repetition of the ending.

501   *Aegypton* PU, *-tum* the rest. Everywhere (except in 871 below) that the nom. or acc. occurs in Lucan there is MS authority for the Greek forms. *-on* is required by metre at X 359.

505   *umbris* MZC, *armis* the rest from 501.

519 sq.   I have removed the full stop which has been placed in various editions either after *gladio* or *dedit*. The reasons for the Egyptian Government lending moral support to Pompey are quite beside the mark. What alone matters now is the *means* they must take to clear themselves from the charge of partisanship. So perhaps C. F. Weber in spite of semicolons after *gladio* and *dedit* (*Classical Quarterly* 9. (1915) 102). Schol. *a* probably took the same view, though the words in italics are rather far from the text 'hoc ergo dicit : gladio hoc crimen purgare debemus *ne uideamur huic aliquando fauisse* quod nobis hoc suadente imperium dedit.'

525   *inertem* Bentley.

530   *Thessalicas* Z.

537   *iubere*] *licere* M, over an erasure, for which IX 1025 sq. 'cui *tantum* fata *licere* | in generum uoluere tuum' has been compared (by Mr Heitland, *Classical Review* 9. 198) ; but the parallel is not close enough, especially as we have *tanta* here.

539   *exultat* V, *excurrit* the rest.

541   *cladisque*, a variant for *gladiisque* in some MSS, would ease the expression somewhat, 'the hideous murder,' *clades* being elsewhere as in 34, VII 795 little different from *caedes*. The words have been confused at VII 489 and probably at VII 748. But the external testimony for *clades* here is weak.

547 sqq.   I have slightly altered the current punctuation to mark that *cognatas praestate manus* refers chiefly to what precedes and *externa monstra pellite* chiefly to what follows.

551   *numinis* Bentley.

555 sq.   I have enclosed *Phario—poterat* in brackets to show that *erat* is to be taken with the nouns of 553 sq. as well as with *Romanus*.

560   *negabat* MZ₁U.

563   *approperat* (Bentley) would get rid of the difficulty in *adpulerat*, but in itself *adcelerat* seems a more likely word. See the examples in the *Thesaurus*, s.u. The homoeographon 'ad*celerat* s*celerat*a' may have caused loss and provoked interpolation.

564   *celsae* MVZ, *celsa* the rest.

567   *adpellere* MVZ, *aduertere* PV, *expellere* G.

575   *classemque*] *sociosque* G. But the appearance of *classe* in the previous line is no valid objection to *classem*, though of course it might have corrupted *socios*; see note on 770.

577   *puppim* PUG, -*em* the rest.

580   *a* GC, om. M₁Z₁, *e* the rest, which cannot mean *a* and is otherwise hardly intelligible.

582   *dura* V, *surda* the rest. The choice is not very easy; for *dura* might be the neuter plural, of a 'harsh prohibition.' as in 238 sq. 'iubenti ardua' of a hard command.

586   *puppem* VPQU₁G, -*im* the rest.

587   *alio* MV, *alto* the rest.

595   *parentem* M₁G₁Q.

601   *uacasset* PUG, an accommodation to *putasset* (600).

614   *indignatur* Bentley (apparently taking *inuoluit* as a present).

615   *monstrare caput* V.   *tum* C.

617 *possit* V.

620 *respexitue* Oudendorp.

624 *ratem*] *uel meam* Ua, a strange variant possibly based on a false reading *ratam*.

628 *auctoremue* PC.

633 *tantum* P.

634 *claude* VUGQ, *clude* the rest.

638 *perferre*] Careful consideration of this line will show that there are two thoughts suggested by the context, to neither of which can *perferre* be easily accommodated. EITHER it may contrast Cornelia's lack of self-control with the stoicism of Pompey (633 sqq.). *She* cannot bear to *see* what *he* endures to *feel*. This is admirably expressed by Heinsius's ingenious conjecture *uir ferre*, the only objection to which is that it is not very near to the MS reading. OR the thought intended may be Cornelia's inability to witness with patience a deed which she would be *prepared* to *suffer* in her own person. With this sense in view I suggest as possible *par ferre*, 'equal to bear,' which would restore the balance of the expression. Prof. Anderson, *Classical Quarterly* 10. (1916) 104, suggests that *non tam patiens* expresses 'an habitual state of Cornelia, who was ever stronger to endure cruel wrong than to witness it,' like *numquam patiens* in 11 650. But on what occasion did Cornelia quail at the sight of a barbarous outrage (saeuum nefas) such as the murder of Pompey?

642 sqq. I have discussed this passage in *Classical Quarterly* 9. (1915) 99 sqq.

644 *prospicies* ed. for *prospiciens* MSS edd. The corruption -*ēs* for -*es* is very easy and common; e.g. in this very book at 559 G has *ten*ens for *ten*es. In *Classical Quarterly* l.c. I have also suggested that the MS reading might be retained (*si tanti est*) by punctuating '*quisquis*— *prospiciens nescis, crudelis,—Magni, properas*' etc., so providing a finite verb for *quisquis* in *nescis*.

645 *sint* U (Enk) VPGQ, *sunt* the rest. There seems to be no justification for the indicative here.

660 *arcersere* MZ, *arcessere* PQ.

665 *iratamque.* For this unsatisfactory reading Bentley proposed *certantemque*, Madvig *aequatamque*, Francken *placatamque*. In *Classical Quarterly* 1. (1907) 218 sq. I have suggested and defended *mirandamque.*   *diis* V (Enk).   *aciem* PU.   *nihil* VUPQ, and so at VI 819 where the other MSS have *nil*.

681   *comprensa* V, *conpressa* the rest.   But the hair was 'grasped,' not 'squeezed.'   Cf. Suetonius *Galba* 20 quoted above in n. 3 p. lix.

693   *sororis* VG.

695   *extructa mole* Cortius.

696   *ptolemaeorum* M_1Z_1, *ptolom.* the rest.   The fact that 'the spelling with *e* has been removed from these two MSS by correction, coupled with the fact that there are traces of the same spelling at V 59 MN (fragment of 5th cent.) PZ and X 427 (U), has led me to restore this for the non-literary *Ptolom.* in 448, 512, 528, 550.

702   *dea* Sandstroem.

714   *sepulcro*]   The MSS mostly appear to spell this word *sepulchrum.*

715   *cordus* (*u* ex *i*) Z, *codrus* the rest.

716   *Idalio* Micyllus, *icario* the MSS and scholia, a mistake which is conceivably Lucan's.   Idalium was in the interior of Cyprus. *Cinyreae* has been corrupted in several MSS to *cireneae* (*cyrenei*). On the termination *-eae*, which has considerable MS support, see Prof. Housman, *Journal of Philology* 33. p. 64.   *-aeae* editors.

720   In *Classical Quarterly* 1. 219 sq. I attacked this line for its tautology and proposed *reducemque in l. M.*   In *Classical Quarterly* 8. (1914) 110 sq. Prof. W. B. Anderson has defended it on the ground that *Magnum* used significantly (see explanatory notes on 102, 455) will redeem the words from being a sheer repetition.   I am now disposed to agree, as I do not find the tautology worse than that in Ov. *M.* 10. 245 sq. 'sine coniuge caelebs | uiuebat thalamique diu consorte carebat,' where *diu* is all that saves the situation, or Val. Fl. 8. 453 sq. 'tunc tota *querellis* | egeritur *questu*que dies' (if *questu* is not corrupt). As for the 'suspicious' agreement of 720 and 570 this, as he says, may be due to Lucan's repeating himself; cf. my note on VIII 377.

727   *effudit* VUG.

735   Hosius proposes *protentis*, but *proiectis* may give the same sense.   See explanatory note.

739   *satis*] *tantis* Z_1.   Does this come from *tanti*?

741   *a funere* MZ, but *munere busti*=*funere.*

742   *neque* Q, *nec* U (Enk) the rest.

745   *semustaque* MSS : see above p. c.

749   *relictum est* GU.   See note on 141 supra.

752   *fatur* V, but *fatus* is a participle.

753   *prouolat* Schrader, the reverse of an improvement.   The

construction of *peruolat* with *ad truncum* need be no difficulty in view of Cic. *Rep.* 6. 29 'quibus (curis) agitatus et exercitatus animus uelocius *in* hanc sedem et domum suam *peruolabit.*'

757 *premit* a corrector in A, Burman, *premunt* the MSS, which seems to have no sense, as corpses were not 'enclosed' in wood (coffins) but placed uncovered on the piled logs.

758 *arripit* Burman, an elegant conjecture.

761 *funere nudo*, apparently the original reading of UGQ (compare *mundo* in P) may well be right in the sense of 'the non-burial of your corpse.' For *nudo* cf. 434 n. and for *funus* Prop. 1. 17. 8 'haecine parua meum *funus* harena *tegat?*' and elsewhere. *f. nullo* may be a copyist's reminiscence of v 668 where it is differently used.

765 *uolucris* MZ₁.

766 *potest* M₁ZC, *potis* Waddel.

767 *succense* VGU (*-nse* in ras.) with voc. as in 338, *succensa* the rest, a much more obvious and less elegant expression.   *manu* VPUG, *manu est* the rest.

770 *nostroque sinu* ed., *nostraque* (over an *erasure* G)—*manu* the MSS from 767. The passage is discussed in *Classical Quarterly* 1. (1907) 220 sq. *nota—manu* Burman, and Prof. Anderson recently in *Classical Quarterly* 9. (1916) p. 105.

779 *praemissa* UG, *promissa* the rest.

786 *semusta* most MSS, *semusta* (*m* in ras.) M, *semiusta* Z (*mius* in ras.), *sed iusta* Q₁G. Cf. 792.

792 *semiusto* C, *semusto* the MSS.

802 *magni* PUV, *magni est* G, *est magno* (*-i*) the rest. But Lucan omits this verb if some part of it is in the immediate neighbourhood. So 395, 409, 630.

803 *arua* PUV, as in 164, 443, *rura* the rest; cf. IX 130 'Nilotica rura.'   *potest*, ed., *potest*. vulg. See *Classical Quarterly* 9. (1915) 101 sq.

807 *maxuma* M₁Z₁, *maxima* the rest.

808 *truces* PUV, *trucis* the rest.

812 *barbariam* M₁Q₁Z₁ and probably U₁, *barbariem* the rest, which agrees with VII 273 *barbaries*.

816 *sordet* Bentley, with insufficient reason. For, if the *miserabile bustum* can 'fall' (*cadet* 868), it must first have 'risen.' In 866, where a lofty tomb is in question, *ardua* is added to *surrexit*.

817 *non illis* Bentley's excellent correction, reinforcing the correspondence of the two parts of the line; *non ullis* the MSS, a harsh

discordance with *plenum*, not excused by VII 404 sq. ' *nullo*que frequentem | *ciue* suo Romam sed mundi faece repletam.'

831   *accepimus*] ita V (Enk).

836   *o Roma*] Bentley wished to read *Romane*, as in Verg. *A.* 6. 852 and elsewhere, on the ground that Lucan does not prefix *o* to *Roma*. The vocative occurs alone some 18 times (three times within 25 lines in VI 302—326); the instances with *o* are this passage and I 199 'summique *o* numinis instar | Roma.' See commentary.

840   *timebit?* some editors, not so well.

843   *beati*, genitive after *sinu*, would give an easier and more elegant construction.

848   *imbribus* Withof.

851   *iam* Francken.

857   *iuuabit* PUVQ, *iubebit* the rest. Either will stand; and *libebit* (or *lubebit*), which is a variant in G and preferred by Oudendorp, is also possible.

860   *est* (in ras. M) the MSS except U, which has *es*, adopted by several editors, generally with a full stop after *summo*. I follow Cortius.

871   *aegyptus* all the MSS; but probably Lucan wrote *Aegyptos*; for the Latin form has no metrical advantage over the Greek; and *Aegyptos* is the best attested lection in the only other passage of Lucan (supra 444) where the nominative occurs.

NOTE ON THE TEXT.

In the footnotes italics are used for a conjectural reading.

Lines 309 sq. are given twice, in their proper place after 288 and for the convenience of the reader also after 308 in italics.

M. ANNAEI LVCANI

DE BELLO CIVILI

LIBER OCTAVVS.

Pompey's flight to the coast and melancholy reflexions.

Iam super Herculeas fauces nemorosaque Tempe,
Haemoniae deserta petens dispendia siluae,
cornipedem exhaustum cursu stimulisque negantem
Magnus agens, incerta fugae uestigia turbat
inplicitasque errore uias. pauet ille fragorem   5
motorum uentis nemorum, comitumque suorum
qui post terga redit trepidum laterique timentem
exanimat. quamuis summo de culmine lapsus
nondum uile sui pretium scit sanguinis esse,
seque memor fati tantae mercedis habere   10
credit adhuc iugulum, quantam pro Caesaris ipse
auolsa ceruice daret. deserta sequentem
non patitur tutis fatum celare latebris
clara uiri facies. multi, Pharsalica castra
cum peterent, nondum fama prodente ruinas,   15
occursù stupuere ducis, uertigine rerum
attoniti; cladisque suae uix ipse fidelis
auctor erat. grauis est Magno quicumque malorum

testis adest. cunctis ignotus gentibus esse
mallet et obscuro tutus transire per urbes   20
nomine ; sed poenas longi Fortuna fauoris
exigit a misero, quae tanto pondere famae
res premit aduersas fatisque prioribus urguet.
nunc festinatos nimium sibi sentit honores
actaque lauriferae damnat Sullana iuuentae ;   25
nunc et Corycias classes et Pontica signa
deiectum meminisse piget. sic longius aeuum
destruit ingentis animos et uita superstes
imperio ; nisi summa dies cum fine bonorum
adfuit et celeri praeuertit tristia leto,   30
dedecorist fortuna prior. quisquamne secundis
tradere se fatis audet nisi morte parata ?

*Pompey reaches Lesbos. Cornelia's forebodings. Her
distress at seeing him. Pompey bids her take heart.*

Litora contigerat per quae Peneius amnis,
Emathia iam clade rubens, exibat in aequor.
inde ratis trepidum uentis ac fluctibus inpar,   35
flumineis uix tuta uadis, euexit in altum.
cuius adhuc remis quatitur Corcyra sinusque
Leucadii, Cilicum dominus terraeque Liburnae,
exiguam, uector pauidus, correpsit in alnum.
conscia curarum secretae in litora Lesbi   40
flectere uela iubet, qua tunc tellure latebas
maestior, in mediis quam si, Cornelia, campis
Emathiae stares. tristes praesagia curas
exagitant, trepida quatitur formidine somnus,
Thessaliam nox omnis habet ; tenebrisque remotis   45
rupis in abruptae scopulos extremaque curris
litora ; prospiciens fluctus nutantia longe

40 secreta

semper prima uides uenientis uela carinae,
quaerere nec quidquam de fato coniugis audes.
en ratis ad uestros quae tendit carbasa portus,   50
quid ferat, ignoras; et nunc tibi summa pauoris
nuntius armorum tristis rumorque sinister.
uictus adest coniunx. quid perdis tempora luctus?
cum possis iam flere, times? tunc puppe propinqua
prosiluit crimenque deum crudele notauit,   55
deformem pallore ducem uoltusque prementem
canitiem atque atro squalentis puluere uestes.
obuia nox miserae caelum lucemque tenebris
abstulit, atque animam clausit dolor; omnia neruis
membra relicta labant, riguerunt corda, diuque,   60
spe mortis decepta, iacet. iam, fune ligato
litoribus, lustrat uacuas Pompeius harenas.
quem postquam propius famulae uidere fideles,
non ultra gemitus tacitos incessere fatum
permisere sibi, frustraque attollere terra   65
semianimem conantur eram; quam pectore Magnus
ambit et astrictos refouet conplexibus artus.
coeperat, in summum reuocato sanguine corpus,
Pompei sentire manus maestamque mariti
posse pati faciem; prohibet succumbere fatis   70
Magnus et inmodicos castigat uoce dolores:
'Nobile cur robur fortunae uolnere primo,
femina tantorum titulis insignis auorum,
frangis? habes aditum mansurae in saecula famae:
laudis in hoc sexu non legum iura nec arma,   75
unica materiast coniunx miser. erige mentem,
et tua cum fatis pietas decertet, et ipsum,
quod sum uictus, ama; nunc sum tibi gloria maior,
a me quod fasces et quod pia turba senatus

57 canitie

tantaque discessit regum manus. incipe Magnum   80
sola sequi. deformis, adhuc uiuente marito,
summus et augeri uetitus dolor: ultima debet
esse fides lugere uirum. tu nulla tulisti
bello damna meo: uiuit post proelia Magnus,
sed fortuna perit. quod defles, illud amasti?'   85

Cornelia upbraids herself as the cause of his disaster.

   Vocibus his correpta uiri uix aegra leuauit
membra solo, tales gemitu rumpente querellas:
'O utinam in thalamos inuisi Caesaris issem,
infelix coniunx et nulli laeta marito!
bis nocui mundo; me pronuba ducit Erinys   90
Crassorumque umbrae, deuotaque manibus illis
Assyrios in castra tuli ciuilia casus,
praecipitesque dedi populos cunctosque fugaui
a causa meliore deos. o maxime coniunx,
o thalamis indigne meis, hoc iuris habebat   95
in tantum Fortuna caput! cur inpia nupsi,
si miserum factura fui? nunc accipe poenas,
sed quas sponte luam. quo sit tibi mollius aequor,
certa fides regum, totusque paratior orbis,
sparge mari comitem. mallem felicibus armis   100
dependisse caput: nunc clades denique lustra,
Magne, tuas. ubicumque iaces, ciuilibus armis
nostros ulta toros ades huc atque exige poenas,
Iulia, crudelis placataque paelice caesa
Magno parce tuo.' sic fata iterumque refusa   105
coniugis in gremium cunctorum lumina soluit
in lacrimas. duri flectuntur pectora Magni,
siccaque Thessaliae confudit lumina Lesbos.

                  108 Thessalia

*The Mytilenaeans beg Pompey to stay in Lesbos. He thanks
them but declines. Their sorrow at losing Cornelia.*

Tunc Mytilenaeum, pleno iam litore, uolgus
adfatur Magnum : 'Si maxima gloria nobis   110
semper erit tanti pignus seruasse mariti,
tu quoque deuotos sacro tibi foedere muros,
oramus, sociosque lares dignere uel una
nocte tua : fac, Magne, locum quem cuncta reuisant
saecula, quem ueniens hospes Romanus adoret.   115
nulla tibi subeunda magis sunt moenia uicto :
omnia uictoris possunt sperare fauorem ;
haec iam crimen habent.   quid quod iacet insula ponto,
Caesar eget ratibus ? procerum pars magna coibit
certa loci ; noto reparandumst litore fatum.   120
accipe templorum cultus aurumque deorum,
accipe : ne Caesar rapiat, tu uictus habeto,   124
accipe, si terris, si puppibus ista iuuentus   122
aptior est ; tota, quantum ualet, utere Lesbo.   123
hoc solum crimen meritae bene detrahe terrae,   125
ne nostram uideare fidem felixque secutus
et damnasse miser.' tali pietate uirorum
laetus in aduersis et mundi nomine gaudens
esse fidem 'Nullum toto mihi' dixit 'in orbe
gratius esse solum non paruo pignore uobis   130
ostendi ; tenuit nostros hac obside Lesbos
adfectus ; hic sacra domus carique penates,
hic mihi Roma fuit.   non ulla in litora puppim
ante dedi fugiens, saeui cum Caesaris iram
iam scirem meritam seruata coniuge Lesbon,   135
non ueritus tantam ueniae committere uobis
materiam.   sed iam satis est fecisse nocentes ;
fata mihi totum mea sunt agitanda per orbem.

heu nimium felix aeterno nomine Lesbos,
siue doces populos regesque admittere Magnum,   140
seu praestas mihi sola fidem.   nam quaerere certumst,
fas quibus in terris, ubi sit scelus.   accipe, numen,
si quod adhuc mecum es, uotorum extrema meorum :
da similes Lesbo populos, qui Marte subactum
non intrare suos infesto Caesare portus,   145
non exire uetent.'   dixit maestamque carinae
inposuit comitem.   cunctos mutare putares
tellurem patriaeque solum : sic litore toto
plangitur, infestae tenduntur in aethera dextrae ;
Pompeiumque minus, cuius fortuna dolorem   150
mouerat, ast illam, quam toto tempore belli
ut ciuem uidere suam, discedere cernens
ingemuit populus ; quam uix, si castra mariti
uictoris peteret, siccis dimittere matres
iam poterant oculis : tanto deuinxit amore   155
hos pudor, hos probitas castique modestia uoltus,
quod summissa nimis nulli grauis hospita turbae
stantis adhuc fati uixit quasi coniuge uicto.

*Pompey converses with the steersman on navigation by
the stars.   Their course is bent to the south.*

Iam pelago medios Titan demissus ad ignes
nec quibus abscondit, nec si quibus exerit orbem,   160
totus erat : uigiles Pompei pectore curae
nunc socias adeunt Romani foederis urbes
et uarias regum mentes, nunc inuia mundi
arua super nimios soles Austrumque iacentis.
saepe labor maestus curarum odiumque futuri   165
proiecit fessos incerti pectoris aestus ;

rectoremque ratis de cunctis consulit astris,
unde notet terras, quae sit mensura secandi
aequoris in caelo, Syriam quo sidere seruet,
aut quotus in plaustro Libyam bene derigat ignis. 170
doctus ad haec fatur taciti seruator Olympi :
'Signifero quaecumque fluunt labentia caelo,
numquam stante polo, miseros fallentia nautas,
sidera non sequimur ; sed qui non mergitur undis
axis inocciduus, gemina clarissimus Arcto, 175
ille regit puppes. hic cum mihi semper in altum
surget et instabit summis minor Vrsa ceruchis,
Bosporon et Scythiae curuantem litora Pontum
spectamus. quidquid descendet ab arbore summa
Arctophylax propiorque mari Cynosura feretur, 180
in Syriae portus tendet ratis. inde Canopos
excipit, Australi caelo contenta uagari
stella, timens Borean : illa quoque perge sinistra
trans Pharon ; in medio tanget ratis aequore Syrtim.
sed quo uela dari, quo nunc pede carbasa tendi 185
nostra iubes?' dubio contra cui pectore Magnus
'Hoc solum toto' respondit 'in aequore serua,
ut sit ab Emathiis semper tua longius oris
puppis, et Hesperiam pelago caeloque relinquas ;
cetera da uentis. comitem pignusque recepi 190
depositum ; tum certus eram quae litora uellem,
nunc portum Fortuna dabit.' sic fatur ; at ille
iusto uela modo pendentia cornibus aequis
torsit et in laeuum puppim dedit, utque secaret
quas Asinae cautes et quas Chios asperat undas, 195
hos dedit in proram, tenet hos in puppe rudentes.
aequora senserunt motus aliterque secante
iam pelagus rostro nec idem spectante carina

     195 *Oenusae* cautes

mutauere sonum. non sic moderator equorum,
dexteriore rota laeuum cum circumit axem,   200
cogit inoffensae currus accedere metae.

Next day Pompey is joined by his son Sextus and
other devoted followers.

Ostendit terras Titan et sidera texit;
sparsus ab Emathia fugit quicumque procella,
adsequitur Magnum ; primusque a litore Lesbi
occurrit natus, procerum mox turba fidelis,   205
nam neque deiecto fatis acieque fugato
abstulerat Magno reges fortuna ministros ;
terrarum dominos et sceptra Eoa tenentes
exul habet comites.

Pompey dispatches King Deiotarus on a hazardous
mission to Parthia.

                    iubet ire in deuia mundi
Deiotarum, qui sparsa ducis uestigia legit.   210
' Quando' ait 'Emathiis amissus cladibus orbis
qua Romanus erat, superest, fidissime regum,
Eoam temptare fidem populosque bibentis
Euphraten et adhuc securum a Caesare Tigrim.
ne pigeat Magno quaerentem fata remotas   215
Medorum penetrare domos Scythicosque recessus
et totum mutare diem uocesque superbo
Arsacidae perferre meas : "Si foedera nobis
prisca manent, mihi per Latium iurata Tonantem,
per uestros astricta magos, inplete pharetras   220
Armeniosque arcus Geticis intendite neruis ;
si uos, o Parthi, peterem cum Caspia claustra
et sequerer duros aeterni martis Alanos,
passus Achaemeniis late decurrere campis

in tutam trepidos numquam Babylona coegi　　225
(arua super Cyri Chaldaeique ultima regni,
qua rapidus Ganges et qua Nysaeus Hydaspes
accedunt pelago, Phoebi surgentis ab igne
iam propior quam Persis eram; tamen omnia uincens
sustinui nostris uos tantum desse triumphis,　　230
solusque e numero regum telluris Eoae
ex aequo me Parthus adit) nec munere Magni
stant semel Arsacidae (quis enim post uolnera cladis
Assyriae iustas Latii conpescuit iras?),
tot meritis obstricta meis nunc Parthia ruptis　　235
excedat claustris uetitam per saecula ripam
Zeugmaque Pellaeum. Pompeio uincite, Parthi:
uinci Roma uolet."' regem parere iubenti
ardua non piguit, positisque insignibus aulae
egreditur, famuli raptos indutus amictus.　　240
in dubiis tutumst inopem simulare tyranno:
quanto igitur mundi dominis securius aeuum
uerus pauper agit!

Pompey proceeds to Cilicia. His route described.

　　　　　dimisso in litore rege
ipse per Icariae scopulos, Ephesonque relinquens
et placidi Colophona maris, spumantia paruae　　245
radit saxa Sami; spirat de litore Coo
aura fluens; Cnidon inde fugit claramque relinquit
sole Rhodon magnosque sinus Telmessidos undae
conpensat medio pelagi. Pamphylia puppi
occurrit tellus, nec se committere muris　　250
ausus adhuc ullis te primum, parua Phaseli,
Magnus adit; nam te metui uetat incola rarus

251 Phaselis

exhaustaeque domus populis, maiorque carinae
quam tua turba fuit. tendens hinc carbasa rursus,
iam Taurum Tauroque uidet Dipsunta cadentem. 255

He calls a Council at Syhedra and addresses his followers.
    He bids them not despair and proposes that they should
    seek aid from the Parthians.

    Crederet hoc Magnus, pacem cum praestitit undis,
et sibi consultum? Cilicum per litora tutus
parua puppe fugit. sequitur pars magna senatus
ad profugum collecta ducem; paruisque Syhedris,
quo portu mittitque rates recipitque Selinus,   260
in procerum coetu tandem maesta ora resoluit
uocibus his Magnus : 'Comites bellique fugaeque
atque instar patriae, quamuis in litore nudo,
in Cilicum terra, nullis circumdatus armis,
consultem rebusque nouis exordia quaeram,   265
ingentis praestate animos. non omnis in aruis
Emathiis cecidi, nec sic mea fata premuntur
ut nequeam releuare caput cladesque receptas
excutere. an Libycae Marium potuere ruinae
erigere in fasces et plenis reddere fastis :   270
me pulsum leuiore manu Fortuna tenebit?
mille meae Graio uoluuntur in aequore puppes,
mille duces; sparsit potius Pharsalia nostras,
quam subuertit, opes. sed me uel sola tueri
fama potest rerum, toto quas gessimus orbe,   275
et nomen quod mundus amat. uos pendite regna
uiribus atque fide, Libyam Parthosque Pharonque,
quemnam Romanis deceat succurrere rebus.
ast ego curarum uobis arcana mearum
expromam mentisque meae quo pondera uergant.   280
aetas Niliaci nobis suspecta tyrannist ;

ardua quippe fides robustos exigit annos.
hinc anceps dubii terret sollertia Mauri;
namque, memor generis, Carthaginis inpia proles
inminet Hesperiae, multusque in pectore uanost   285
Hannibal, obliquo maculat qui sanguine regnum
et Numidas contingit auos; iam supplice Varo
intumuit uiditque loco Romana secundo.
effundam populos alia tellure reuolsos   309
excitosque suis inmittam sedibus ortus.   310
quare agite Eoum, comites, properemus in orbem.   289
diuidit Euphrates ingentem gurgite mundum,   290
Caspiaque inmensos seducunt claustra recessus,
et polus Assyrias alter noctesque diesque
uertit; et abruptumst nostro mare, discolor unda,
oceanusque suus.   pugnandi sola uoluptas;
celsior in campo sonipes et fortior arcus,   295
nec puer aut senior letales tendere neruos
segnis, et a nulla mors est incerta sagitta.
primi Pellaeas arcu fregere sarisas
Bactraque Medorum sedem murisque superbam
Assyrias Babylona domos.   nec pila timentur   300
nostra nimis Parthis, audentque in bella uenire,
experti Scythicas Crasso pereunte pharetras.
spicula nec solo spargunt fidentia ferro,
stridula sed multo saturantur tela ueneno;
uolnera parua nocent, fatumque in sanguine sum-
    most.   305
o utinam non tota mihi fiducia saeuis
esset in Arsacidis! fatis nimis aemula nostris
fata mouent Medos, multumque in gente deorumst.
effundam populos alia tellure reuolsos   309
excitosque suis inmittam sedibus ortus.   310

294 regnandi   306 tanta

quod si nos Eoa fides et barbara fallent
foedera, uolgati supra commercia mundi
naufragium fortuna ferat.   non regna precabor
quae feci ; sat magna feram solacia mortis
orbe iacens alio, nihil haec in membra cruente,   315
nil socerum fecisse pie.   sed, cuncta reuoluens
uitae fata meae, semper uenerabilis illa
orbis parte fui, quantus Maeotida supra,
quantus apud Tanaim toto conspectus in ortu !
quas magis in terras nostrum felicibus actis   320
nomen abit aut unde redit maiore triumpho ?
Roma, faue coeptis ; quid enim tibi laetius umquam
praestiterint superi quam, si ciuilia Partho
milite bella geras, tantam consumere gentem
et nostris miscere malis ? cum Caesaris arma   325
concurrent Medis, aut me fortuna necessest
uindicet aut Crassos.'

*The ex-consul Lentulus vehemently opposes this project
and recommends an appeal to Egypt instead. The
Council agrees with Lentulus.*

                          sic fatus murmure sensit
consilium damnasse uiros ; quos Lentulus omnis
uirtutis stimulis et nobilitate dolendi
praecessit dignasque tulit modo consule uoces :   330
'Sicine Thessalicae mentem fregere ruinae ?
una dies mundi damnauit fata ? secundum
Emathiam lis tanta datur ? iacet omne cruenti
uolneris auxilium ? solos tibi, Magne, reliquit
Parthorum Fortuna pedes ? quid transfuga mundi, 335
terrarum totos tractus caelumque perosus,
auersosque polos alienaque sidera quaeris,

                    336 *notos*

Chaldaeos culture focos et barbara sacra,
Parthorum famulus? quid causa obtenditur armis
libertatis amor? miserum quid decipis orbem,   340
si seruire potes? te, quem Romana regentem
horruit auditu, quem captos ducere reges
uidit ab Hyrcanis Indoque a litore siluis,
deiectum fatis, humilem fractumque uidebit
extolletque animos Latium uaesanus in orbem,   345
se simul et Romam Pompeio supplice mensus?
nil animis fatisque tuis effabere dignum ;
exiget, ignorans Latiae commercia linguae,
ut lacrimis se, Magne, roges.   patimurne pudoris
hoc uolnus, clades ut Parthia uindicet ante   350
Hesperias quam Roma suas? ciuilibus armis
elegit te nempe ducem : quid uolnera nostra
in Scythicos spargis populos cladesque latentes?
quid Parthos transire doces? solacia tanti
perdit Roma mali, nullos admittere reges,   355
sed ciui seruire suo? iuuat ire per orbem
ducentem saeuas Romana in moenia gentes
signaque ab Euphrate cum Crassis capta sequentem?
qui solus regum, fato celante fauorem,
defuit Emathiae, nunc tantas ille lacesset   360
auditi uictoris opes aut iungere fata
tecum, Magne, uolet? non haec fiducia gentist.
omnis in Arctois populus quicumque pruinis
nascitur, indomitus bellis et mortis amator :
quidquid ad Eoos tractus mundique teporem   365
ibitur, emollit gentes clementia caeli.
illic et laxas uestes et fluxa uirorum
uelamenta uides.   Parthus per Medica rura,
Sarmaticos inter campos effusaque plano

Tigridis arua solo nulli superabilis hostist   370
libertate fugae ; sed non, ubi terra tumebit,
aspera conscendet montis iuga nec per opacas
bella geret tenebras, incerto debilis arcu,
nec franget nando uiolenti uerticis amnem
nec, tota in pugna perfusus sanguine membra,   375
exiget aestiuum calido sub puluere solem.
non aries illis, non ullast machina belli,
aut fossas inplere ualent, Parthoque sequenti
murus erit quodcumque potest obstare sagittae.
pugna leuis bellumque fugax turmaeque uagantes,   380
et melior cessisse loco quam pellere miles ;
inlita tela dolis, nec Martem comminus usquam
ausa pati uirtus, sed longe tendere neruos
et quo ferre uelint permittere uolnera uentis.
ensis habet uires, et gens quaecumque uirorumst   385
bella gerit gladiis.   nam Medos proelia prima
exarmant uacuaque iubent remeare pharetra.
nulla manus illis, fiducia tota uenenist.
credis, Magne, uiros, quos in discrimina belli
cum ferro misisse parumst ? temptare pudendum   390
auxilium tantist, toto diuisus ut orbe
a terra moriare tua ? tibi barbara tellus
incumbat ? te parua tegant ac uilia busta,
inuidiosa tamen Crasso quaerente sepulcrum ?
sed tua sors leuior, quoniam mors ultima poenast   395
nec metuenda uiris. at non Cornelia letum
infando sub rege timet. num barbara nobis
est ignota uenus, quae ritu caeca ferarum
polluit innumeris leges et foedera taedae
coniugibus, thalamique latent secreta nefandi ?   400
inter mille nurus epulis uaesana meroque

395 melior   400 patent

regia non ullis exceptos legibus audet
concubitus; tot femineis conplexibus unum
non lassat nox tota marem. iacuere sorores
in regum thalamis sacrataque pignora matres.   405
damnat apud gentes sceleris non sponte peracti
Oedipodionias infelix fabula Thebas:
Parthorum dominus quotiens sic sanguine mixto
nascitur Arsacides! cui fas inplere parentem,
quid rear esse nefas? proles tam clara Metelli   410
stabit barbarico coniunx millesima lecto?
quamquam non ulli plus regia, Magne, uacabit
saeuitia stimulata uenus titulisque uirorum.
nam quo plura iuuent Parthum portenta, fuisse
hanc sciet et Crassi; ceu pridem debita fatis   415
Assyriis trahitur cladis captiua uetustae.
haereat Eoae uolnus miserabile sortis;
non solum auxilium funesto ab rege petisse,
sed gessisse prius bellum ciuile pudebit.   419
nam quod apud populos crimen socerique tuumque
maius erit quam quod, uobis miscentibus arma,
Crassorum uindicta perit? incurrere cuncti
debuerant in Bactra duces et, ne qua uacarent
arma, uel Arctoum Dacis Rhenique cateruis
imperii nudare latus, dum perfida Susa   425
in tumulos prolapsa ducum Babylonque iaceret.
Assyriae paci finem, Fortuna, precamur;
et, si Thessalia bellum ciuile peractumst,
ad Parthos, qui uicit, eat. gens unica mundist
de qua Caesareis possim gaudere triumphis.   430
non tibi, cum primum gelidum transibis Araxen,
umbra senis maesti Scythicis confixa sagittis
ingeret has uoces? "Tu, quem post funera nostra

428 Thessaliae

ultorem cinerum nudae sperauimus umbrae,
ad foedus pacemque uenis?" tum plurima cladis   435
occurrent monimenta tibi, quae moenia trunci
lustrarunt ceruice duces, ubi nomina tanta
obruit Euphrates et nostra cadauera Tigris
detulit in terras ac reddidit. ire per ista   439
si potes, in media socerum quoque, Magne, sedentem
Thessalia placare potes. quin respicis orbem
Romanum? si regna times proiecta sub Austro
infidumque Iubam, petimus Pharon aruaque Lagi.
Syrtibus hinc Libycis tutast Aegyptos; at inde
gurgite septeno rapidus mare summouet amnis.   445
terris suis contenta bonis, non indiga mercis
aut Iouis; in solo tantast fiducia Nilo.
sceptra puer Ptolemaeus habet tibi debita, Magne,
tutelae commissa tuae. quis nominis umbram
horreat? innocuast aetas. ne iura fidemque   450
respectumque deum ueteris speraueris aulae:
nil pudet adsuetos sceptris; mitissima sors est
regnorum sub rege nouo.' non plura locutus
inpulit huc animos. quantum, spes ultima rerum,
libertatis habes! uictast sententia Magni.   455

Pompey arrives at Mount Casius in Egypt.

Tum Cilicum liquere solum Cyproque citatas
inmisere rates, nullas cui praetulit aras
undae diua memor Paphiae, si numina nasci
credimus aut quemquam fas est coepisse deorum.
haec ubi deseruit Pompeius litora, totos   460
emensus Cypri scopulos quibus exit in Austrum,
inde maris uasti transuerso uertitur aestu;

451 ueteri—aula

nec tenuit gratum nocturno lumine montem
infimaque Aegypti pugnaci litora uelo
uix tetigit, qua diuidui pars maxima Nili   465
in uada decurrit Pelusia septimus amnis.
tempus erat quo Libra pares examinat horas,
non uno plus aequa die, noctique rependit
lux minor hibernae uerni solacia damni.
conperit ut regem Casio se monte tenere,   470
flectit iter; nec Phoebus adhuc nec carbasa languent.

*The Egyptian king's Council meets in haste.   Acoreus
proposes that Pompey shall be welcomed.*

Iam rapido speculator eques per litora cursu
hospitis aduentu pauidam conpleuerat aulam.
consilii uix tempus erat; tamen omnia monstra
Pellaeae coiere domus, quos inter Acoreus   475
iam placidus senio fractisque modestior annis
(hunc genuit custos Nili crescentis in arua
Memphis uana sacris; illo cultore deorum
lustra suae Phoebes non unus uixerat Apis)
consilii uox prima fuit, meritumque fidemque   480
sacraque defuncti iactauit pignora patris.

*Pothinus argues that they have no option except
to kill Pompey.*

sed melior suadere malis et nosse tyrannos,
ausus Pompeium leto damnare Pothinus:
'Ius et fas multos faciunt, Ptolemaee, nocentes;
dat poenas laudata fides, cum sustinet' inquit   485
'quos fortuna premit. fatis accede deisque
et cole felices, miseros fuge. sidera terra
ut distant et flamma mari, sic utile recto.
sceptrorum uis tota perit, si pendere iusta

incipit, euertitque arces respectus honesti.   490
libertas scelerumst quae regna inuisa tuetur,
sublatusque modus gladiis. facere omnia saeue
non inpune licet, nisi cum facis. exeat aula
qui uolt esse pius. uirtus et summa potestas
non coeunt; semper metuet quem saeua pudebunt. 495
non inpune tuos Magnus contempserit annos,
qui te nec uictos arcere a litore nostro
posse putat. neu nos sceptris priuauerit hospes,
pignora sunt propiora tibi ; Nilumque Pharonque,
si regnare piget, damnatae redde sorori.   500
Aegypton certe Latiis tueamur ab armis.
quidquid non fuerit Magni dum bella geruntur,
nec uictoris erit. toto iam pulsus ab orbe,
postquam nulla manet rerum fiducia, quaerit
cum qua gente cadat. rapitur ciuilibus umbris,   505
nec soceri tantum arma fugit : fugit ora senatus,
cuius Thessalicas saturat pars magna uolucres ;
et metuit gentes, quas uno in sanguine mixtas
deseruit, regesque timet, quorum omnia mersit,
Thessaliaeque reus, nulla tellure receptus,   510
sollicitat nostrum, quem nondum perdidit, orbem.
iustior in Magnum nobis, Ptolemaee, querellae
causa datast. quid sepositam semperque quietam
crimine bellorum maculas Pharon aruaque nostra
uictori suspecta facis ? cur sola cadenti   515
haec placuit tellus, in quam Pharsalica fata
conferres poenasque tuas ? iam crimen habemus
purgandum gladio quod nobis sceptra senatus
te suadente dedit, uotis tua fouimus arma.
hoc ferrum, quod fata iubent proferre, paraui   520
non tibi, sed uicto; feriam tua uiscera, Magne ;
malueram soceri : rapimur quo cuncta feruntur.

tene mihi dubitas an sit uiolare necesse,
cum liceat? quae te nostri fiducia regni
huc agit, infelix? populum non cernis inermem   525
aruaque uix refugo fodientem mollia Nilo?
metiri sua regna decet uiresque fateri.
tu, Ptolemaee, potes Magni fulcire ruinam,
sub qua Roma iacet? bustum cineresque mouere
Thessalicos audes bellumque in regna uocare?   530
ante aciem Emathiam nullis accessimus armis:
Pompei nunc castra placent, quae deserit orbis?
nunc uictoris opes et cognita fata lacessis?
aduersis non desse decet, sed laeta secutos;
nulla fides umquam miseros elegit amicos.'   535

The Council assents and Achillas is deputed to carry out
the sentence. He persuades Pompey to leave his
galley and enter a small boat.

Adsensere omnes sceleri. laetatur honore
rex puer insueto, quod iam sibi tanta iubere
permittant famuli. sceleri delectus Achillas,
perfida qua tellus Casiis excurrit harenis
et uada testantur iunctas Aegyptia Syrtes,   540
exiguam sociis monstri gladiisque carinam
instruit. o superi, Nilusne et barbara Memphis
et Pelusiaci tam mollis turba Canopi
hos animos? sic fata premunt ciuilia mundum?
sic Romana iacent? ullusne in cladibus istis   545
est locus Aegypto, Phariusque admittitur ensis?
hanc certe seruate fidem, ciuilia bella,
cognatas praestate manus, externaque monstra
pellite, si meruit tam claro nomine Magnus

      539 exultat   541 cladisque

Caesaris esse nefas. tanti, Ptolemaee, ruinam   550
nominis haud metuis, caeloque tonante profanas
inseruisse manus, inpure ac semiuir, audes?
non domitor mundi nec ter Capitolia curru
inuectus regumque potens uindexque senatus
uictorisque gener, (Phario satis esse tyranno   555
quod poterat) Romanus erat. quid uiscera nostra
scrutaris gladio? nescis, puer inprobe, nescis,
quo tua sit fortuna loco ; iam iure sine ullo
Nili sceptra tenes ; cecidit ciuilibus armis
qui tibi regna dedit. iam uento uela negarat   560
Magnus et auxilio remorum infanda petebat
litora ; quem contra non longa uecta biremi
adpulerat scelerata manus Magnoque patere
fingens regna Phari celsae de puppe carinae
in paruam iubet ire ratem, litusque malignum   565
incusat bimaremque uadis frangentibus aestum,
qui uetet externas terris adpellere classes.
quod nisi fatorum leges intentaque iussu
ordinis aeterni miserae uicinia mortis,
damnatum leto, traherent ad litora Magnum,   570
non ulli comitum sceleris praesagia derant :
'quippe fides si pura foret, si regia Magno
sceptrorum auctori uera pietate pateret,
uenturum tota Pharium cum classe tyrannum.'
sed cedit fatis classemque relinquere iussus   575
obsequitur, letumque iuuat praeferre timori.

Cornelia vainly tries to accompany her husband.

Ibat in hostilem praeceps Cornelia puppim,
hoc magis inpatiens egresso desse marito
quod metuit clades. 'Remane, temeraria coniunx,

563 *adproperat : adcelerat*   567 aduertere

et tu, nate, precor, longeque a litore casus   580
expectate meos et in hac ceruice tyranni
explorate fidem' dixit.   sed surda uetanti
tendebat geminas amens Cornelia palmas :
'Quo sine me crudelis abis? iterumne relinquor
Thessalicis summota malis? numquam omine laeto 585
distrahimur miseri.   poteras non flectere puppim,
cum fugeres, alio latebrisque relinquere Lesbi,
omnibus a terris si nos arcere parabas?
an tantum in fluctus placeo comes?' haec ubi frustra
effudit, prima pendet tamen anxia puppe,   590
attonitoque metu nec quoquam auertere uisus
nec Magnum spectare potest.

Pompey is stabbed by Achillas and Septimius, a former
  officer of his own.   His heroism in death and dying
  reflexions.

                              stetit anxia classis
ad ducis euentum, metuens non arma nefasque,
sed ne summissis precibus Pompeius adoret
sceptra sua donata manu.   transire parantem   595
Romanus Pharia miles de puppe salutat
Septimius, qui, pro superum pudor, arma satelles
regia gestabat posito deformia pilo,
inmanis uiolentus atrox nullaque ferarum
mitior in caedes.   quis non, Fortuna, putasset   600
parcere te populis, quod bello haec dextra uacaret,
Thessaliaque procul tam noxia tela fugasses?
disponis gladios, ne quo non fiat in orbe,
heu, facinus ciuile tibi.   uictoribus ipsis
dedecus et numquam superum caritura pudore   605

fabula, Romanus regi sic paruit ensis,
Pellaeusque puer gladio tibi colla recidit,
Magne, tuo. qua posteritas in saecula mittet
Septimium fama? scelus hoc quo nomine dicent
qui Bruti dixere nefas? iam uenerat horae   610
terminus extremae, Phariamque ablatus in alnum
perdiderat iam iura sui. tum stringere ferrum
regia monstra parant. ut uidit comminus enses,
inuoluit uoltus atque indignatus apertum
fortunae praebere caput; tunc lumina pressit   615
continuitque animam, ne quas effundere uoces
uellet et aeternam fletu corrumpere famam.
sed, postquam mucrone latus funestus Achillas
perfodit, nullo gemitu consensit ad ictum
respexitque nefas, seruatque inmobile corpus   620
seque probat moriens atque haec in pectore uoluit:
'Saecula Romanos numquam tacitura labores
attendunt, aeuumque sequens speculatur ab omni
orbe ratem Phariamque fidem: nunc consule famae.
fata tibi longae fluxerunt prospera uitae;   625
ignorant populi, si non in morte probaris,
an scieris aduersa pati. ne cede pudori
auctoremque dole fati; quacumque feriris,
crede manum soceri. spargant lacerentque licebit,
sum tamen, o superi, felix, nullique potestas   630
hoc auferre deo. mutantur prospera uita:
non fit morte miser. uidet hanc Cornelia caedem
Pompeiusque meus. tanto patientius, oro,
claude, dolor, gemitus; natus coniunxque peremptum
si mirantur, amant.' talis custodia Magno   635
mentis erat, ius hoc animi morientis habebat.

614 *indignatur*

Cornelia's anguish and lamentations.

At non tam patiens Cornelia cernere saeuum
quam perferre nefas miserandis aethera conplet
uocibus: 'O coniunx, ego te scelerata peremi:
letiferae tibi causa morae fuit auia Lesbos,   640
et prior in Nili peruenit litora Caesar.
nam cui ius alii sceleris? sed quisquis, in istud
a superis inmisse caput, uel Caesaris irae
uel tibi prospicies, nescis, crudelis, ubi ipsa
uiscera sint Magni; properas atque ingeris ictus,   645
qua uotumst uicto. poenas non morte minores
pendat et ante meum uideat caput. haud ego culpa
libera bellorum, quae matrum sola per undas
et per castra comes, nullis absterrita fatis,
uictum, quod reges etiam timuere, recepi.   650
hoc merui, coniunx, in tuta puppe relinqui?
perfide, parcebas? te fata extrema petente
uita digna fui? moriar, nec munere regis.
aut mihi praecipitem, nautae, permittite saltum,
aut laqueum collo tortosque aptare rudentis,   655
aut aliquis Magno dignus comes exigat ensem;
Pompeio praestare potest quod Caesaris armis
inputet. o saeui, properantem in fata tenetis?
uiuis adhuc, coniunx, et iam Cornelia non est
iuris, Magne, sui: prohibent accersere mortem;   660
seruor uictori.' sic fata interque suorum
lapsa manus rapitur trepida fugiente carina.

*Septimius hacks off Pompey's head which is carried to
the king and afterwards embalmed.*

At Magni cum terga sonent et pectora ferro,
permansisse decus sacrae uenerabile formae

iratamque deis faciem, nil ultima mortis   665
ex habitu uoltuque uiri mutasse, fatentur
qui lacerum uidere caput. nam saeuus in ipso
Septimius sceleris maius scelus inuenit actu,
ac retegit sacros scisso uelamine uoltus
semianimis Magni spirantiaque occupat ora   670
collaque in obliquo ponit languentia transtro.
tunc neruos uenasque secat nodosaque frangit
ossa diu ; nondum artis erat caput ense rotare.
at, postquam trunco ceruix abscisa recessit,
uindicat hoc Pharius dextra gestare satelles.   675
degener atque operae miles Romane secundae,
Pompei diro sacrum caput ense recidis,
ut non ipse feras? o summi fata pudoris !
inpius ut Magnum nosset puer, illa uerenda
regibus hirta coma et generosa fronte decora   680
caesaries conprensa manust, Pharioque ueruto,
dum uiuunt uoltus atque os in murmura pulsant
singultus animae, dum lumina nuda rigescunt,
suffixum caput est quo numquam bella iubente
pax fuit; hoc leges Campumque et rostra mouebat,   685
hac facie Fortuna tibi Romana placebas.
nec satis infando fuit hoc uidisse tyranno ;
uolt sceleris superesse fidem. tunc arte nefanda
summotast capiti tabes, raptoque cerebro
adsiccata cutis, putrisque effluxit ab alto   690
umor, et infuso facies solidata uenenost.

Indignant apostrophe to 'Ptolemy.

Vltima Lageae stirpis perituraque proles,
degener, incestae sceptris cessure sorori,
cum tibi sacrato Macedon seruetur in antro,

665 *mirandamque*   681 conpressa

et regum cineres extructo monte quiescant,   695
cum Ptolemaeorum manes seriemque pudendam
Pyramides claudant indignaque mausolea,
litora Pompeium feriunt, truncusque uadosis
huc illuc iactatur aquis? adeone molesta
totum cura fuit socero seruare cadauer?   700
hac Fortuna fide Magni tam prospera fata
pertulit, hac illum summo de culmine rerum
morte petit cladesque omnes exegit in uno
saeua die quibus inmunes tot praestitit annos,
Pompeiusque fuit qui numquam mixta uideret   705
laeta malis, felix nullo turbante deorum
et nullo parcente miser; semel inpulit illum
dilata Fortuna manu. pulsatur harenis,
carpitur in scopulis hausto per uolnera fluctu,
ludibrium pelagi; nullaque manente figura   710
una notast Magno capitis iactura reuolsi.

Cordus, a former quaestor of Pompey, rescues the
body from the sea.

Ante tamen Pharias uictor quam tangat harenas
Pompeio raptim tumulum Fortuna parauit,
ne iaceat nullo uel ne meliore sepulcro.
e latebris pauidus decurrit ad aequora Cordus;   715
quaestor ab Idalio Cinyreae litore Cypri
infaustus Magni fuerat comes. ille, per umbras
ausus ferre gradum, uictum pietate timorem
conpulit, ut mediis quaesitum corpus in undis
duceret ad terram traheretque in litora Magnum.   720
lucis maesta parum per densas Cynthia nubes
praebebat; cano sed discolor aequore truncus

conspicitur. tenet ille ducem conplexibus artis,
eripiente mari ; tunc uictus pondere tanto
expectat fluctus pelagoque iuuante cadauer   725
inpellit.

His soliloquy by the side of the corpse.

postquam sicco iam litore sedit,
incubuit Magno lacrimasque effudit in omne
uolnus et ad superos obscuraque sidera fatur :
'Non pretiosa petit cumulato ture sepulcra
Pompeius, Fortuna, tuus ; non, pinguis ad astra   730
ut ferat e membris Eoos fumus odores,
ut Romana suum gestent pia colla parentem,
praeferat ut ueteres feralis pompa triumphos,
ut resonent tristi cantu fora, totus ut ignes
proiectis maerens exercitus ambiat armis.   735
da uilem Magno plebei funeris arcam,
quae lacerum corpus siccos effundat in ignes ;
robora non desint misero nec sordidus ustor.
sit satis, o superi, quod non Cornelia fuso
crine iacet subicique facem, conplexa maritum,   740
imperat, extremo sed abest a munere busti
infelix coniunx nec adhuc a litore longest.'

He collects wood from an old boat's wreck to burn the
body, lighting it by faggots taken from an abandoned
pyre.

sic fatus paruos iuuenis procul aspicit ignes
corpus uile suis, nullo custode, crementis.
inde rapit flammas semiustaque robora membris   745
subducit. 'Quaecumque es,' ait 'neclecta nec ulli
cara tuo, sed Pompeio felicior umbra,
quod iam conpositum uiolat manus hospita bustum,

da ueniam ; si quid sensus post fata relictumst,
cedis et ipsa rogo paterisque haec damna sepulcri,
teque pudet, sparsis Pompei manibus, uri.'   751
sic fatus plenusque sinus ardente fauilla
peruolat ad truncum qui, fluctu paene relatus,
litore pendebat.   summas dimouit harenas
et collecta procul lacerae fragmenta carinae   755
exigua trepidus posuit scrobe.   nobile corpus
robora nulla premit, nulla strue membra recumbunt ;
admotus Magnum, non subditus, accipit ignis.

He asks forgiveness of the dead man's spirit for the
inadequate rite.

ille, sedens iuxta flammas, ' O maxime ' dixit
' ductor et Hesperii maiestas nominis una,   760
si tibi iactatu pelagi, si funere nullo
tristior iste rogus, manes animamque potentem
officiis auerte meis ; iniuria fati
hoc fas esse iubet.   ne ponti belua quidquam,
ne fera, ne uolucres, ne saeui Caesaris ira   765
audeat, exiguam, quantum potes, accipe flammam,
Romana succense manu.   Fortuna recursus
si det in Hesperiam, non hac in sede quiescent
tam sacri cineres ; sed te Cornelia, Magne,
accipiet nostroque sinu transfundet in urnam.   770
interea paruo signemus litora saxo,
ut nota sit busti, si quis placare peremptum
forte uolet, plenos et reddere mortis honores,
inueniat trunci cineres et norit harenas,
ad quas, Magne, tuum referat caput.'

At the approach of dawn he hurriedly buries the
ashes in a humble grave.

haec ubi fatus,   775
excitat inualidas admoto fomite flammas.
carpitur et lentum Magnus destillat in ignem,
tabe fouens bustum. sed iam percusserat astra
Aurorae praemissa dies ; ille, ordine rupto
funeris, attonitus latebras in litore quaerit.   780
quam metuis, demens, isto pro crimine poenam,
quo te fama loquax omnis accepit in annos ?
condita laudabit Magni socer inpius ossa :
i modo securus ueniae fassusque sepulcrum
posce caput. cogit pietas inponere finem   785
officio. semiusta rapit resolutaque nondum
ossa satis, neruis et inustis plena medullis,
aequorea restinguit aqua congestaque in unum
parua clausit humo. tunc, ne leuis aura retectos
auferret cineres, saxo conpressit harenam,   790
nautaque ne bustum religato fune moueret,
inscripsit sacrum semiusto stipite nomen
HIC SITVS EST MAGNVS.

To think that after all his deeds Pompey the Great
should be buried thus!

placet hoc, Fortuna, sepulcrum
dicere Pompei, quo condi maluit illum
quam terra caruisse socer ? temeraria dextra,   795
cur obicis Magno tumulum manesque uagantis
includis ? 'situs est' qua terra extrema refuso
pendet in oceano ; Romanum nomen et omne
imperium Magno tumulist modus : obrue saxa

crimine plena deum. si totast Herculis Oete   800
et iuga tota uacant Bromio Nyseia, quare
unus in Aegypto Magni lapis? omnia Lagi
rura tenere potest si nullo caespite nomen
haeserit; erremus populi cinerumque tuorum,
Magne, metu nullas Nili calcemus harenas.   805
quod si tam sacro dignaris nomine saxum,
adde actus tantos monimentaque maxuma rerum,
adde trucis Lepidi motus Alpinaque bella
armaque Sertori reuocato consule uicta
et currus quos egit eques, commercia tuta   810
gentibus et pauidos Cilicas maris; adde subactam
barbariem gentesque uagas et quidquid in Euro
regnorum Boreaque iacet. dic semper ab armis
ciuilem repetisse togam, ter curribus actis
contentum multos patriae donasse triumphos.   815
quis capit haec tumulus? surgit miserabile bustum
non illis plenum titulis, non ordine tanto
fastorum, solitumque legi super alta deorum
culmina et extructos spoliis hostilibus arcus
haud procul est ima Pompei nomen harena   820
depressum tumulo, quod non legat aduena rectus,
quod, nisi monstratum, Romanus transeat hospes.

*The poet inveighs against the criminality of Egypt and
against the ingratitude of Rome which still allows
the ashes of its greatest to rest in a foreign soil.*

   Noxia ciuili tellus Aegyptia fato,
haud equidem inmerito Cumanae carmine uatis
cautum, ne Nili Pelusia tangeret ora   825
Hesperius miles ripasque aestate tumentis.

quid tibi saeua precer pro tanto crimine tellus?
uertat aquas Nilus, quo nascitur orbe, retentus,
et steriles egeant hibernis imbribus agri,
totaque in Aethiopum putres soluaris harenas.   830
nos in templa tuam Romana accepimus Isim
semideosque canes et sistra iubentia luctus
et quem tu plangens hominem testaris Osirim :
tu nostros, Aegypte, tenes in puluere manes.   834
tu quoque, cum saeuo dederis iam templa tyranno,
nondum Pompei cineres, o Roma, petisti ;
exul adhuc iacet umbra ducis. si saecula prima
uictoris timuere minas, nunc excipe saltem
ossa tui Magni si, nondum subruta fluctu,
inuisa tellure sedent. quis busta timebit,   840
quis sacris dignam mouisse uerebitur umbram ?
imperet hoc nobis utinam scelus et uelit uti
nostro Roma sinu : satis o nimiumque beatus,
si mihi contingat manes transferre reuolsos
Ausoniam, si tale ducis uiolare sepulcrum.   845
forsitan, aut sulco sterili cum poscere finem
a superis aut Roma uolet feralibus Austris
ignibus aut nimiis aut terrae tecta mouenti,
consilio iussuque deum transibis in urbem,
Magne, tuam, summusque feret tua busta sacerdos.
nam quis ad exustam Cancro torrente Syenen   851
ibit et imbrifera siccas sub Pliade Thebas,
spectator Nili, quis Rubri stagna profundi
aut Arabum portus, mercis mutator Eoae,
Magne, petet, quem non tumuli uenerabile saxum
et cinis, in summis forsan turbatus harenis,   856
auertet manesque tuos placare iubebit
et Casio praeferre Ioui? nil ista nocebunt

857 iuuabit : libebit

famae busta tuae. templis auroque sepultus
uilior umbra fores; nunc est pro numine summo   860
hoc tumulo fortuna iacens, augustius aris
uictoris Libyco pulsatur in aequore saxum.
Tarpeis qui saepe deis sua tura negarunt,
inclusum Tusco uenerantur caespite fulmen.
proderit hoc olim, quod non mansura futuris   865
ardua marmoreo surrexit pondere moles.
pulueris exigui sparget non longa uetustas
congeriem, bustumque cadet, mortisque peribunt
argumenta tuae. ueniet felicior aetas
qua sit nulla fides saxum monstrantibus illud ;   870
atque erit Aegyptus populis fortasse nepotum
tam mendax Magni tumulo quam Creta Tonantis.

APPENDIX

LIBER IX.   1—18.

*The spirit of Pompey escapes to the starry spheres; and
descends to earth again to animate Brutus and Cato.*

At non in Pharia manes iacuere fauilla,
nec cinis exiguus tantam conpescuit umbram.
prosiluit busto, semiustaque membra relinquens
degeneremque rogum, sequitur conuexa Tonantis,
qua niger astriferis conectitur axibus aer   5
quodque patet terras inter lunaeque meatus
semidei manes habitant, quos ignea uirtus,
innocuos uita, patientes aetheris imi
fecit, et aeternos animam collegit in orbes :
non illuc auro positi nec ture sepulti   10
perueniunt.   illic postquam se lumine uero
inpleuit stellasque uagas miratus et astra
fixa polis, uidit quanta sub nocte iaceret
nostra dies, risitque sui ludibria trunci.
hinc super Emathiae campos et signa cruenti   15
Caesaris ac sparsas uolitauit in aequore classes,
et, scelerum uindex, in sancto pectore Bruti
sedit et inuicti posuit se mente Catonis.

167—214.

*Last tributes of wife and friends.   The tempered eulogy
of Cato.*

Interea, totis audito funere Magni
litoribus, sonuit percussus planctibus aether,
exemploque carens et nulli cognitus aeuo
luctus erat, mortem populos deflere potentis.   170
sed magis, ut uisast, lacrimis exhausta, solutas
in uoltus effusa comas, Cornelia puppe
egrediens, rursus geminato uerbere plangunt.
ut primum in sociae peruenit litora terrae,
collegit uestes miserique insignia Magni   175
armaque et inpressas auro, quas gesserat olim,
exuuias pictasque togas, uelamina summo
ter conspecta Ioui, funestoque intulit igni.
ille fuit miserae Magni cinis. accipit omnis
exemplum pietas, et toto litore busta   180
surgunt Thessalicis reddentia manibus ignem.
sic, ubi depastis summittere gramina campis
et renouare parans hibernas Apulus herbas
igne fouet terras, simul et Garganus et arua
Volturis et calidi lucent buceta Matini.   185
non tamen ad Magni peruenit gratius umbras
omne quod in superos audet conuicia uolgus
Pompeiumque deis obicit, quam pauca Catonis
uerba sed a pleno uenientia pectore ueri.
'Ciuis obit' inquit 'multum maioribus inpar   190
nosse modum iuris, sed in hoc tamen utilis aeuo
cui non ulla fuit iusti reuerentia; salua

libertate potens, et solus plebe parata
priuatus seruire sibi, rectorque senatus,
sed regnantis, erat. nil belli iure poposcit,   195
quaeque dari uoluit, uoluit sibi posse negari.
inmodicas possedit opes, sed plura retentis
intulit. inuasit ferrum, sed ponere norat ;
praetulit arma togae, sed pacem armatus amauit ;
iuuit sumpta ducem, iuuit dimissa potestas.   200
casta domus luxuque carens corruptaque numquam
fortuna domini. clarum et uenerabile nomen
gentibus, et multum nostrae quod proderat urbi.
olim uera fides Sulla Marioque receptis
libertatis obit : Pompeio rebus adempto   205
nunc et ficta perit. non iam regnare pudebit,
nec color imperii nec frons erit ulla senatus.
o felix, cui summa dies fuit obuia uicto
et cui quaerendos Pharium scelus obtulit enses !
forsitan in soceri potuisses uiuere regno.   210
scire mori sors prima uiris, sed proxima cogi.
et mihi, si fatis aliena in iura uenimus,
fac talem, Fortuna, Iubam ; non deprecor hosti
seruari, dum me seruet ceruice recisa.'

EXPLANATORY NOTES

['Schol. C' means the Scholia published by Usener, 'Schol. a' those published by Endt, 'Schol. W' those published in Weber's edition. See the Critical Apparatus pp. xcix sq.

References given thus VI 342 without name of author are to books of Lucan.

An asterisk affixed to the number of a line, thus 32*, refers the reader to a note in the Critical Apparatus.]

1. **super** 'beyond'; cf. 164, 226, 'supra' 312 n.

Herculeas. The gorge of Tempe, acc. to one legend, made by Hercules, Diodorus 4. 18. 6, Lucan VI 343 sqq., Sen(eca) *Herc. F.* 286 sqq. Heracleum was a town 5 Roman miles from Phila, Livy 44. 8 fin.

-que, unlike the Eng. *and*, but like the Greek τε, often means 'that is to say.' Exx. in 5, 46, 148, 190, 655, 696 and elsewhere. The English idiom is to leave the copula out altogether 'the gorge of Hercules, wooded Tempe,' the pause between the words giving the relation. In some cases, as in Verg. *A.* 1. 672, 5. 447 (with Henry's notes in *Aeneidea*), Plaut. *Stich.* 7, it adds nothing to the sense. *et* is similarly used, Verg. *A.* 2. 99. Cf. 647, 798, 858, with notes.

2. **Haemoniae.** This is said by Dionysius of Halicarnassus (1. 17) to be the old name of Thessaly; and so it is used by Apollonius Rhodius 3. 1090, cf. 4. 1000 and elsewhere. In strictness it would seem to have been that of the northern portion, as recognised by the second account given by Strabo 9, fin. p. 443 ἔνιοι δὲ διελόντες δίχα τὴν μὲν πρὸς νότον λαχεῖν φασι Δευκαλίωνι καὶ καλέσαι Πανδώραν ἀπὸ τῆς μητρός, τὴν δ' ἑτέραν Αἵμονι ἀφ' οὗ Αἱμονίαν λεχθῆναι. This agrees with the statement of Baton of Sinope in his treatise 'on Thessalia and Haemonia,' quoted by Athenaeus 14. 45 p. 639, that the Vale of Tempe was the result 'of violent earthquakes in Haemonia'

(ἐν τῇ Αἱμονίᾳ σεισμῶν μεγάλων γιγνομένων). The extension of the name of a people or district is a common phenomenon in language : Ἑλλάς and England are two well-known instances. In such cases the original limited signification frequently remains and may be detected by careful scrutiny. Compare what is said upon *Thessalia*, *Introd.* pp. xcii sq.

deserta, a 'transferred epithet,' in its sense applying to *siluae* ; cf. *tota* 375, *commissa* 449, 568, 591, 636, 671, 807 with notes.

dispendia 'a détour.' It properly means '*dis*bursements' ' losses,' the opposite of '*com*pendia' 'gains.' Hence of losses of time and what causes them, as a circuitous route etc.: Verg. *Aen.* 3. 453 'morae —*dispendia*,' Mart. 9. 99. 5 'tu qui longa potes *dispendia* ferre uiarum.'

3. **negantem** 'saying No to,' refusing to obey; cf. Propertius 4. 5. 5 'docta uel Hippolytum Veneri mollire *negantem*.' Statius *Theb.* 4. 123 sq. 'dexter Iaccho | collis, at Hennaeae Cereri *negat*,' ib. 3. 457 sq. 'pauidis maculosa bidentum | corda *negant*' and elsewhere.   Compare Browning in *The Laboratory* 'This never will free | The soul from those masculine eyes,—say " no " | To that pulse's magnificent come and go.' For the facts see *Introd.* p. xxvi.

4. **incerta,** proleptic. Cf. *hibernas* ix 183 n.

turbat, i.e. confuses the trail. Cf. Ovid *Met.* 8. 160 sq. (of Daedalus making the Labyrinth) '*turbat*que notas et lumina *flexum* | ducit in *errorem* uariarum ambage *uiarum*.'

5. **-que** explanatory as supra 1 n.

uias 'tracks'; cf. Ov. l.c. 166 sq. 'ita Daedalus implet | innumeras *errore uias*.'

fragorem should mean the crack of snapping branches, Ov. *M.* 8. 340 sq. 'sternitur incursu (the rush of the wild boar) nemus et propulsa *fragorem* | *silua* dat,' which to the unnerved Pompey (*Introd.* p. xxvi) would suggest horsemen pursuing him through the forest.

6. **comitum** may mean the companions of his flight *or* his staff.

7. **qui,** quisquis comitum.

redit 'returns,' rejoins his leader ; but whether he is supposed to have been scouting and to have come in from the rear or to have followed Pompey from the battle-field is not made clear.

lateri...timentem. For the construction (dative=' for') cf. Valerius Flaccus 1. 490 sq. 'uenator cum lustra fugit domin*o*que *timentem* | urguet equum' and Verg. *A.* 2. 728 sq. (which Lucan is following) 'nunc omnes terrent aurae, sonus excitat omnis | suspensum et pariter comit*i*que oner*i*que *timentem*'; so also in prose Sen. *Dial.* 10. 17. 2. Contrast VII 678 'non terg*o* tela *pauentem*' with my note. The side (like the back) was without armour, cf. 618.

8. **summo de culmine.** *rerum* is added in 702; cf. VII 594 n. Pompey is 'fallen from his high estate,' Dryden *Alexander's Feast.*

lapsus in strictness does not qualify *scit* but the infinitival clause in dependence on *scit*—an incoherence of the same kind as *reuoluens* 316 n. inf. The similar looseness in the use of English participles is apt to blind us to the irregularity.

9. **uile.** 'That not as yet is the fee for his life-blood low.' Somewhat differently Martial 1. 76. 1 'o mihi curarum pretium non uile mearum.'

10. **fati**, *his former* lot ('fatis—prioribus' 23, 'stantis adhuc fati' 158); cf. 'in fata redire' VII 719 n. It is a noticeable feature in Lucan's style to omit qualifiers in his phrases. Cf. 13 n., 85 n.

11. **adhuc** with **habere.**

12. **ceruice**, the head with its neck. In this connexion *ceruix*, or *collum*, and *caput* (647) are used with little difference. IX 1023 sq. 'accipe quidquid | pro *Magni ceruice* dares,' X 518 'gladio *ceruix* male caesa pependit,' ib. 423 sq. 'poteratque cruor per regia fundi | pocula Caesareus mensaeque incumbere *ceruix*,' IX 281 '*ceruicis* pretio ('risking their heads'), ib. 1089 sq. 'uos condite tanti | *colla* ducis,' X 1 'Pompei *colla* secutus'; cf. Claudian *Bell. Gild.* 465 quoted on 673 and 'de*collare*' 'to de*capitate.*' Even in prose we have 'gladio ceruices subiectas' followed by 'eidem caput suum subiecerat' Val(erius) Max(imus) 4. 7 Ext. 1, and in Greek ἀποκόψαι τὸν τράχηλον Plutarch *Cato Maior* 17. Compare also 436 n., 581.

The Pompeian admission that no mercy would be shown to Caesar should be noted. As Cicero knew well, Pompey's victory would have been celebrated by a 'Sullan' proscription '*Sullano* more exemploque uincet' *ad Att.* 10. 7. 1 for which cf. 25 n.

13. **fatum**, here his *present* lot; 10 n., 85 n.

14. **clara**, contrasted with **celare** (13), unites the senses of 'unmistakable,' 'plain' and 'illustrious.' For the first cf. Quintil(ian) *Inst.* 8. 3. 63 'cetera quae nobis illam pugilum congredientium *faciem* ita ostendunt ut non *clarior* futura fuerit spectantibus.'

Pharsalica 'Pompeiana' Schol. C.

15. **ruinas**, *Pompey's* fall, 10 n.

16. **uertigine** 'turn,' 'revolution,' here used as the verbal noun of *uertere* in a metaphorical sense, cf. Prop. 2. 8. 7 'omnia *uertuntur*,'

as at VI 460 'torti magica *uertigine* fili.' The phrase is copied by
Ammianus Marcellinus 31. 19 fin. 'in ipsa *uertigine* pereuntium
rerum' and Maximianus 3. 3 'mentem *rerum uertigine* fractam.'

18. erat, with what we may call the 'subjective' use of *esse* which
differs little from *uideri*. Pompey was scarcely regarded as a trust-
worthy witness of a disaster which had happened to himself. Cf.
317, 378 sq., 871, IX 179.

grauis, 'aut quoniam pudebat illum aut quoniam sollicitum faciebat'
Schol. C. The first explanation seems right. For *grauis* compare 157,
IX 64 'officium graue manibus.'

20. tutus (with **obscuro nomine**) 'protected,' cf. IX 732 'nec *tutus*
spatiost elephas.' See also 225.

21. The thought is expanded in 701 sqq.

22. tanto pondere famae 'with all the weight of his glory'; cf.
'*pondere* fati' VII 686 n.

23. premit, 486, 544.

urguet, of a heavy load; Ov. *F.* 4. 515 'quamuis onus urguet,'
Plaut. *Poen.* 857.

24. honores, here not 'offices' but 'distinctions,' Pompey having
triumphed (*lauriferae* 25) twice before holding any magistracy.

festinatos 'accelerated,' gained before the time; cf. Plin. *Pan.* 69
'quin immo (Caesar illos) *festinatis honoribus* amplificat atque auget et
maioribus suis reddit.'

25. acta l. Sullana i., 'the Sullan feats of his laurelled youth,'
i.e. as a supporter of Sulla. *Sullanus* usually has a sinister sense in
Lucan and Pompey is represented as being his apt pupil in cruelty,
I 330 '*Sullanum* solito tibi *lambere ferrum*,' ib. 326 'docilis *Sullam*
scelerum uicisse *magistrum*,' ib. 335 'ille tuus—Sulla,' VII 307 n. 'cum
duce Sullano gerimus ciuilia bella,' II 171 'omnia *Sullanae* lustrasse
cadauera *pacis*.' Similarly Lucan's uncle Seneca, from whom the
poet's estimate of Sulla and much besides was doubtless derived,
'*Sullana* crudelitas' Sen. *Dial.* 4. 34. 3; '*Sullano*—saeculo' ib. 1.
20. 4, cf. on Sulla's tyranny id. *Dial.* 1. 3. 7 sqq., *de Clem.* 1. 12.
Livy's condemnation of both can hardly have been less severe; see the
periochae to books 88 and 89.

damnat 'gives judgment against,' 'reprobates,' 127, 328. His
'laurelled youth' is of course an allusion to his first triumph, 81.

26. Corycias...classes refers to the naval war with the pirates of
Cilicia, of which Corycus was a promontory with a famous cave described
by the geographer Mela 1. 72 sqq.

Pontica signa, i.e. the land campaigns against Mithridates.

27.   **deiectum** ; cf. 206 n., 344. The phrasing of the whole passage strongly resembles that of Sen. *N. Q.* 4. *praef.* 22 'quae illi ingenti spectaculo interfuit ex quo liquere mortalibus posset quam uelox foret ad imum *lapsus e summo* (v. 8) quamque diuersa uia magnam potentiam Fortuna *destrueret.* uno enim tempore uidit Pompeium Lepidumque *ex maximo fastigio* aliter ad extrema *deiectos* cum Pompeius alienum exercitum fugeret, Lepidus suum.'

longius aeuum '*protracted* life.' For the thought cf. Livy 9. 17. 6 'Cyrum…quid nisi *longa uita*, sicut Magnum modo *Pompeium*, uertenti praebuit fortunae?'

28 sq.   **superstes imperio** (dat.), 'outlasting power.' Cf. v 688 '*fatis* non posse *superstes* | esse *tuis*,' and Florus 4. 2. 51 quoted in *Introd.* p. xxxviii n. 2.

29.   **fine bonorum** echoes perhaps consciously VII 19 (n.).

30.   **praeuertit** 'forestalls' (perf.) ; cf. Sen. *Phaedr.* 259 '*morte praeuertam* nefas.'

32*.   **tradere se fatis** 'to put himself in the hands of Fate.'

nisi morte parata ' unless death is within his reach' as was the case with Hannibal, 'uenenum, quod multo ante *praeparatum* habebat ad tales casus, poposcit' Livy 39. 50. 8.   The phrase occurs, in a different sense, at V 773.

33.   **Peneius amnis** 'Peneus' stream'='*Penei* amnis' Grattius 501 ; probably a gen. of the 'possessor,' cf. Roby *Lat. Gr.* 1277, though the poets use adjectives for genitives with considerable freedom (compare 866 n. and 'uictor Herculeus' 'Sen.' *Herc. Oet.* 1355 = 'uictor Herculis' objective gen.) and an 'amnis Penei,' like 'urbs Romae' is possible. The 'Hypaneius amnis' of the Christian poet Licentius *ad Augustinum* 62 has probably been modelled on Lucan's phrase.

34.   **Emathia,** i.e. *Thessalica* or *Pharsalica*; so in 188, 203, 211 'Emathiis cladibus,' 267, 531.   *Emathia* is the battle of Pharsalia in 333, 360.   'Macedonian' and 'Thessalian' are not discriminated in this connexion.   The reasons are given in my note on VII 872.

clade = *caede*; cf. Crit. App. on 541.

35 sqq.   See Crit. App. and for the facts *Introd.* pp. xxvi sq.

36*.   **flumineis…uadis,** 'nedum maris' Schol. C.   For the contrast between the river boat and the sea-going vessel cf. Prop. 3. 9. 35 sq. 'non ego uelifera tumidum *mare* findo carina : | tota (*or* tuta) sub exiguo flumine nostra morast.'

37.   **quatitur,** filled with alarm ; of the moral effect of the presence

of Pompey's powerful fleet under M. Bibulus whose main station was off Corcyra; cf. Verg. *Aen.* 9. 608 '*quatit* oppida bello,' Florus 2. 7. 8 'Rhodii nauticus populus, qui *nauibus* a mari, consul a terris *omnia* equis uirisque *quatiebat.*'

38 sq. **Cilicum,** cf. Caesar *B. C.* 3. 3. 1.

terrae...Liburnae would be *Liburniae,* or *terrae Liburnicae,* in prose. But *Liburnae* suggests the swift Liburnian triremes (*Liburnae,* 'rostra *Liburna*' (adj. as here) Prop. 3. 11. 44) of which we know from Caesar *B. C.* 3. 5. 3, cf. ib. 9. 1, Pompey's fleet included a contingent. For the turn of the phrase cf. Florus 4. 2. 20 quoted on 257 and id. 4. 8. 9 (of Sextus Pompeius) 'quippe modo trecentarum quinquaginta nauium *dominus* cum sex septemue *fugiebat*,' and Justin 2. 13. 9 sq. (of Xerxes crossing the Hellespont after his defeat) 'piscatoria scapha *trepidus* traiecit, erat res spectaculo digna et ad aestimationem sortis humanae rerum uarietate miranda *in exiguo latentem* uidere *nauigio* quem paulo ante uix aequor omne capiebat.'

uector, emphatic, a mere 'passenger.' The word (cf. 'et qui uehit et qui *uehitur*' Schol.) shows an isolated sense of the suffix *-tor*, probably induced by the middle use of the part. *uehens* 'riding.'

40*. **conscia curarum** with **litora,** cf. Cic. *Verr.* 2. 5. 160 'hanc iste *urbem* delegerat quam haberet adiutricem scelerum, furtorum receptricem, *flagitiorum* omnium *consciam.*' Lesbos shares Pompey's affection and solicitude for Cornelia. Cf. *Introd.* p. xxxi n. 4.

secretae 'sequestered,' 'out of the way,' like '*sepositam*—Pharon' 513 sq.

43. **Emathiae,** in the centre of the field of Pharsalia, 34 n.

stares; stant uicti, uictor sedet, cf. 440 n.

44. **exagitant** 'rouse,' 'exacerbate'; properly of stirring up wild beasts from their lairs. Cf. Cic. *Att.* 3. 7. 2 'ne et meum *maerorem exagitem* et te in eundem luctum uocem.' Sallust *Cat.* 48. 5 'tanta *uis* hominis magis leniunda quam *exagitanda* uidebatur.'

45. **Thessaliam,** i.e. dreams of Pharsalia, the battle as in 510. On Lucan's uses of *Thessalia* see Excursus C p. lxxxix.

habet 'is filled with,' used for a more distinctive verb; cf. 385 n.

46. **scopulos,** σκοπέλους from σκοπ-εῖν, appropriately used of the high points of the cliff from which the furthest view could be obtained; cf. 'scopulosae rupis' 11 619.

extrema, to the very edge; for the **que** cf. 1 n. and for the narrative *Introd.* p. xxx.

47. **nutantia,** 'swaying' or rocking with the ship's motion under a press of canvas.

48. **prima uides,** apparently a reminiscence of Ovid *M.* 11. 466, though there in a scene of departure.

carinae 'cuiuscumque,' Schol. C.

49. **nec** 'nor yet.' For the sense cf. v 781 (Cornelia speaks) 'et *puppim,* quae fata feret tam laeta, *timebo,*' Sen. *Dial.* 11. 13. 4 '*ad omnem nauium conspectum pauent.*'

50*. **en** is to be carried on to **tendit carbasa.**

uestros, not for *tuos,* which would be absurd, as the *portus* did not belong to Cornelia, but implying 'in which you are allowed a share,' 'common to you and your hosts of Lesbos.' So in Prop. 3. 15. 44 (addressed to Cynthia) 'nescit *uestra* ruens ira referre pedem' (the passion of your sex). For the overlapping usages of *tuus* and *uester* see *Hermathena* no. 40. (1914) pp. 91 sqq.

51*. **summa pauoris,** the total of your fears, your utmost fear; III 497 '*summa* fuit Grais, starent ut moenia, *uoti,*' the subject is the next line. The substantive verb (*est* here) is not inserted. So 364, 762, 802 n. *sum* is left out in 648.

53. The several words have each a marked and almost unnatural emphasis to be rendered by a pause after each, **uictus—adest—coniunx.** This is not a simple check but a final defeat, not a rumour of disaster but its actual presence, not a mere *nuntius* but your wretched husband himself; cf. *Classical Quarterly* 1. p. 220 and notes on 105, 209, 257, 367, 371, 455 inf.

In these lines Lucan is closely following Ovid *M.* 11. 666 sqq. 'non haec tibi *nuntiat* auctor | ambiguus, non ista uagis *rumoribus* audis; | *ipse ego* fata tibi praesens mea naufragus edo.'

perdis tempora l., cf. x 595 sq. 'nec *tempora cladis* | *perdidit* in somnos.'

luctus paves the way for the apophthegm in 83 '*lugere.*'

54. The sense is 'Your fear is too late; it is time to mourn.' The seasons for *metus* and *dolor* are similarly opposed in II 27, Val(erius) Fl(accus) 1. 327.

propinqua, cf. v 678 'iam luce propinqua.'

55. **notauit** 'marked.'

crimen...deum, cf. 800 infr., Seneca quoted on 651.

56. **prementem** 'hiding,' '*premunt* tentoria gazas,' VII 742 n. For Pompey's luxuriant hair see 680 infr.

57*. **puluere.** Then Fauonius must have been an inefficient valet, see *Introd.* p. xxviii.

58. **obuia,** ἐπελθοῦσα 'rushing upon her'; cf. IX 338 sq. 'terraque saepit | *obuia* consurgens,' ib. 208 'o felix, cui summa dies fuit *obuia* uicto.'

nox, the darkness of unconsciousness; cf. III 735 '*nox subit* atque oculos uastae obduxere tenebrae,' Stat. *Theb.* 9. 40 infr., Ov. *Am.* 3. 5. 45 sq. 'gelido mihi sanguis ab ore | fugit et ante oculos *nox* stetit alta meos'; of sleep, IX 674. So νύξ in Greek.

59*. **animam cl.,** 'imprisoned,' i.e. stopped her breath. So IV 370. **neruis,** abl. after **relicta.**

60. **riguerunt** from rig*esco* (682) 'stiffened,' i.e. ceased to beat. Cf. Stat. *Theb.* 9. 40 'nox oculos mentemque rapit; tum *sanguine fixo* | membra simul, simul arma ruunt.'

61. **decepta** 'mocked,' 'befooled'; cf. VII 8 'uana *decepit* imagine somnos,' Suet(onius) *Tib.* 65 '*spe* adfinitatis ac tribuniciae potestatis *deceptum*' (of Seianus being outwitted by Tiberius). Cornelia had hoped for death to release her. Cf. IX 99, where she says, referring to her own safe return after her husband's murder, 'insidiae ualuere tuae *decepta*que *uixi*.' Schol. C notes ' παραδόξως spes in malis.'

62. **litoribus,** abl. with **ligato,** whether of ' place where ' or ' place whence' is undeterminable ; cf. note on VII 860 'religasset litore.'

uacuas, 'adhuc sine turba dolentium et consolantium' Schol. C. The Lesbians do not as yet know of his arrival. Contrast '*pleno* iam *litore*' 109 when they have assembled.

64 sq. The order is *non permisere sibi fatum incessere ultra gemitus tacitos.*

non ultra, not going beyond ; cf. Suet. *Vesp.* 14 'in hunc postea deprecantem *non ultra uerba* excanduit.' For the sense cf. I 257 sq. 'gemitu sic quisque latenti, | non ausus timuisse palam.' Here the attendants are restrained by a feeling of delicacy.

tacitos, not so much 'stifled' as 'without words,' 'inarticulate'; cf. II 20 sq. 'tum questus tenuere suos magnusque per omnes | errauit sine uoce dolor.'

incessere 'incusare Pompei fortunam' Schol. C. Cf. V 680 sq. 'circumfusa duci fleuit gemituque suorum | et non ingratis *incessit* turba *querellis*.'

66. **pectore ambit,** a strained phrase ; folds to his breast, 'encircles' in his embrace ; 'amplexibus ambit' Ov. *M.* 12. 328.

67. **astrictos** 'rigid,' 'frozen,' 'pariterque toris exhorruit omnis | mater et *adstricto* riguerunt ubere nati' Val. Fl. 2. 203 sq.

refouet, warms back to life.

68. **summum...corpus**, the surface of the body; cf. Ov. *M.* 2. 235 '*sanguine* tum credunt in *corpora summa uocato*' etc.; cf. inf. 305 n. Verg. *Aen.* 12. 376.

69. **manus** 'touch' as we say.

70. **pati** 'endure the sight of'; cf. *patimur* 349.

71. **uoce** 'aloud,' not merely by look.

72. **robur** 'stout-heartedness,' 'fortitude'; Sen. *Dial.* 6. 1. 1 'fiduciam mihi dedit exploratum iam *robur animi* et magno experimento adprobata uirtus tua,' id. *Oed.* 77 sq. 'pectus antiquum aduoca | uictasque magno *robore* aerumnas doma.'

74. **frangis**, i.e. allow to be broken; cf. 1 103 '(Isthmos) Ionium Aegaeo *franget* mare,' Sen. *Herc. F.* 806 sq. 'domitus *infregit minas* | et cuncta lassus capita submisit canis' (of Cerberus), 111 484 sq. 'postquam *uirtus incerta* uirorum | perpetuam *rupit defesso milite* cratem.' These usages are not strictly actives but rather what we may call 'inverted passives,' inasmuch as the effect is not produced by an action but only by a failure to act. The Stoic notion that τὸ μὴ κωλῦον (non-prevention) was a cause, αἴτιον, is similar.

aditum 'avenue,' 'entrance to'; Cic. *pro leg. Manil.* 1 'hoc *aditu laudis*...me...meae rationes...prohibuerunt,' *de Or.* 1. 98 'rerum aditum.'

mansurae, cf. 865 infr., Sen. *Dial.* 3. 20. 2, 'duraturo' ib. 11. 18. 2.

75. **hoc**, i.e. your ; *isto* would be more usual, but these pronouns were not carefully distinguished in Silver Latin. See notes on 122, 545, 762.

legum iura seems to mean the 'rights given by the law,' civil as opposed to military powers. So in the sing. IX 560 '*iure* suo populis uti *legum*que licebit?' For the contrast cf. Claudian *IV Cons. Hon.* 5 sq. 'cernis ut *armorum* proceres *legum*que *potentes* | patricios sumunt habitus?'

76. **materia**, properly 'stuff,' 137 n.; cf. Sen. *Dial.* 11. 3. 2 'in illo *pietas tua* idoneam nacta *materiam* multo se liberius exercuit'; cf. ib. 12. 6. 2 '*laxam* ostendendae uirtuti nacta *materiam*.' We should say 'field' here.

coniunx miser, a husband in distress, the distress of a husband. The thought in these verses is the same as in Ovid's addresses to his

wife *Tr.* 4. 3. 71—84 'sed magis in curam nostri consurge tuendi |
exemplumque mihi coniugis esto bonae, | *materiam*que tuis tristem
uirtutibus inple ; | ardua per praeceps gloria uadat iter…dat tibi *nostra
locum tituli fortuna* caputque | conspicuum *pietas* qua tua tollat habet. |
utere temporibus quorum nunc munere factast | et patet in *laudes* area
lata tuas,' cf. ib. 5. 14. 23 sq.

78. **quod sum uictus,** the very fact that I am a beaten man.
Compare Deianira's words in 'Sen.' *Herc. Oet.* 361 sqq. 'fortuna amorem
peior inflammat magis ; | *amat* uel *ipsum quod* caret patrio lare, | quod
nudus auro crinis et gemma iacet.'

79. **fasces,** the consuls and so forth in his train ; v 12 sq. 'nam
quis castra uocet tot strictas iure secures, | tot *fasces* ?'

  pia 'loyal,' apparently ironical.   Pompey's complaints (if we regard
Lucan's words in 205 sqq., 258) are somewhat premature ; and *discessit*
(80) ludicrously inappropriate from a fugitive.

  senatus appears to be gen., as in the imitation by Sidonius
Apollinaris *Carm.* 7. 572 sq. 'quo forte loco *pia turba senatus* |
detulerat uim uota preces,' though it might be nom., *p. turba* being
in apposition as in v 333.

81. **deformis** 'unsightly' (56) ; here in a moral sense ; cf. 598
'*deformis* fugae,' Val(erius) Max(imus) 5. 8. 4.

82. **uetitus =** 'incapacitated ' is here used to supply a participle to
nequire; cf. IV 73, VII 316 n. '*uetita* uirtute *moueri*' 'unable to stir,'
ib. 371.

83. **fides,** exhibition, proof of loyalty.

  lugere 'mourn,' i.e. 'mourn for '; so Schol. C 'quid ingeris *officia
mortis* adhuc *uiuo* ?'   Cf. VII 631 'nullos *lugere* uacamus' following on
' *mors* nulla querella | digna suast,' so *luctus* 832 infr.

85*. **fortuna.**   *eius* would be inserted in ordinary Latin.   But
Lucan often omits the 'qualifier' whether a genitive or possessive
adjective (15, 293, 423, 426, 454) or defining adjective (10, 13) or the
object of a verb (170, 182, 381, cf. 137) or its complement as a
dative (294, 331, 417).   In this way verbs have their meanings modified
(*transire* 354, 595, *reuocare* 809); cf. 10 supra n.

  quod d., i. amasti ?   See *Introd.* p. xxx n. 5.   The tone of Pompey's
speech to Cornelia, and its motive, may be illustrated from a passage
in a modern novel which I have come across since the *Introduction*
was written.

  "Stop !". [sobbing] cried Mrs Murray sternly.   Mabel stopped
abruptly and looked up at her mother with sudden anger, complaining :

" You shouldn't speak like that. I can't explain, but you don't understand." " My dear, I only spoke harshly because it's the way to stop
such tears." *Two Generations*, by F. Niven (1916), pp. 187 sq.

illud means *fortunam*. For the expression cf. Cic. *Att.* 12. 14. 3
' non enim iam idem esse poteris ; *perierunt illa quae amabas*.'

86. **correpta** 'chidden,' 'pulled up,' as we say; cf. VII 190 sq.
' animumque dolentem | *corripit*.'

87. **rumpente.** Cf. V 151 sq. ' *rupta* trementi | *uerba* sono.'

88. **utinam...issem,** 'ut ipsum (Caesarem) perimerem' Schol. C.
The wish is illogical but none the less true to nature.

89. **laeta** active, ' bringing joy to '; in this sense usually of things
as in 322, Val. Fl. 1. 30 ' uirtusque haud *laeta* tyranno,' Sil(ius)It(alicus)
11. 201 ' haud ulli *laeta* (neuter) profatur.' For the thought cf. III 22
(quoted on 104).

90. **nocui,** a strong word, 'ruined,' 'destroyed': cf. 305 'nocent.'

pronuba...Erinys, i.e. not ' pronuba *Iuno*,' whose place Erinys is
supposed to take, as the goddess of war does in Verg. *A.* 7.319 'et *Bellona*
manet te *pronuba*.' Cf. Ov. *Her.* 2. 117 '*pronuba Tisiphone*,' ib. 6.
43 sq. 'non ego sum furto tibi cognita: *pronuba Iuno* | adfuit et sertis
tempora uinctus Hymen. | an (*so read for* at) mihi nec Iuno nec Hymen
sed tristis *Erinys* | praetulit infaustas sanguinolenta faces ? '

91 sq. The sense is that she has passed completely into the power
of the dead Crassi, and thus brings death and disaster to any cause she
espouses; cf. 505 and 516 infr. The thought is from Livy, according
to Schol. C, *Introd.* p. xxx n. 4.

ciuilia. This adj., which properly means ' belonging to citizens,'
has, as Francken points out, in Lucan become specially associated
with the wars of citizens. So in 604 ' facinus ciuile,' VII 432 'ciuile
nefas,' 823 inf. ' ciuili...fato.'

92. **Assyrios,** at Carrhae (Assyriae, 1 104 sq. ' miserando funere
Crassus | *Assyrias* Latio maculauit sanguine *Carrhas*'), cf. 234, 416 infr.

93. **praecipites...dedi.** So in the passive Sall. *Iug.* 63. 6 ' postea
ambitione *praeceps datus* est,' and in a literal sense Sen. *Tro.* 630 'quem
mors manebat saeua *praecipitem datum* ' ('hurled from the heights'), and
other passages from Terence onwards. It is a variant from *in praeceps
dare, dari,* e.g. Livy 27. 27. 11 'tum inprouide se conlegamque et prope
totam rempublicam *in praeceps dederat*,' and elsewhere.

94. Apparently a reminiscence of Pompey's words in VII 349 '*causa*
iubet *melior superos* sperare *secundos*.'

maxime, i.e. more than MAGNE to which title there is an allusion,

as we may see from the passage from Livy whom Schol. C tells us
Lucan is following here. Cf. notes on 102, 455, 550, 711, 760, 796.
' Magnus' seems to have become a recognised addition to Pompey's
names after his third and greatest triumph 61 B.C.; cf. Livy *periocha*
103, Dio C. 37. 21. 3.

95. **indigne**, deserving better than to be wedded to me; cf. 697.

hoc iuris 'so *much* power.' This is the force of the partitive gen.
For *ius* cf. 636 and 642 with the notes.

97. **sed** 'and that too.'

98. **mollius...certa...paratior.** For the positive and comparative
side by side cf. Sen. *de Benef.* 2. 29. 1 'queruntur—quod *solida* sit cutis
beluis, *decentior* dammis, *densior* ursis, *mollior* fibris,' Mart. 10. 35. 16
' esses *doctior* et *pudica* Sappho.'

paratior 'ad parendum tibi' Schol. C.

100. **sparge** 'fling,' or 'scatter.' In the latter case there might be
an allusion to the story of Medea and her dismemberment of Absyrtus,
Sen. *Med.* 132 sqq. 'nefandae uirginis paruus *comes* | diuisus ense, funus
ingestum patri | *sparsum*que *ponto* corpus.' But the first sense is equally
possible; cf. VI 102 sq. 'miseros ultra tentoria ciues | *spargere* funus
erat,' IX 748 '*spargere* signa' 'to throw away their standards,' and
203 n., 629 infr. Cornelia has in mind a sacrifice like that of
Iphigenia.

armis with **dependisse** is apparently dative, 'to have paid (offered
up) my life to a prosperous campaign'; cf. X 80 'tempora Niliaco
turpis *dependit* amori.'

101. **denique** 'as that cannot be,' faute de mieux.

lustra 'purge' (wipe out the effect of) 'thy disasters.'

102*. **Magne.** Lucan avoids the vocative of *Pompeius*; seemingly
because of its doubtful scansion: Pompēī Hor(ace) *C.* 2. 7. 5, Pompēī
Ov. *Pont.* 4. 1. 1; cf. Priscian 7. 19 (p. 303 Keil) who declares that it.
must be a disyllable. In the other cases he uses both names indifferently,
regard being had to the greater metrical convenience of the shorter
word. Compare e.g. 794 and 796, 802 and 820. *Magnus* is of course
employed if Pompey's 'greatness' is in point, e.g. 207, 455.

ubicumque iaces 'wherever you may be.' For this nearly colour-
less use of *iacere* cf. 813 infr., I 20 'et gens si qua *iacet* nascenti
conscia Nilo,' IV 119 'et pigras, *ubicumque iacent*, effunde paludes,'
' Sen.' *Herc. Oet.* 1109 'quicquid per Libyam *iacet*' (1112 'quicquid
subiacet axibus'), cf. *adiacet* VII 188 n. The participle corresponding
is *positus* VII 704 n., Sen. *Phaedr.* 943. The relation of *iacere* to *ponere*

is the same as that of τιθέναι to κεῖσθαι, or of *constiti* (e.g. Verg. *G.* 4.
483 '*uento* rota *constitit*') to *constituo*, or of *careo* to *priuo* (Juv. 1. 59).
It may also be taken 'wherever you are laid' *sita es, posita es.* As a
matter of fact Iulia was buried in the Campus Martius, against Pompey's
wishes, Livy *periocha* 106.

ciuilibus armis. To Cornelia's excited fancy the enmity of
Pompey and Caesar is due to the malign influence of the jealous
spirit of Iulia.

103.   **nostros...toros,** as *thalamis—meis* 95.

104*.   **crudelis,** cf. Verg. *A.* 6. 501 'quis tam *crudelis* optauit
sumere poenas?' ib. 585 '*crudelis* dantem Salmonea *poenas*,' Ov. *M.* 2.
612 *poenae crudelis*, VII 431 '*saeuas* debet tibi Parthia *poenas.*'

paelice, of a second wife; compare the objurgations of Iulia's
apparition, III 21 sqq. 'fortunast mutata toris semperque potentis |
detrahere in cladem fato damnata maritos | innupsit tepido *paelex*
Cornelia busto.' The expression is extravagant, as Iulia had been
buried two years before Pompey married Cornelia.

105.   **tuo** takes the chief emphasis, 'now thine own.' On Iulia's
affection for Pompey see *Introd.* p. xxx n. 5.

refusa 'sinking back.' In the sense of physical prostration the
simple *fusus* is more common; VII 753 'tot corpora *fusa*' 'stretched
out,' 'spilt' as we say with a similar metaphor.

108*.   **sicca...Thessaliae,** appy. dative 'dry for Thessalia,' i.e.
facing Pharsalia without tears. See also Crit. App. For the expression
cf. IX 1044 sq. 'qui *sicco lumine* campos | uiderat *Emathios*' (applied
to Caesar).

confudit 'spoiled,' i.e. dimmed, obscured, with tears. Cf. Ov. *Tr.*
3. 5. 11 sq. 'uidi ego *confusos* uoltus uisosque notaui | osque madens
fletu pallidiusque meo,' and in a medical sense Sen. *Dial.* 5. 9. 2
(of impaired vision) '*confusis oculis* prosunt uirentia.' So *turbare,
conturbare* Juv(enal) 6. 7 sq. 'cuius | *turbauit nitidos* extinctus passer
ocellos,' Sen. *Dial.* 11. 5. 3 'si *oculos* tuos, indignissimos hoc malo, sine
ullo flendi fine et *conturbat* idem et exhaurit.'

Lesbos. The '*place where*' is treated as if it were the agent or
cause of the action, the real cause being suppressed. A harsh but
instructive example is Val. Fl. 6. 186 'uoluit ager galeas.' This
poetical artifice may be viewed as an 'inverted passive.' See notes
on 74, 269, 698.

109.   **pleno** 'filled,' cf. 752 n., and note on *uacuas* 62.

111.   **pignus,** 130, '*pignus* depositum' 190 sq.

112. **tu quoque** corresponds to *nobis* (110), i.e. do you too play your part and show you appreciate our conduct.

deuotos, bound religiously (*sacro foedere*), not as in 91.

113. **socios**, i.e. sociorum.

dignere, dignos existimes; Tac(itus) *A*. 4. 74 'quos non sermon*e*, non uis*u dignatus* erat.'

uel una nocte, even a single night's *stay*; cf. 1 520 '*nox una* tuis non credita muris.' A characteristic feat\ure of Lucan's style is its curt use of nouns for nominal phrases. So 197 'motus' '*change of* motion,' 249 'medio pelagi' 'a *course thro*' the middle of the sea,' 335 'pedes' '*falling at* their feet,' 473 'aduentu' '*news of* his coming,' 647 'caput' 'head *severed*,' 872 'tumulo' '*claiming* the grave.'

114. **reuisant** etc., cf. 821 sq., 850 sqq. infr.

116. **magis**, *potius*. So poets not unfrequently, e.g. Calpurnius Siculus *Ecl*. 6. 65 'si placet, antra *magis* uicinaque saxa petamus.'

117. **omnia** = *cetera omnia*, IV 824 'emere *omnes*, hic uendidit Vrbem,' Verg. *Aen*. 10. 301 sq. 'sedere carinae, | *omnes* innocuae; sed non puppis tua Tarchon,' Liv. 1. 55. 3 'eum *omnium* sacellorum exagurations admitterent aues, in Termini fano non addixere,' Tac. *A*. 1. 74, Sen. *Dial*. 11. 7. 1 'cum uoles *omnium* rerum obliuisci, Caesarem cogita.' Cf. *totos* 336 n.

118*. **crimen habent** 'have incurred guilt,' 517.

iacet, 102 n. For the juxtaposition of clauses with asyndeton (Cr. App.) cf. 519 (553 sqq.), 603, 664 sqq., 772.

120. **loci** 'of the rendezvous,' as we might say.

noto, 'probato in fide' Schol. C; perhaps, rather, from a military point of view, 'where there are no unexplored dangers.' IV 586 'tenuit stationis *litora notae*,' Caesar *B. G*. 4. 24. 3 'cum illi aut ex arido aut paulum in aqua progressi omnibus membris expeditis *notissimis locis* audacter tela conicerent.'

fatum, cf. VII 719 quoted on 10.

121. **cultus**, signs of worship, i.e. adornments, X 17 sq. 'nulla captus dulcedine rer\um, | non auro *cultu*que *deum*.'

122. For the repetition of **accipe** see X 1022 sq.

For the rare doubling of **si** compare Cato *de Re Rustica* 139 '*si* deus, *si* dea es,' and n. on 156 infr., Ov. *Her*. 10. 93 sq. '*si* freta, *si* terras porrectaque litora uidi, | multa mihi terrae, multa minantur aquae.' Other particles are so repeated, e.g. *ne* Hor. *A. P*. 152.

ista (cf. 762) would be *haec* in Ciceronian Latin. Cf. IX 417 where it is opposed to *ille*. An early example of this use, so common in Silver

Latin, is Verg. *Aen.* 9. 138 sq. 'nec solos tangit Atridas | *iste* dolor.'
How easy is the slide from the one pronoun to the other we may see
from Sen. *Dial.* 12. 6. 2 'aspice agedum *hanc* frequentiam cui uix urbis
immensae tecta sufficiunt ; maxima pars *istius* turbae patria caret':
cf. 75 n. Ovid *Pont.* 1. 2. 87 sq. 'ira uiri mitis non me misisset in
istam | si satis *haec* illi nota fuisset *humus.*'

iuuentus, of men of military age, cf. 'iuuenis' 743.

124*. **uictus,** though conquered.

126 sq. For the sense cf. 534.

secutus...damnasse. For this variety of construction cf. Cic. *Cael.*
51 'emers*isse* iam e uadis et scopulos praeter*uecta* uidetur oratio mea.'
It is not uncommon in poets, O**v**. *M.* 14. 149 sq. 'nec *amata* uidetur |
nec *placuisse* deo,' *F.* 2. 551 sq. 'bustis ex*isse* feruntur | et tacitae
ques*ti* tempore noctis aui.' Compare also 'inuolu*it*...indigna*tus*' 614 n.

128. **mundi nomine** 'on the world's account,' i.e. not on his own.
The priggish vanity is true to life, cf. VII 664, 708.

129. **esse,** emphatic 'was not dead.'

132. **adfectus,** a favourite word in Silver Latin, used also by Ovid,
and once by Cicero in translating from the Greek.

133. **hic m. Roma fuit,** cf. v 28 sq. 'Veiosque habitante Camillo |
illic Roma fuit.'

non ulla, 'alia littora fugiens non attigi praeter uestra' Schol. C.

134. **dedi** 'set' or 'turned' my vessel, cf. 194. The use is a strained
extension of *dare uela* (185) but not as harsh as that in Florus 4. 11. 8
'prima dux fugae regina *cum* aurea *puppe ueloque* purpureo in altum
dedit'='put to sea.' The statement is not strictly true ; see *Introd.*
pp. xxvii sq.

135. **iam** with **meritam.**

137*. **materiam** with **ueniae,** cf. 76 n. Pompey means that he
did not shrink from putting it in the power of the Mytilenaeans to make
their peace with Caesar by surrendering him.

iam satis est go together. The implication is 'we must now part
company, you and I.' The contrast is pointed by **mihi—mea** in the
following line. In such contrasts it is sufficient in poetry if the personal
pronoun appears in one of the members ; cf. 653 n., Hor. *Epod.* 6. 7 sqq.
'agam per altas aure sublata niuis | quaecumque praecedet fera: | *tu*
cum timenda uoce complesti nemus, | proiectum odoraris cibum,'
Mart. 5. 62. 8 '*emi* hostes: plus est: *instrue tu* ; minus est' are good
examples. In Lucan IX 1103 sq. neither the *ego* nor the *tu* of emphasis
is inserted.

nocentes, sc. 'uos.' The omission is in Lucan's manner. Schol. C has 'quid in uobis delicta congemino?' which Usener suggests may be from Livy.

138. **fata,** my destined course.

agitanda, lit. 'driven,' i.e. 'plied' or 'pursued.' Schol. C 'experienda fortuna est per totum mundum.' The expression is unusual. Perhaps there is nothing nearer than Vergil's 'mutas *agitare* inglorius *artes*' *A.* 12. 397.

139. **nimium,** cf. 848. So too in English 'In a drear-nighted December | *Too happy, happy* Tree, | Thy branches ne'er remember | Their green felicity.' For **heu** cf. Stat. *Silu.* 2. 7. 24 '*felix, heu nimis et beata tellus*,' probably a reminiscence or reproduction of Lucan's turn (cf. 550 infr. n.). Markland in his note on Statius points out that *heu* (instead of *o*) *nimium* is more usual in melancholy reflexions, as in Verg. *Aen.* 4. 657 (Dido) 'felix, heu nimium felix si litora tantum | numquam Dardaniae tetigissent nostra carinae!' But Pompey's tone is here distinctly despondent.

140 sq. Schol. C ' si receptus fuero, tua laus est quam imitantur ; si non ero receptus, tua laus est quae sola recepisti.'

141*. **praestas...fidem,** cf. VII 721 n.

142. **fas** ' fides,' Schol. C.

scelus ' perfidia,' Schol. C.

143. **uotorum...meorum.** The gen. (partitive) is more emphatic than the adj. in agreement as in ' ulli—*tuo*' 746 sq., 'the last out of all my prayers.'

144. **Lesbo,** the *people* of Lesbos, 123.

Marte, i.e. in the open field.

145 sq. Cf. Schol. C 'nam intrare etiam inimici permittunt ut capiant.' There is the same point in III 368 sq. ' iam non *excludere* tantum, | *inclusisse* uolunt.'

148. **patriae solum,** subjoined by **que** to make **tellurem** clearer. *solum uertere* is a technical term for going into exile.

149. **plangitur.** The impersonal passive is often, very effectively, used in Latin to give the impression of an aggregation of separate but similar actions or movements, and so to convey a notion of vagueness or immensity, as in Verg. *Aen.* 6. 179 '*itur* in antiquam siluam, stabula alta ferarum ; | procumbunt piceae, sonat icta securibus ilex,' id. *G.* 3. 341 sqq. ' saepe diem noctemque et totum ex ordine mensem | *pascitur*; itque pecus longa in deserta sine ullis | hospitiis,' where the picture of the ' league-long pasturing' is injured by making *pecus* the subject to *pascitur*.

infestae, of angry or threatening gestures; cf. Prop. 1. 8. 15 sq. 'et me defixum uacua patiatur in ora | crudelem *infesta* saepe uocare *manu.*' Compare Sen. *Clem.* 1. 25. 5 'ubi crebris mortibus pestilentiam esse adparuit, conclamatio ciuitatis ac fuga est et *dis ipsis manus intentantur,*' and the similar scene at Pompey's departure from Larisa, VII 724 sq.

150. **Pompeium,** like *illam* infr., is acc. after **ingemuit,** as in Stat. *Theb.* 9. 2 sq. 'ipsi etiam *minus ingemuere* iacentem | Inachidae' (very likely a reminiscence of Lucan).

minus is very near to *non* in sense as in *si minus* and in other connexions, Cic. *de Diu.* 1. 24 'nonnumquam ea quae praedicta sunt *minus* eueniunt'; cf. Stat. *Theb.* l.c.

151. **ast** is rare except at the beginning of a fresh sentence. Exx. are Verg. *Aen.* 4. 487 sq. 'haec se carminibus promittit soluere mentes | quas uelit, *ast* aliis duras immittere curas,' Plaut. *Merc.* 246. The collocation *minus—ast* is apparently unexampled.

152. The order is *ut ciuem suam uidere.* The expression is cramped, **uidere** being curtly used for a more specific phrase, e.g. *apud se uersari uiderant.* It seems hardly possible to give the verb the sense 'regarded.' In Quintilian *Inst.* 12. 10. 65 'hunc, ut deum, homines intuebuntur' the verb means 'turn their gaze on.' The perf. is used here as *uiderant* would not fit the verse; *deuinxit* 155 and *uixit* 158 cannot plead this excuse.

154. **peteret** 'if she *had been going* to,' a perfectly normal use of the imperfect subjunctive in an imaginary supposition referring to the *past.*

The student will do well to observe that the obscurities in these conditional statements may be at once cleared up if the form of what is *implied* in them is considered, as recommended in the *New Latin Primer* §§ 242, 243. Thus here *peteret* implies 'non *petebat*' 'she *was* not *going,*' and the tense is seen to be correct. Compare also note on 602.

154. **dimittere** 'let go,' 'bid good bye,' Cic. *Att.* 12. 18. 4 'est enim longum iter discedentemque te...non sine magno dolore *dimittam.*'

156. **hos...hos.** Instead of *et,* we have the pronoun repeated for emphasis; cf. II 565 sq. '*hinc* consul uterque, | *hinc* acies statura ducumst' and *si...si* 122 supra.

probitas, female 'virtue'; so Stat. *Silu.* 5. 1. 117 sqq. 'nec tamen hinc mutata quies *probitas*ue secundis | intumuit rebus; tenor idem animo moresque *modesti* | fortuna crescente manent,' ib. 154 'quid *probitas* aut casta fides?' and Lucan's forerunner Ovid *Tr.* 5. 5. 48 sq., 14. 22, *Pont.* 2. 11. 17, 3. 1. 93 sq.

modestia, *not* 'modesty' (*pudor*) but rather 'self-control,' 'un-assumingness,' as opposed to 'forwardness' or 'self-assertion'; so *modestior,* 476, 'more restrained.'

157*. 'A humble sojourner with a retinue overburdensome to none.' **grauis** agrees with **turbae,** forming a genitive of description (223, 245). The variant *turba* would be ablative of 'cause,' and *grauis* would then agree with **hospita.** For the phrase *nulli grauis* cf. *Anth. Epigr.* (Buecheler) 1313. 4 'namque *grauis nulli* uita fuit pueri,' ib. 1321. 3 'qui *nulli grauis* extiteram dum uita manebit.'

158. **stantis a. fati** would be most simply taken as a Graecism for the abl., but this appears impossible. It is probably an extension of the genitive of 'description' which, through *esse*'s lack of participles, has attached itself to the verbal predicate, 'she lived (as one) of a still unfallen fortune.' Other harsh examples are 1 98 '*temporis angusti mansit* concordia discors,' Sen. *Herc. F.* 853 sqq. 'pars tarda graditur senecta | tristis et longa satiata uita, | pars adhuc currit *melioris aeui.*' Cf. also Livy 30. 26. 7 'eodem anno Q. Fabius Maximus moritur *exactae aetatis*' (ὤν), Sallust *Iug.* 91. 5 'ad hoc pars ciuium extra moenia *in hostium potestate* [ὄντες] coegere uti deditionem facerent.' A somewhat different though cognate use is Mela 1. 16. 53 'Caria sequitur: *habitant incertae originis,*' where *habitant* is a substitute for *habitatores* (*incolae*) *sunt.* For the sense of *stantis* 'unfallen' cf. 'stant' 233, Ov. *Tr.* 5. 14. 21 'dum stetimus' 'before my downfall.'

On Cornelia's character see the *Introd.* p. xxxi n. She did not display the feminine arrogance and corruption which necessitated an enactment that governors' wives should not accompany their husbands to the provinces, Tac. *A.* 3. 33.

159 sqq. For the subject-matter see *Introd.* pp. xxx sq.

pelago, abl. of place; cf. VII 621 '*demissum fauci̇bus* ensem.' But *in* with acc. is more usual.

demissus, *middle* = *cum se demisisset* (Caesar), IX 625 'Oceanum *demisso sole* calentem.'

ad, as far as the middle of his blaze; Q(uintus) Curt(ius) 6. 5. 27 '(corporis) laeua pars *ad* pectus est nuda.'

160*. **quibus...si quibus.** The difference in expression is not necessarily designed to raise doubts as to the existence of Antipodes; cf. Prop. 2. 24. 47 sq. 'dura est *quae* multis simulatum fingit amorem, |

et se plus uni *si qua* parare potest,' id. 4. 1. 105 sq. 'aut *si quis* motas cornicis senserit alas | umbraue *quae* magicis mortua prodit aquis.'

exerit 'pushes out,' from the eastern horizon ; cf. v 598 sq. 'primus *ab Oceano caput exeris* Atlanteo, | Core, mouens aestus,' Sen. *Herc. F.* 598 'inlustre latis *exeris* terris *caput*' (of the sun).

162. **adeunt** 'travel to.'

socias...R. f. urbes, periphrasis for the *ciuitates foederatae* such as Rhodes. See *Introd.* p. xxxii.

163 sq. **regum mentes.** For the outcome of these reflexions see 276 sqq. infr.

The following words seem to apply to *Parthia*, in spite of the loose geography ; cf. 292 n. In themselves they would suit *Africa*, cf. IX 382 sqq. 'qua *nimius Titan*... | per mediam Libyen ueniant atque *inuia* temptent.'

164. **super,** 1 n.

iacentis, 102 n.

165. The sense is : 'Oft, in the sad toilings of his anxious thoughts and his recoiling from the future, he threw off the weary turmoil of his wavering heart.' As *consulit* (167) shows, the virtual, though not the grammatical, subject is Pompey ; cf. Schol. W. '*labor*] ipse laborans.' There are similar slides in 490 and 720, where see notes.

166. **proiecit,** cf. IX 952, quoted on 210 below. Sen. *Dial.* 11. 5. 5 '*proice* omnem ex toto *dolorem*.'

168. **unde** 'from (by) which of them he marks (identifies) the lands.'

quae sit mensura, i.e. 'what means of measuring his path through the sea he has in the sky.' *mensura* retains some of its verbal meaning ; cf. IX 846 sq. 'nec quae *mensura* uiarum | quisue modus norunt caelo duce,' Ov. *Ars* 3. 265 'ne possit *fieri mensura* cubantis.' For the general sense Val. Fl. 1. 168 'aequoreos caelo duce tendere cursus' is an instructive parallel ; cf. also Florus 3. 5. 28 'Scythicum (through Scythia) *iter*, tamquam in mari, *stellis secutus*.'

169. **Syriam...seruet,** keeps Syria in view ; so 'steers for Syria.' Pompey has his ultimate destination in mind, whether Parthia (*Introd.* p. xxxii n. 2) or Numidia (170).

170. 'Which of all the lights in the Wain keeps him just straight for Libya.' The object of **derigat** is omitted, 85 n.

Libyam, a poetical extension of the acc. of motion to a place. Cf. 1 686 sq. 'dubiam super aequora Syrtim | arentemque feror *Libyen*' and *Ausoniam* 845 infr.

ignis, *stella*: cf. Hor. *C.* 1. 12. 47 sq. 'uelut inter *ignis* | luna minores,' 1 652 'stella nocens nigros Saturni accenderet *ignes.*'

171. **doctus** 'trained,' 'skilled' professionally, its usual sense.

taciti, of the night stillness ; 'it *tacitis* ratis ocior horis' Val. Fl. 2. 60, in a passage imitated from this.

seruator 'watcher,' the agent-noun of *seruare* (with its primitive meaning ; cf. Verg. *Aen.* 6. 338 'dum sidera *seruat*,' v 395 'nec caelum *seruare* licet '), apparently only here in this sense.

172 sqq. The gliding constellations of the zodiac (*signifer orbis* Cicero, *signifer polus* III 254), however useful to others (as astrologers), are no guides for steersmen (*nos*).

caelo, as apparently **polo** in the next line, means a region or part of the sky.

miseros...nautas (cf. Val. Fl. 1. 573 '*miseris* olim implorabile *nautis* '), used here because of *fallentia.*

175. **axis,** the pole, explained by **gemina...Arcto** ; cf. Ov. *Tr.* 2. 190 'Parrhasiae uirginis *axe* premor.'

inocciduus 'unsetting,' also used by Statius and Claudian, Lucan's constant imitators, but by both metaphorically.

176. **puppes,** emph.

This and the following lines answer Pompey's question. A glance at the map shows that from Mytilene our course to the Bosporus is due north and to Syria in the first instance due south, and so the circumpolar stars will rise above the masthead or sink towards the sea in the same degree as we steer for the one or the other; while to reach Numidia we must (when we are in the southern Mediterranean) keep the south polar constellations on our left.

177. **summis...ceruchis,** used again in X 494. The word is taken from the Greek κεροῦχος (Pherecrates quoted by the Schol. on Ar. *Eq.* 759) and means the ropes by which the extremities (κέρατα, *cornua*) of the yard arm were attached to the top of the mast. So that *summi ceruchi* is practically the same as *summus malus.*

178. **curuantem.** This does not mean 'indenting the coast line with bays,' for which the Black Sea is nowise remarkable, but 'bending it into a curve' or 'curves,' as Hor. *C.* 1. 33. 15 sq. 'Hadriae | *curuantis* Calabros sinus' expresses the hollow curve of the gulf of Tarentum ; cf. Verg. *A.* 3. 533 'portus ab Euroo fluctu *curuatus* in arcum.' The geographer Mela compares it to the double-curved Scythian bow, 1. 102 'hic iam sese ingens *Pontus* aperit, nisi qua promunturia sunt, huc atque illuc longo rectoque limite extentus,

sinuatus cetera, sed quia contra minus quam ad laeuam et dextram abscessit mollibusque fastigiis donec angustos utrimque angulos faciat inflectitur, ad formam Scythici arcus maxime *incuruos.*'

Pontum. In the same sense Pliny *N. H.* 2. 178, advancing proofs for the curvature of the earth, has 'adeoque manifesto adsurgens fastigium curuatur ut Canopus quartam fere partem signi unius supra terram eminere Alexandriae intuentibus uideatur, eadem a Rhodo quodammodo ipsam terram stringere, in Ponto omnino non cernatur ubi maxime sublimis septentrio.'

179. **spectamus** 'we head for'; of the ship's direction, as in 198. So in Greek ὁρᾶν of direction.

quidquid, as in 365, infr., VII 387 n. 'whatever amount,' acc. of extent (internal).

arbore, the ship's 'tree' is the mast, cf. IX 337.

180. **Arctophylax,** the Bearward or Bootes, while **Cynosura** is the Little Bear, by which the Phoenicians steered, the Greeks, less well, using the Great Bear (*Helice*); cf. Ov. *F.* 3. 107 sq. 'esse duas Arctos, quarum *Cynosura* petatur | Sidoniis, *Helicen* Graia carina notet,' *Tr.* 4. 3. 1 sq., Val. Fl. 1. 18 (Langen).

propior, in ordinary prose, would be 'prop*ius*' with *acc.*

181. **inde,** from that point; Antioch in Syria is almost on the same latitude as Rhodes, where Canopus first comes in sight according to Pliny *N.H.* l.c. on 178 and Manilius 1. 217, if Mr Housman is right, with other places cited by him there.

Canopos, a very bright star in the constellation Argo near the South Pole.

182. **excipit** 'succeeds,' takes the ship from the charge of the Little Bear. The object of the verb is again omitted.

uagari 'content to range the southern sky.' We need not suppose, with Scaliger, that Lucan thought Canopus was a planet. For *uagari* is not the same as *errare* 'to stray,' though both verbs may be used of the planets as in Hor. *Ep.* 1. 12. 17 'stellae sponte sua iussaene *uagentur* et errent' unless this refers to all stars, Cic. *Rep.* 1. 22 'earum quinque stellarum quae *errantes* et quasi *uagae* (notice the qualification) nominarentur.'

183. **timens Borean,** cf. 'nec *metuens* imi *Borean* habitator Olympi' VI 341. Lucan amuses himself with the fancy that the star is afraid of the northern cold.

quoque 'also,' to complete the answer to Pompey's second question. For Numidia you must steer S. and then W.

illa...sinistra 'with it on your left'; an abl. like that in 54.

184. **trans** 'past,' 'beyond.' So *transire* sometimes means 'to pass by,' 822 n. 'limen *transire*' 'to pass by the threshold' Ovid *Rem.* 785 after Prop. 2. 7. 9; cf. *transcurrente* VII 74 n.

medio...aequore, that is without striking land previously.

185. **uela dari**, of *setting* sail; but *uela negare* (infr. 560) shows the Romans associated the use with *dare* 'to give.'

quo...pede 'with *which* sheet?' on the port or the starboard tack? *utro* would be more exact. So '*quis* iustius arma | sumpserit' 1 126, of Caesar and Pompey. The first **quo**, however, may simply mean 'whither.'

187. **hoc...serua** 'see to this.'

188 sq., as an answer to the skipper's question, mean 'Do not steer to the W. or the S.W., to Thessaly or Italy.'

Emathiis, 34 n.

189. **pelago caeloque**, your sky-and-sea-course, explained by 168 n.

190. **cetera** 'all else let the winds dispose.'

191. **tunc,** i.e. previously.

192. At this point the vessel is supposed to have reached a point a little to the N.E. of Chios. See the *Introd.* p. xxxii.

193. 'He turned the sails as they hung in due balance from the level yard-arms.'

iusto, cf. '*iusta* libra' *Pan. Messall.* 41 'a true balance.'

194. **dedit puppim** 'set' or 'put' the ship to the left; cf. 134 n.

195*. **Asinae.** *Introd.* p. xxxii and n. 3.

196. **hos...hos,** sc. *dextros...laeuos.* For the contrasted *hos* cf. Verg. *G.* 4. 84 sq. 'usque adeo obnixi non cedere dum grauis aut *hos* | aut *hos* uersa fuga uictor dare terga subegit,' Lucr. 3. 83 'hunc... hunc,' Val. Fl. 6. 362 sq. '*hi* tendere contra, | *hi* contra.'

dedit, let those ropes go towards the bows while holding taut these from his place in the stern. The student should notice how in these few lines *dare* shifts between the senses of 'giving' and 'putting' or 'setting.'

197. **motus,** the (altered) motions (of the vessel). The expression is again cut down.

198. **idem,** the same quarter, acc. as in 178.

spectante. The ship can 'look' because it has a face; cf. Hor. *Epod.* 4. 17 sq. 'quid attinet tot *ora nauium* graui | *rostrata* duci pondere?' and in Greek πρόσωπον νεώς Achilles Tatius 3. 1. 2; cf. Philostratus *Imagg.* 1. 18 (ναῦς) βλοσυροῖς κατὰ πρῶραν ὀφθαλμοῖς οἷον βλέπει 'what a look it has with fierce eyes on its bows.' Ships are so represented on ancient monuments. Compare Ov. *M.* 11. 504 sqq. '(puppis) et nunc sublimis ueluti de uertice montis | *despicere* in ualles imumque Acheronta *uidetur*, | nunc, ubi demissam curuum circumstetit aequor, | *suspicere* inferno summum de gurgite caelum.' And even Caesar speaks of ships 'seeing' or 'sighting' other vessels, *conspicatae*, *B. C.* 2. 6. 4, 22. 3.

199. They 'changed their sound' because the ship's course had been turned through a right angle and the waves would now strike it broadside. The description is vivid and accurate. For the expression cf. Seneca *Ep.* 56. 1 'audio crepitum illisae manus umeris quae, prout plana peruenit aut concaua, ita *mutat sonum.*'

moderator. So in Ovid *M.* 4. 345 the sun is called 'uolucrum *moderator equorum.*'

200. 'The charioteer, when taking the turning-post, makes his right wheel circle round the stationary left.' This is the only simile in book VIII.

dexteriore. The comparative may perhaps be employed to draw particular attention to the active wheel ; but in view of Ov. *M.* 7. 241 the change is more likely to be metrical. The origin of the use may have been the idea that the Greek δεξιτερός (and ἀριστερός) were comparatives.

201. **inoffensae** takes the main stress of the sentence, and has a full verbal force 'to approach the turning-post, but *not to strike it.*'

202. This curt description of sunrise may be compared with that of Ovid *M.* 5. 444 'rursus ubi alma dies hebetarat sidera.' Lucan took no interest in natural phenomena as such. Cf. VII 479 n.

texit, 'covered' or withdrew from sight; 'put out' ('restinxit stellas' Lucr. 3. 1044) would be a more natural expression; but cf. IX 1006 'orta dies nocturnam lampada *texit*' of the light in the Pharos of Alexandria. Rutilius 1. 400 'dum tegit astra dies' is not so strange.

203. **sparsus.** The predominant notion here seems to be 'flung to a distance' as in Val. Fl. 5. 487 sq. 'suus ut magnum rex *spargat* ab Argis | Alciden, Sthenelo ipse satus,' id. 2. 595 sq. 'iterum Aeolios Fortuna nepotes | *spargit* et infelix Scythicum gens quaeritis amnem.' Compare note on 100.

procella, of disasters in war; Ov. *M.* 13. 656, Florus 2. 6. 12 'hic secunda belli Punici *procella* desaeuit.'

205. **natus,** Sextus. For the difficulties in this passage see the *Introd.* pp. xiv, xxix.

206. **nam**. The connexion of thought appears to be this: ' I need not dwell on the fidelity of Roman nobles; why, kings themselves were still willing to be the servitors of Pompey.' *proceres* can scarcely include the *reges*; cf. VII 69 sq. '*proceres*que tuorum | castrorum *reges*que tui,' X 450 '*Hesperiae* cunctos *proceres* aciemque senatus,' II 277 sqq. 'pars magna senatus | et duce priuato gesturus proelia consul | sollicitant *proceres*que alii.'

neque 'not even.' So Livy 40. 20. 6 apparently the earliest instance; *nec* is more usual except in Tacitus.

deiecto fatis, as in 344, 'cast down from his (previous) destiny.' Compare the places cited on 27, and for the simple abl. Stat. *Theb.* 5. 47 'regno *deiecta*,' and for *fatis* 10 n. and VII 719 quoted there.

207. **ministros**, predicate. For the sense cf. VII 584 sq. '*regum* | saepe *duces*.'

208. **terrarum dominos**, a phrase applied to the gods by Horace and Ovid, but here to terrestrial rulers; cf. 38, 242.

sceptra E. tenentes. The participle of the present not uncommonly, especially in Silver Latin, takes a substantival force in which the sense of time disappears; cf. Sen. *Dial.* 6. 26. 1 '*proscribentis* (the proscribers) in aeternum ipse proscripsit,' and exactly as here *Benef.* 4. 28. 5 '*percussores et* domi *ferrum exercentes* murus ab hoste defendit,' *Dial.* 4. 8. 3 'hoc omnino ab animalibus mutis differunt quod illa mansuescunt *alentibus*, horum rabies ipsos *a quibus est nutrita* depascitur.'

209. **exul...comites** have the Lucanian emphasis, 'Lords of the world, wielders of the sceptres of the East, hath this exile in his train.' Compare 53 n.

iubet. Upon this despatch of one of 'the monarchs on the staff' on a distant and perilous mission see *Introd.* pp. xiii, xxxiv. There is reason to believe that at a somewhat earlier period Pompey had opened negotiations with Orodes; but the Parthian king demanded Syria as the fee for his assistance (Dio Cassius 41. 55. 4), an impossible stipulation, and threw the envoy into prison (*Introd.* p. xxxiv). Justin's statement, 42. 4. 6, that the Parthians 'Pompeianarum partium fuere,' lacks all corroboration; cf. Lucan III 264 sq. 'inter Caesareas acies diuersaque signa | pugnaces dubium Parthi tenuere fauorem,' and the 'amicitia cum Pompeio bello Mithridatico iuncta' is a phantom.

Though this message to Parthia is an invention of the poet's, as a disclosure of what its inventor thought in keeping with his hero's character, it is highly instructive. The selfishness, the callousness and the prodigious vanity which we can descry in the arguments of 224 sq., 233 sq., and 237 sq. are only too true to life. In all Pompey's career there was little more discreditable than his relations with Parthia.

deuia mundi, cf. IX 382 'exusta mundi.'

210. **Deiotarum.** The *i* is consonantal and to be pronounced *y*, as the *e* is long, Gr. Δηιόταρος.

Lucan perverts the facts, for which see *Introd.* p. xxvii.

sparsa u. legit. For the expression cf. IX 950 sqq. 'Caesar ut Emathia satiatus clade recessit, | cetera curarum proiecit pondera, soli | intentus genero; cuius *uestigia* frustra | terris *sparsa legens* fama duce tendit in undas' etc. The perf. *legit* is in sense equivalent to a *pluperf.* as it is in contrast to the historic *pres. iubet*; cf. 712 n.

211. **amissus.** The non-insertion of *est* is rarer in subordinate than in principal sentences, because the declaring force in the former is weaker. For examples see note on 614.

212. **Romanus erat,** it is Caesar's now; cf. VII 164 'usque ad Thessaliam Romana et publica signa,' and note.

fidissime regum. According to Strabo, 12. 3. 13, Deiotarus received the title of king from Pompey who also largely increased his hereditary dominions. On the adjective see *Introd.* xxxiv n. 4.

213. **temptare,** i.e. 'make appeal to'; cf. 390, II 632 sq. 'mundi iubeo *temptare* recessus; | Euphraten Nilumque moue.'

Eoam...fidem, cf. 311.

214. **securum a,** lit. without anxiety from the side of Caesar; so *securus ab hac parte* in prose. Compare '*timere a* suis' Cicero (*Phil.* II 216).

215. **fata,** cf. 10, 206 supr. For the sense compare 265.

216. **penetrare.** Bentley on Hor. *C.* 1. 37. 24 compares inter alia Ammianus 29. 5. 34 'Caprarienses montes longe *remotos penetrauit.*'

Scythicos...recessus, of the far off provinces of Parthia (302 and n.), 291, and 353 n. and II 632 (above).

217*. 'To change the whole day,' i.e. the day-lighted sky, is a variant on 'mutare *caelum*' ('*caelum* non animum *mutant* qui trans mare currunt' Hor. *Ep.* 1. 11. 27); cf. VII 189 '*sub quocumque die,* quocumquest sidere mundi' and note. *Dies* in this sense might be thought to preserve its original sense as seen in the Sanskr. *Dyaŭs* (Ζεύς, *Dies*piter); but as there is no early example of the use in Latin literature, it is probably an innovation of the post-Augustan poets. On Lucan's ideas of the position of Parthia see 337 n.

218. Arsacidae, the king of Parthia as descendant of Arsaces I, the reputed founder of the monarchy.

foedera, a reference to the treaty which Pompey, on behalf of Rome, concluded with Phraates in 66 B.C. Lucan's authority is no doubt Livy; cf. the *periocha* of lib. 100 'Cn. Pompeius ad gerendum bellum aduersus Mithridaten profectus cum rege Parthorum Phraate amicitiam renouauit.' Compare Florus 3. 5. fin. 'exceptis quippe Parthis qui *foedus* maluerunt et Indis qui adhuc nos nec nouerant omnis Asia inter Rubrum mare et Caspium et Oceanum Pompeianis domita signis tenebatur,' and 3. 11. 5, the envoys sent to Crassus when he attacked Parthia in 54 B.C. 'appealed to this treaty 'missi ab Orode rege legati nuntiauere, *percussorum cum Pompeio foederum* Sullaque meminisset.' Cf. Dio 36. 45. 3, 37. 5. 2. Relations between the Roman general and the Parthian king soon became strained, and the next year Pompey sent his lieutenant Afranius to expel the Parthians from Gordyene (Plut. *Pomp.* 36). The claim of Pompey that this treaty still subsisted (**manent**) might be called impudent if anything were impudent in politics.

219. iurata implies 'iurare *foedus*,' '*in* foedus iurare' being the usual phrase. So we have in English 'gone to *swear a peace*,' Shakespeare *K. John* III 1. 1. IV 228 sq. 'sceleri *iurata* nefando | *sacramenta*' is easier.

220. uestros. *uobis* would have given a more symmetrical expression; but the adjective was chosen to balance *Latium*.

astricta, lit. 'drawn tight.' The verb is used with *foedus* on the analogy of *astringere fidem*, Ter. Cic. etc.

magos. The Magians or priestly caste among the Persians continued to be held in high esteem by the Parthians, and seem to have taken an important part in the ritual of treaties down to late times. Cortius quotes Sidonius Apollinaris *Carm.* 2. 82 sq. 'partibus at postquam statuit noua formula foedus | Procopio dictante *Magis*, iuratur ab illis | ignis et unda deus.' So Claudian *Cons. Stil.* 1 58 sqq. of a treaty struck with Parthia, 'turis odorati cumulis et messe Sabaeo | pacem conciliant arae. penetralibus ignem | sacratum rapuere adytis rituque iuuencos | Chaldaeo strauere *Magi*.'

221. Armenios. Armenia was no part of Parthia but was not always distinguished from it, and so the author of the *Consol. ad Liuiam* means the Parthians by his '*Armenius*que *fugax*' 389.

Geticis, on the other hand, seems to be used for *Scythicis* (that is 'Parthian' again). Compare Sen. *Oed.* 476 sq. 'laxauit uictos arcus

*Geticas*que sagittas | lactea *Massagetes* qui pocula sanguine miscet.' Similarly in Val. Fl. 6. 340 *Edonis* means ' Scythian' and not, as usual, ' Thracian.' Poets, especially Latin poets of the post-republican period, allow themselves great liberties in the use of adjectives from proper and especially gentile names as quasi-synonyms. See Excursus B p. lxxviii. The line appears to be only a grandiose way of saying ' have your bows ready strung.' To make a parallel we might say ' On *English* guns fix *British* bayonets.'

intendite, like ' *tendunt neruis* melioribus *arcus,* VII 141.

222* sqq. On the punctuation of this passage see Cr. App. The **si** resumes the *si* of 218, the conclusion to both coming in 235—7. The argument of the whole passage is as follows : ' If, Parthians, a mutual compact binds us both, then arm now (218—221) ; if, in the midst of my Eastern conquests, I forbore to push you to extremities 222—5)—I had every temptation to do so but I stopped in my victorious career and allowed your king to approach me as an equal (225—*adit* 232)—*and* if on a second occasion I saved your dynasty (for who else held Rome's hand after the defeat of Carrhae ?), then let Parthia now perform her part and cross the frontier in my cause' (232—7).

o Parthi is an appeal, ' ye Parthians '; not ' Parthians ' simply, still less ' O Parthians'; see on 836.

Caspia claustra. There are three famous mountain passes to which the name ' Caspian' has been, whether correctly or incorrectly, applied. **1.** In Asia the important ' Caspian Gates ' at the division of Parthia and Media not far from the Median town of *Rhagae*, through which Alexander passed in his pursuit of Darius (Arrian 3. 20). These are the ' *Caspia claustra* ' intended here as in 291. **2.** The Caspian or *Albanian* Gates on the borders of the Caspian Sea near Albana (now *Derbent*) formed by a spur of the Caucasus. These last are sometimes confused with **3,** the inland pass called the *Caucasian* or Sarmatic Gates, now the *Pass of Dariel.*

223*. aeterni martis, gen. of description, cf. 245, 374, 676, 678, Sen. *Tro.* 1114 ' *sedis incertae* Scytha.'

Alanos, see Excursus B p. lxxx. Ammianus Marc., 31. 2. 22, says of them ' utque hominibus quieti et placidis otium est uoluptabile, ita illos pericula iuuant et bella.'

224*. passus. Contrast Hor. *C.* 1. 2 fin. ' *neu sinas Medos equitare* inultos, | te duce, Caesar.' This magnanimity of Pompey was purely selfish. He shrank from engaging in an inconvenient war; according to Dio c. 37. 7. 2 he was afraid of the Parthian power.

Achaemeniis, *Persicis*, from Achaemenes, the mythical progenitor of the elder Cyrus and founder of the Persian dynasty (Herodotus 1. 125, 7. 11).

decurrere, of the Parthian cavalry; cf. 11 49 sq. 'Achaemeniis *decurrant* Medica Susis | agmina.'

225. **in tutam...B.** 'to the shelter of Babylon'; cf. 11 504 'ad *tutas* hostis *compellitur* arces.' On *tutus* 'protected' cf. 20 n. The notion of '*safety*' need not be present; see Prop. 2. 12. 11 'ante ferit quoniam, *tuti* quam cernimus hostem.'

226. **super,** 1 n.

Chaldaei...regni. 'Chaldaea' meant originally the country on the extreme south of Babylonia adjoining Arabia Deserta, but it was applied later to the whole of Babylonia. In connexion with **Cyri** the Chaldaean empire should mean the empire of the conqueror of Babylon, which extended as far east as the Indus and the Iaxartes.

ultima may agree with **arua,** or be used as a subst. as in IV 147, X 273.

227. **Nysaeus Hydaspes.** Nysa, said in legend to have been the birthplace of Bacchus, is usually identified with *Nagara* and placed on the hills between the Indus and the Cophen (now the *Kabul* river): the Hydaspes (Jelum) falls into the Acesines (Chenab), another tributary of the Indus.

228. **accedunt pelago** 'join the sea,' cf. Ov. *Tr.* 5. 7. 2 'aequoreis *additur* Hister aquis.' The Hydaspes does not fall into the sea. The Ganges does, but more than 1000 miles away. As a representation of Pompey's movements in the East the expression is grotesquely extravagant.

ab. We say 'to.' The Latin idiom is on the analogy of *procul*, *longe abesse ab*.

229. **Persis** probably means 'Parthia,' not Persia or Persis proper. Compare III 258, of Armenia regarded as a province of Parthia, and Excursus B p. lxxix. But the reference to the Sun is specially suitable to the Persae proper.

uincens. The participle is used for a subordinate clause 'cum omnia uincerem.' Cf. 316 n.

232. **ex aequo** 'on level terms.' This phrase occurs twice in Pliny in reference to the Parthians *N. H.* 6. 50, 112 'pertinent ad Scythas cum quibus ex aequo degunt.' Addressed to Orodes it would

not be particularly felicitous, recalling, as it might, the fact that Pompey had refused to his father Phraates the customary title of 'King of Kings' (Plut. *Pomp.* 38, Dio C. 37. 6).

adit, probably perfect ; cf. 321, IX 347.

233. **stant,** i.e. have been preserved from falling.

234. It is not easy to say what this refers to, unless, may be, to the retention in Italy (50 B.C.) of the two legions which had been intended for use against the Parthians.

236. **excedat.** Verbs compounded with *ex* often take an accusative in the sense of getting clear of or beyond anything. An extreme extension of the use is 'erupere Capuam,' Florus 3. 20. 3, where 'Capua' would be usual.

237. **Zeugma,** Ζεῦγμα, on the right bank of the Euphrates opposite Apamea, and the chief crossing-place in Lucan's time, so named from a bridge of boats which according to one account was first built by Alexander. Pliny *N.H.* 34. 150 'They say that there still exists by the river Euphrates in the city called Zeugma an iron chain used by Alexander the Great in constructing the bridge there ('qua Alexander Magnus ibi iunxerit pontem') the restored links of which are attacked by rust, from which the original ones are free'; and Dio C. 40. 17. 3 says it was so named from Alexander's crossing the river here. But the consensus of other authorities makes Alexander cross at *Thapsacus* ; and Pliny *N.H.* 5. 86 makes the river bridged and Zeugma and Apamea founded by Seleucus Nicator 'Zeugma LXXII p. a Samosatis, transitu Euphratis nobile. ex aduerso Apameam, Seleucus, *idem utriusque* conditor, ponte iunxerat.' (Hence in strictness the town on the right bank would seem to have been called Σελεύκεια ἡ ἐπὶ τοῦ Ζεύγματος Polybius 5. 43. 1 or Σελεύκεια ἡ πρὸς τῷ Εὐφράτῃ *Corp. Inscr. Graec.* 2548.) Pausanias, 10. 29. 4, makes the god Dionysus the first to bridge the Euphrates on his expedition against India. What view Lucan adopted is not clear, as **Pellaeum** might refer to Alexander himself (III 233) or to one of his successors, as to a Seleucid (298 infr.) or a Ptolemy (infr. 475, 607). In X 20 it is applied to Alexander's father Philip, who made Pella the capital of Macedonia.

239. **ardua,** acc. after **iubenti.**

aulae. This borrowed Greek word is properly applied to Eastern monarchs' Courts, and apparently not used of Roman Emperors' before Statius.

240. **egreditur,** sc. *naue.*

famuli…amictus, cf. Val. Max. 9. 8. 2 'maiestate sua seruili ueste occultata' (of Caesar's attempt to cross from Apollonia to Brundisium agreeing with Plut. *Caes.* 38), id. 5. 6. ext. 1 (of Codrus king of Athens) 'depositis insignibus imperii *famularem cultum* induit.'

raptos, 'raptim sumptos' (VII 330); cf. 689.

241. 'At critical times it protects a king to wear the mask of poverty.'

inopem simulare is literally 'to represent' or 'reproduce a poor man,' cf. Hor. *Ep.* 1. 19. 12 'siquis uoltu toruo ferus et pede nudo | exiguaeque togae *simulet* textore *Catonem.*'

243. **dimisso**, having taken leave of the king, 154.

in litore. See *Introd.* p. xxxiii.

244, 245. **per Icariae scopulos.** Lucan appears to represent Pompey as passing between Samos and Icaria, or Icarus, which is 'in reality a continuation of the range of hills traversing Samos from east to west' (Smith's *Dict. of Geography* under *Icarus*) and which Strabo says was without harbours though it had anchorage stations (ἀλίμενος πλὴν ὑφόρμων) and was uninhabited in his time, being only used by the Samians for pasturage (14. 1. 19 p. 639, cf. id. 10. 5. 13 p. 488), and *per* seems to be used as in 'Cilicum *per litora*' (257) of the coasting voyage along Cilicia. But we may doubt if he took this route, see p. 146.

Ephesonque to **maris** is practically a parenthesis; cf. *Introd.* l.c.

Colophona. *Old Colophon* was really two miles from the coast; but the name is also applied to the new town *Notium*, Livy 37. 26. 5.

placidi…maris. For the gen. cf. 223 n.

paruae, see Excursus B p. lxxxviii.

246. **saxa.** Cf. the description in Smith's *Dict. of Geography* under *Samos.* 'The westernmost extremity of the island, opposite Icaria, was anciently called Cantharium. Here the cliffs are very bare and lofty.'

247. **fluens**, of air in motion; IV 71 'in solam Calpen *fluit umidus aer*,' Vitruuius 1. 6. 2 'uentus autem est *aeris fluens unda* cum certa motus redundantia,' Lucr. 1. 280 'fluunt' (of the winds).

fugit…relinquit. See *Introd.* pp. xxxv, xxxvi.

248. **sole**, a pregnant use; 'glorious with its Sun' includes the worship, the famous Colossus and the light; cf. Hor. *C.* 1. 7. 1 *claram Rhodon.*

249. **compensat** said to mean 'abridges' 'saves' here and in Seneca *Phaedra* 88 sq. 'hac hac pergam | qua (?quae) uia longum

compensat iter' only. But it is doubtful if *compensare* can be used for *compendium facere* with a gen. It is better taken as 'makes up for' 're-places,' that is substitutes for a long in and out coasting voyage an open-sea route; cf. Calpurnius *Ecl.* 3. 83 'cocto *pensare* legumine panem,' 5. 111 'sitis est *pensanda* tuorum, | Canthe, gregum uiridante cibo.'

medio pelagi, again a compression ; ' by (taking) the middle of the sea,' a genitive like *mundi* in 209.

250. **occurrit** 'meets,' a very natural image, the reverse of *decedit, fugit* and the like as in Stat. *Ach.* 2. 308 'incipit et Scyros longo *decedere* ponto,' Val. Fl. 5. 101 sq. '*fugit* omne | Crobiali latus,' though mis-understood by a Scholiast (W) 'ciuitas cuius habitatores *uenerunt ei obuiam.*'

251*. **Phaseli** (voc., Cr. App.) according to Lucan, Pliny *N. H.* 5. 96 and Mela 1. 79 in Pamphylia, of which it was the last town, but placed in Lycia by Strabo, who makes Pamphylia begin at Olbia, 14. 4. 1, p. 667, cf. Livy 37. 23. 1 '*in confinio Lyciae et Pamphyliae* est ; prominet penitus in altum (so Cic. *Verr.* II 4. 21 'proiecta in altum') conspiciturque prima terrarum Rhodum a Cilicia petentibus et procul nauium praebet prospectum.' On the disagreement between Lucan and Plutarch *Pomp.* 76 see *Introd.* xxxvi n. 4. The verbal agreement between Lucan and the passage of Livy quoted above may be noted.

253. **exhaustae** 'drained of,' with abl. as in v 333 '*exhausta*que sanguine turba.' The depopulation of Phaselis is mentioned only here. Strabo says it was a πόλις ἀξιόλογος. Perhaps Lucan is pointedly contradicting a predecessor, *Introd.* p. xxxvi n. 4.

populis 'population,' 'multitude.' Lucan uses the word vaguely of a number of people trying to board a ship in III 665 'nutaretque ratis *populo* peritura recepto.' See also on 871 infr.

255*. See *Introd.* p. xxxvi and Excursus B pp. lxxxii sqq.

256. **hoc**, apparently abl. neuter, referring to the action of *pacem praestitit*; cf. Sen. *Dial.* 6. 22. 1 'unde enim scis an diutius illi expedierit uiuere ? an *illi hac* morte *consultum* sit ?'

undis, the seas and all on them. Compare the *pax maris* of IV 437.

257 sq. **Cilicum** *e.q.s.* There is staccato emphasis in Lucan's manner on almost every word ' *Cilicum* p. l. —*tutus—parua* puppe— *fugit*' and ' ad *profugum* c. *ducem.*' Compare 53 and note. A good commentary is Florus 4. 2. 20 (on Pompey's flight from Italy) 'turpe dictu, modo princeps patrum, pacis bellique moderator, per trium-phatum a se mare lacera et paene inermi naue fugiebat.'

260. An inexplicable line. **1.** The obvious meaning of the Latin is that Syhedra was the port of departure and return for the shipping of Selinus, which is false to fact. **2.** W. Judeich *Caesar im Orient* takes *rates* of Pompey's vessels (for which we may compare 457 'inmisere rates') and understands 'quo *ex* portu et mittit rates (*Pompeius*) et recipit eos Selinus.' This would give an intelligible sense, and the fleet would naturally go to Selinus before starting for Cyprus (*Introd.* p. xl n. 6); but it cannot be extracted from the Latin. **3.** If **quo** could be separated from *portu* and understood as ' whither ' and **portu** taken closely with **mittitque** and **recipitque**, a zeugmatic use of the abl. '*from...in*' to which parallels may easily be found, e.g. with the dat.-abl. plural in ' opportunum et opulentum uiti*is*' Sen. *Dial.* 12. 6. 2 (' *uitiis* is dat. with *opportunum* and abl. with *opulentum* ' Duff), we should also get a reasonable sense ; but the inattention to intelligibility it presupposes may be more than we should attribute to Lucan. Comp. 818 n.

261. **ora resoluit**, a Vergilian phrase, *G.* 4. 452 'sic fatis *ora resoluit*,' *A.* 3. 457 'uocemque uolens atque *ora resoluat*'; cf. VII 609.

263. **instar patriae**, the equivalent of our country; with the regular meaning of *instar*, Cic. *Brut.* 191 'Plato enim mihi unus *instar centum milium*,' 1 199 sq. 'summique o numinis instar, | Roma, faue coeptis,' VII 571 note. See E. Wölfflin's paper in *Archiv f. Lat. Lexicographie* 2. 581 sqq. Schol. α well explains 'qui de uobis *magnitudinem ciuitatis* adfertis.'

266. **omnis** 'all of me,' 'wholly'; cf. Hor. *C.* 3. 30. 5 'non *omnis* moriar multaque pars mei | uitabit Libitinam.' Pompey identifies himself with his side, as a general with his army VII 652 n., infr. 608.

267. **Emathiis**, 34 n. supr.

268. **receptas**, a variation of Lucan's on the usual *acceptas*.

269. A feature of artificial poetry is the freedom with which it turns a ' relation' into a ' subject.' It makes a principle of the fallacy ' quod *post* hoc, ergo *propter* hoc,' and in the same way of ' quod *cum* hoc ' (or ' *in* hoc '), ' ergo *ab* hoc.' This is a good example. Because, from sitting on the ruins of Carthage (II 88 sqq. ' pelago delatus iniquo | hostilem in terram uacuisque mapalibus actus | nuda triumphati iacuit per regna Iugurthae | et Poenos pressit cineres ') Marius afterwards rose to the consulship, these ruins are said to *raise* him thereto ; cf. Manilius 4. 47 sq. ' adiacuit Libycis compar iactura ruinis | eque *crepidinibus* cepit *Karthaginis* Vrbem.' In this way we get an ' inverted passive' as I have called it, notes on 74 and 108 supra.|

270. **plenis r. fastis**, a difficult expression, which seems to mean 'to restore to the fasti that he had filled' with his name, i.e. as consul for six times. For the adj. as a part. cf. 773. The thought is illustrated by Sen. *Dial.* 3. 21. 3 '(ambitio magni animi) non est contenta honoribus annuis; si fieri potest, *uno nomine occupare fastuus uult*, per omnem orbem titulos disponere.'

271. **pulsum**, 'struck' down or 'defeated'; cf. *impulit* 707 infr.

leuiore manu 'with a lighter stroke'; cf. 708.

tenebit, keep me where I am, i.e. *down*; compare 834, VI 300 'ipse furentis | dux *tenuit* gladios,' 'kept back.'

272. **mille**, the same round number in IX 32. It would recall the popular figure for the great armada which conquered Troy. Verg. *Aen.* 2. 198, Sen. *Troad.* 717, Stat. *Ach.* 1. 34.

uoluuntur, i.e. 'toss' as we say. The opposite is *stant* 592. The form of the verse may, as Haskins says, be derived from Vergil, *Ecl.* 2. 21 'mille meae Siculis errant in montibus agnae.'

273. **duces**; cf. IV 540 '*dux* ipse *carinae.*'

Cf. Florus 4. 2. 64 '*sparsae* magis quam oppressae *uires* erant.'

276. Cf. VII 694 'Pompei nomen populare per orbem.'

277. **uiribus**, an abl. of the instrument passing into abl. of thing concerned; cf. 'merit*is expendite* causam' Ov. *M.* 13. 150. We may note the variation in the expressions for the three *regna*, viz. a country, a people and a capital; for *Pharos* means *Alexandria*.

278. **quemnam**, singular because the individual monarchs are meant.

Romanis...rebus, cf. VII 110 (quoted on 341 infr.).

280. 'And whither (to which alternative) sinks the balance (lit. the weight in the scales) of my mind.' Sen. *Medea* 394 'quo pondus animi uergat, ubi ponat minas' is a close parallel.

281. **aetas**, i.e. tender age; Ptolemy was now 13 years old, *Introd.* p. xliv n. 3.

282. **ardua...fides**, loyalty 'uphill,' i.e. under a strain; cf. Ov. *Ars* 2. 537 'ardua molimur; sed nulla nisi *ardua uirtus*' and IV 576 'non *ardua uirtus.*'

283. **anceps**, double-fronted, treacherous.

Mauri. This is a 'quasi-synonym' (221 n.) for Numidian or for African, as again at IV 784. The licence requires excuse, as Lucan can use the word correctly, IX 300 sq. 'Libyci *contermina Mauris* | regna Iubae' and *Mauretania* was on *Caesar's* side.

284. **generis,** the family of the 'perfidus Hannibal.'

285*. **inminet,** cf. Val. Max. 9. 15 Ext. fin. 'imperi*o* dementer *inminens*.'

Hesperiae. This 'Italy which he threatens' had long been abandoned to Caesar.

' (The thought of) Hannibal fills his empty head.' For **multus** (an imitation, apparently, of the Greek πολύs) cf. Florus 4. 2. 50 '*multus* in eo proelio Caesar fuit' ' was much in evidence' as we say. Ov. *M.* 11. 562 sq. 'sed *plurima* nantis in ore | Alcyone coniunx.' So Hor. *C.* 1. 7. 8 '*plurimus* in Iunonis honore.'

286 sq. Iuba according to an inscription (*C.I.L.* II 3417), our sole authority, was the son of Hiempsal, and grandson of Gauda (the half-brother of the illegitimate Iugurtha) who was son of Gulussa and grandson of Masinissa. The allusions here are dark ; but thus much is clear. Iuba, Lucan means, does not belong to the genuine royal house of Numidia ; his direct descent is from the 'impius Hannibal.' **qui** must mean *Iuba* ; for with Hannibal's family we are not concerned ; and **contingit sanguine obliquo** must be compared with the use in Sen. *Apocolocyntosis* 9 § 5 'cum diuus Claudius et diuum Augustum *sanguine contingat* nec minus diuam Augustam' etc., and Juvenal 11. 62 '*contingens sanguine* caelum,' descendant of the gods. ' He stains the purple by his indirect descent from Numidian ancestors.' As nothing is known about Iuba's descent which would explain Lucan's allusion, it has been thought that he has confused *Iuba* and *Iugurtha* ; this is 'not proven.'

287. **supplice Varo,** predicatively like 'Pompeio supplice' 346, 'thro' the suppliancy of Varus.' The defeat of P. Attius Varus by Curio and the intervention of Iuba are curtly dealt with by Lucan IV 699 sqq.

288. **Romana,** *res Romanas,* 341 n., 545, IX 124 'the fortunes of Rome' or, as we should say, 'Rome.'

secundo, i.e. 'inferior,' 676.

309—310*.

309. **alia,** i.e. neither Egypt nor Numidia.

reuolsos, cf. I 482 'finibus Arctois patriaque a sede *reuolsos*'; also the bombastic phrase of 'Sen.' *Herc. Oet.* 1222 sq. 'feruida | plaga *reuulsus* cancer.'

310. **inmittam** 'let them go free,' for the compound cf. Verg. *Aen.* 5. 146 sq. '*inmissis* aurigae undantia lora | concussere iugis,' Nepos *Hannibal* 5 'eius generis multitudinem magnam *inmisit*,' Cic.

Or. 190 '*inmittit* imprudens senarium.' In all these cases it closely approaches *emittere* in meaning. The word is very appropriate to the Parthian cavalry.

excitos suis sedibus agrees verbally with Livy 31. 14. 12 'di prope ipsi *exciti sedibus suis*'; cf. Sen. *Dial.* 12. 7. 4 'alios alia causa *exciuit domibus suis.*'

ortus (the lands of) the East, II 642 'totos mea, nate, per *ortus* | bella feres'; cf. ib. 588 '*occasus* mea iura timent.'

289. **Eoum...orbem** takes up *ortus* in *v.* 310.

290*. **diuidit** 'parts' or 'marks off,' usually with *a* or the abl. following; but cf. Tac. *A.* 1. 43 'discedite a contactu ac *diuidite* turbidos.'

mundum, a part or a 'quarter' of the world, as *orbis* above and elsewhere not unfrequently (603, 828).

291. **Caspia...claustra,** 222 n.

seducunt follows the use of *diuidit* above; it generally means 'draw apart,' 'separate.' Ovid *Her.* 19. 143 '*seducit* terras haec breuis unda duas.'

recessus, cf. 216 n.

292. The apparent meaning of this is that Parthia, or some part of it, is in the jurisdiction of the South Pole, i.e. in the Southern Hemisphere, which of course is not the case.

293. **uertit** 'turns,' i.e. causes the revolution of; but the expression is loose, as the pole does not do this.

abruptum, and so not accessible to Caesar; the same idea recurs in *suus* 294.

nostro, an ambiguous form, but probably dat., cf. Plin. *N.H.* 5. 134 'Nisyron *abruptam illi* (sc. Coo) putant,' cf. ib. 141.

mare, the Mare Rubrum or Erythraeum of which the Sinus Persicus and the Sinus Arabicus (now the Red Sea) were the arms, called *Rubrum profundum* in 853.

294. **oceanus**, named *Azanius* from *Azania*, a region of Aethiopia, Plin. *N.H.* 6. 108 '*oceanum* qui influit *Azanium* appellant.'

suus, to be referred to an unexpressed subject *illis* or *Assyriis* to be understood out of *Assyrias*. For such omissions cf. 85 n.

pugnandi, cf. III 265 '*pugnaces*...Parthi,' Prop. 3. 9. 25 'Medorum *pugnaces* ire per hastas,' Ammianus 31. 2. 20 'unde etiam Persae, qui sunt originitus Scythae, *pugnandi* sunt peritissimi.'

295*. **fortior.** So Plutarch *Crassus* 24 says of the Parthian archers at the battle of Carrhae εὐτόνους τὰς πληγὰς καὶ βιαίους διδόντες ἀπὸ τόξων κραταιῶν καὶ μεγάλων. The Parthians kept on the traditions of the Persian bowmen; cf. Xen. *Anab.* 3. 4. 17.

297. **segnis**, with inf. IV 525, X 398.

298. **Pellaeas** (237 n.) of the Syro-Macedonian empire from which the Parthians, under ' Arsaces,' the traditional founder of the Arsacid dynasty, broke away about 240 B.C. The details are obscure; see Bevan *House of Seleucus* vol. 1 pp. 283 sqq.

sarisas, the long Macedonian pike, originally about 24 feet long but later shortened to 20 feet, with an iron head of about 1 ft. : in contrast to the Roman *pilum* X 47 sq. ' pro pudor, Eoi propius timuere *sarisas* | quam nunc *pila* timent populi.'

299. **Bactra**, now *Balkh*. A part of the Greek kingdom of Bactria was subdued about 150 B.C. by Mithridates I (Justin 41. 6) who also completed the subjugation of Media, but Bactra never belonged to the Parthians.

Medorum sedem, cf. *Medorum domos* 216 and Excursus B p. lxxix.

muris, cf. Herodotus 1. 178 sqq.

300. The order of words is *Babylona, Assyrias domos.* Assyria and Babylonia were neighbouring and rival states ; Babylon was first taken by the Assyrians in the 13th century B.C.

domos ' abode,' cf. 216, which shows that *Assyrias* means ' Assyri*orum*.'

301. **nimis** 'greatly,' with a negative as usual in this sense.

Parthis, dat. of the person concerned in a verbal action. It is specially, though not exclusively, used of verbs of emotion or perception ; ' Romanus cunct*is* petitur cruor' VII 511.

302. **Scythicas**, i.e. *suas* (cf. 221 n.), since *Scythicus* means *Parthicus* (Excursus B p. lxxix), cf. 216, 353, 432, VII 435 n., II 552 sq. ' *Parthorum* utinam post proelia sospes | et *Scythicis Crassus* uictor remeasset ab oris.'

Crasso pereunte. Of the younger Crassus this would be exact (Plut. *Crass.* 25), but Lucan means the elder one (432 n.).

303 sq. Lentulus turns this against Pompey, 385 sqq.

fidentia, a semi-personification, cf. Val. Fl. 6. 124 'inceptus iam lancea *temnit* eril*is*.'

305. **nocent** 'are deadly,' cf. VI 485 'omne potens animal leti genitumque *nocere*,' Hor. *Epod.* 3. 3 'edit *cicutis* alium *nocentius*.'

summo, on the surface, 68 n. ; ' it is death if the blood is drawn.'

306*. **tota...fiducia**, Pompey's sole hope is in the Parthians, ' postquam nulla manet rerum *fiducia*' 504.

307. Sen. *Herc. F.* 263 '*ferax deorum* terra, quem dominum tremis?' Ov. *M.* 14. 568 sq. 'perstat *habet*que *deos* pars utraque quodque deorumst | instar, habent animos.'

in Arsacidis depends on **esset.** If it had depended on *fiducia* the gen. would have been used.

311. If the faith that Parthia keeps is no better than a *Punica fides* or a *Pharia fides* 624.

312. **uolgati,** well-known, familiar; cf. III 415 sq. 'non *uolgatis* sacrata figuris | numina sic metuunt; tantum terroribus addit | quos timeant, non nosse deos.'

supra, cf. 318, 'beyond' like *super* 1 n.

commercia, cf. 810.

313. **naufragium.** For the metaphor cf. Cic. *Sest.* 15 'totum superioris anni *rei publicae naufragium* exponere,' Florus 4. 2. 64 'huc reliquias partium *naufragarum* quidam furoris aestus expulerat.'

regna, for *reges,* as *precabor* 'pray to' shows.

314. **solacia** explained by 315 sq.; cf. 354 inf. n.

315. I.e. that I have escaped Caesar's power to kill or to spare.

316. **reuoluens.** This participle is practically out of relation to the rest of the sentence, which should have run '*uideo me* uenerabilem *fuisse*' or the like, but instead has *fui* with the sense pointed out on 18 = 'I find I was.' A very similar incoherence is found in Pliny *N. H.* 32. 144 'fibri quorum generis lutras nusquam mari accepimus mergi, *tantum marina dicentes,*' where the words in italics have nothing to do in time or sense with what precedes (Preface to Bréal's *Semantics,* Eng. edn p. xxxiv n. 1). Compare *lapsus* in 8 supr.

318 sq.* **quantus...conspectus,** a participial clause attached in the Greek manner to *fui,* cf. Cic. *Fin.* 5. 87 'patrimonium neglexit, agros deseruit incultos, *quid quaerens* aliud nisi uitam beatam?' Stat. *Silu.* 2. 6. 80 sq. 'iam litora duri | saeua, Philete, senis durumque Acheronta uidebas, | *quo* domini *clamate sono*!,' Sen. *Dial.* 6. 26. 3 'humilia cuncta et grauia et anxia et quotam partem luminis nostri cernentia!' As a matter of fact, Pompey did not get beyond the Caucasus.

319. **ortu,** in the same sense as the plural 310 n. The number is shifting in such expressions; so Livy 21. 30. 5 'ab occas*u* solis ad exort*us.*'

320. **magis** with **felicibus,** of course, corresponds to **maiore tr.,** the feats of the Mithridatic war being, like the triumph itself, the greatest of Pompey's life.

321. **abĭt...redĭt**; cf. *perīt* 422, *patīt* 703 n., *obīt* ix 190 and Hosius
ed. 3 p. 385.

322. **Roma, faue coeptis**, i 200 quoted on 263; cf. Prop. 4. 1. 67
' Roma, faue ; tibi surgit opus.' For the personification of *Roma* see
VII 373 n.

laetius, 89 n.

324 sq. **consumere...miscere.** This belongs to the class of expressions usually called ' hysteron proteron,' but the two words coupled
form a whole (compare what is said on the conjunctions *que, et* in note
on 1) and the order is merely metrical. Cf. Ovid *Pont.* 4. 12. 38
' hic cumulus nostris *absit abestque* malis ' and *Classical Review* 30
p. 190.

325. **malis**, cf. VII 654 sq. ' nec, sicut mos est miseris, trahere
omnia secum | mersa iuuat gentesque suae miscere ruinae.'

327*. **murmure** goes equally with **sensit** and **damnasse.**

328. **Lentulus.** But see the *Introduction*, p. xxxix.

omnIs with **quos.**

329. **uirtutis stimulis** ' under the spur (goad) of a gallant spirit ';
cf. VII 103 sq. ' si modo *uirtutis stimulis* iraeque calore | signa petunt.'

nobilitate ' distinction '; Schol. C ' quod nobilius et clarius quam
ceteri.' Cf. VI 487 ' *nobilis* ira leonum,' Plautus, *Miles* 1322 sqq.
' nam tu quemuis potis es facere ut afluat facetiis | et quia tecum eram,
propterea animo eram ferocior ; | eam *nobilitatem* amittendam uideo.'

330. **tulit.** For *ferre* in this sense cf. Stat. *Silu.* 3. 1. 165 ' talia *dicta
ferentem*,' Val. Fl. 4. 330, Sil. 8. 264; *misit* or *dedit* would have been
more usual.

modo with the substantive **consule,** ' who was but now a consul.'
Cf. Ovid *M.* 1. 325 ' uirum de tot *modo* milibus unum,' cf. Florus
4. 2. 20, quoted on 257. Other adverbs of time are so used in verse
and poetic prose from Plautus (*Persa* 385 ' non tu *nunc hominum*
mores uides ') onwards. The expression ' lately consul ' agrees with
what Dio (41. 43) tells us about the anxiety of the Pompeians to
observe constitutional forms, the consuls of 49 calling themselves *pro-
consuls* § 3 ; cf. the significant passage of Lucan V 7–11 and *Introd.*
p. xlvi n. 2.

331. **Thessalicae...ruinae**, see note on 45 sup. and cf. IX 1019 sq.
' *Thessalicas* quaerens Magnus reparare *ruinas* | ense iacet nostro.'

mentem, usually *animum* ; but cf. Verg. *Aen.* 12. 609 ' demittunt
mentes,' Ov. *Tr.* 3. 9. 17 ' superest ingens audacia *menti*,' 635 infr. n.

fregere, sc. *tibi*, the qualifier being omitted, 85 n.

332. **damnauit.** Observe that under Roman law there were no appeals.

secundum Emathiam lis datur. This is a legal expression of giving a decision in favour of a litigant's contention or a document or plea. Val. Max. 2. 8. 2 'itaque, Lentule, quamuis adhuc tacueris, *secundum* te *litem do*,' Cic. *Rosc. Com.* 3 'quominus *secundum* eas (tabulas) *lis detur* non recusamus,' Livy 23. 4. 3. Compare '*secundum* legem' Livy 1. 26. 5 'in accordance with the law.' For *Emathiam* 'Pharsalia' cf. 360 n., 34 n.

333. **iacet** 'is prostrate,' i.e. helpless.

334. **auxilium** in a medical sense (as we say ' first *aid*'). So Ovid *Rem. Am.* 48 '*uolneris auxilium* Pelias hasta tulit' and often elsewhere ; cf. also 418 infr.

solos 'only': *solum* would be more logical, but for the adj. 'by themselves' compare e.g. IX 497.

335. **pedes,** i.e. to fall at their feet, a condensed expression. Cf. Sen. *Herc. Fur.* 517 sq. 'lacrimis agendumst : supplicem primus uides ; | hae te precantur *pedibus* intactae manus,' similarly id. *Troad.* 701 sq., id. *Clem.* 1. 21. 2 'ex alto *ad inimici pedes* abiectus.' Cf. VII 372 n.

transfuga mundi 'a deserter from the (known) world.' This world is called *uolgatus* or *Romanus* 312, 212. For the phrase cf. Ov. *M.* 6. 189 '*exul* erat *mundi*.' Statius follows Lucan *Silu.* 1. 2. 203 '*transfuga* Pisae' (of the Alpheus passing under the seas to Sicily) and Claudian both Lucan and Statius, *Eutrop.* 1. 14 sqq. ' Nilusne meatu | deuius et *nostri* temptat iam *transfuga mundi* | se Rubro miscere mari ?'

336*. **totos** is to be understood in the sense of *omnes ceteros* ; cf. 117 and 460 with notes. It is an exaggeration like *toto—orbe* 503. The taunting effect of the repeated *t*'s should be noted, 390 sqq. (n).

337. **auersos...polos** can only mean the S. Pole, the *alter polus* of 292. The '*totum* mutare diem' of 217 agrees with the hypothesis that Lucan conceived Parthia to extend into the Southern hemisphere.

338. **culture.** For the voc. for the nom. (cf. *famulus* in 338) see 643 n.

339. I.e. ' Why do you make a love of freedom an excuse to screen your appeal to force?'

341. **Romana.** *res Romanas* (288 n.); cf. VII 110 '*res* mihi *Romanas* dederas, Fortuna, *regendas*.'

342. **horruit.** The Parthian King is meant, being the subject

uppermost in the speaker's mind at the moment; cf. *quemnam* in 278. The omission of a dominant subject is not uncommon in early and conversational Latin, and adds liveliness to the expression. Varro, *L.L.* 6. 73 '*spes* a sponte potest esse declinata quod tum *sperat* (a man hopes) cum quod uolt fieri putat.'

auditu in antithesis to **uidit** (343) 'quid si uidisset?' Schol. *a*. Compare also '*auditi*' 361, and for the use of the verbal Q. Curt. 5. 4. 10 'hic captiuus expositis interrogatus a rege *auditu*ne an oculis comperta quae diceret.' This use approximates to that of the gerund, *audiendo*.

343*. **ab Hyrcanis...siluis.** For the unusual arrangement of the words (hyperbaton) see the Cr. App. The repetition of the preposition shows that we are to think of Pompey's victorious progress as extending from Hyrcania on the N. (N. E.) to India on the S. (S. E.).

344. **deiectum fatis**, 206 n.

345. **animos**, ambition.

Latium...orbem like *orbem Romanum* 442 the countries under Roman control.

346. **se...mensus**, measuring his own power and Rome's by Pompey's humiliation. Lentulus turns Pompey's own argument (287 sq. which see) against him. For the phrase cf. Sen. *Benef.* 2. 16. 1 'cum ille cui donabatur, *se ipse mensus*, tanti muneris inuidiam refugisset.'

347. **effabere**, i.e. effari poteris.

348. **commercia linguae**, of the 'interchange' of speech, VI 700 sq. 'per quam | Manibus et mihi sunt tacit*ae commercia linguae*.' Compare what Ovid writes of his straits in Tomi *Tr*. 5. 10. 35 sq. ' exercent illi *sociae commercia linguae* : | *per gestum* res est significanda mihi.'

349. **lacrimis**, cf. Sen. *Herc. Fur.* quoted on 335 above.

patimurne ' do we endure?' with the suggestion that we do not, and so 'are we to endure?' Cf. the similar use of the pres. ind. in statements 443.

pudoris uolnus; cf. the stronger expression in IV 231 sq. ' pro, dira *pudoris* | *funera !* ' ' death ' or ' death blow to honour.'

350 replies to Pompey's argument in 326 sq.

351. **armis**, dat.

353*. **Scythicos**, 302 n.

spargis, apparently ' fling wide' 'spread.' ' Quid diuulgas crimina Romanorum ?' Schol. C.

cladesque latentes. In this addition the pres. participle is apparently used because there is no future participle from *lateo* (Priscian) 'a disaster which but for you would not be known.' It must be confessed that the phrasing is harsh, v. Cr. App.

354. **transire** is here used absolutely as in VII 647 and 595 infr., Tac. *Agr.* 12 (of the sun), but in the sense of crossing the boundary or the Euphrates (cf. 236 supr.). Similarly Caelius ap. Cic. *Fam.* 8. 10. 2 speaks of the 'Parthorum *transitus*' in 51 B.C. Compare Pliny *N.H.* 7. 96 'ad solis occasum *transgressus*' (of Pompey).

solacia, explained by the infin. with which it is in a sort of apposition ; cf. 314 supr.

355. **admittere**, as in 546, of letting in intruders ; for **reges** are foreign monarchs.

356*. **suo**, i.e. *Romano*.

358. **ab Euphrate** with **sequentem**, all the way from the Euphrates. Latin nouns from Greek ones in -ης, dative in -ῃ, may have -*ē* in the abl. So *Gangē* Ov. *F.* 3. 729, *Hippomenē* id. *M.* 10. 608.

359 sqq. The argument recurs 531 sqq.

celante = *nondum prodente* 15 supra 'before destiny revealed its preference.'

360. **Emathiae** 333 n. *aciem Emathiam* in 531.

361. **auditi**, intended to recall the *auditu* of 342. Val. Fl. 4. 206 sq. ' etenim *fiducia*, credo, | huc tulit, *auditas* et sponte lacessitis oras' may be a reminiscence of this passage

363. **Arctois**. This adj. is a Roman (and late Greek) formation on the analogy of *Eous* or Ἐῷος, as *Eurous* proves, for the Classical Greek ἀρκτικός 'Arctic.' Similarly Horace's strange *Lesbous* for *Lesbius* (Hor. *C.* 1. 1. 34) seems to follow the analogy of *Myrtous* (which occurs in v. 14 *of the same poem*), *Sardous*, *Cous*. Another example is Nonnus's still stranger Ἰνδῷος.

364. **mortis amator** 'courter of death' ; cf. IV 146 sq. ' indomitos quaerit populos et semper in arma | *mortis amore* feros.' For the non-insertion of *est* cf. 51 n.

365. **quidquid**, acc., 179 n.

366*. **ibitur** 'we travel,' i.e. along the surface of the globe ; cf. Manilius 3. 323 sqq. ' at simul ex illa terrarum parte recedis, | *quidquid ad extremos* temet praeuerteris *axes*' (the words are corrupt, but the sense is clear).

clementia caeli. We say 'the genial climate' as above (365) ' a warmer world '; but Latin prefers the abstract in such cases. For the expression compare the imitation in Florus 3. 3. 13 'in Venetia quo

fere tractu Italia mollissima est, ipsa soli *caeli* que *clementia robur elanguit.*'
For the fact cf. Hippocrates *de aere aquis et locis* § 85 περὶ δὲ τῆς
ἀθυμίης τῶν ἀνθρώπων καὶ τῆς ἀνδρηίης ὅτι ἀπολεμώτεροί εἰσι τῶν
Εὐρωπαίων οἱ Ἀσιηνοὶ καὶ ἡμερώτεροι, αἱ ὧραι αἴτιαι μάλιστα. For
the effect of climate on temperament see also Aristotle *Pol.* 4 (7). 7. 2,
Vitruuius 6. 1. 9 sqq. Livy 38. 17. 17 and Seneca *Dial.* 12. 7. 1,
quoted on 724 inf.

367. **laxas**, *non adstrictas.* **fluxa**, *fluentia.* Both epithets refer
to the ample ungirded robes of Orientals. Cf. Ammianus Marcellinus
23. 6. 84 (of the Persae) 'indumentis plerique eorum lumine colorum
fulgentibus uario ut (licet sinus lateraque dissuta relinquunt flatibus
agitari uentorum) inter calceos tamen et uerticem nihil uideatur in-
tectum.' For the expression cf. Seneca *Oed.* 428 sq. 'inde tam molles
placuere cultus | et sinus *laxi fluidumque* syrma.'

uirorum with strong emphasis 'on the limbs *of men.*' It should
follow *uelamenta* as it depends on both the nouns. Compare the
remarks on hyperbaton in *Classical Review* 30 p. 144 *a*.

368. **uelamenta** 'coverings' as in Seneca *Dial.* 12. 11. 2, in this
sense usually *uelamina.* The alliteration reinforces the disapproval;
cf. 336, 384, 390, 414, 606, 652.

uides. The indicative present is more vivid than the subjunctive
present usual in prose.

rura often used by Lucan with proper names of stretches of country.
Hence *ruricolae* 'inhabitants' simply in Val. Fl. 5. 142.

369. **Sarmaticos...campos**. On this see Excursus B p. lxxix. In
view of *Medica* (368) it is worth noting that Pliny *N.H.* 6. 19 has
'*Sarmatae, Medorum*, ut ferunt, *suboles.*'

inter. Cf. 'inter agros' Tib. 2. 1. 67, Priap. 83. 16 (attributed by
some to Tibullus) 'iacebis *inter arua* pallidus situ,' Val. Fl. 6. 434 sq.
'flammiferos uidet *inter* regia tauros | *pascua.*'

effusa 'stretched out'; cf. IV 19 sq. 'explicat hinc tellus campos
effusa patentis | uix oculo prendente modum' and elsewhere.

370. **Tigridis**. In Greek the gen. of the river appears to have
been Τίγριδος (Aristotle) or Τίγρητος from Τίγρης (Xenophon, cf. the
modern name *Diglito*), but of the animal τίγριος. The Latin of
ordinary speech however (Pliny, Tacitus) seems to have used the
non-increasing form *tigris* for both.

371. **libertate fugae** (cf. 491), 'for their flight is free,' abl. of
Cause. The phrase takes a strong emphasis, cf. 367 n.

tumebit 'rises,' cf. 11 397 sq. 'nulloque a uertice *tellus* | altius intumuit,' IV 11 sq. 'colle *tumet* modico lenique excreuit in altum | pingue solum tumulo' (from the same root), Ovid *Her.* 5. 138 'in immensis qua *tumet* Ida iugis,' id. *Am.* 2. 16. 51 sq. 'at uos, qua ueniet, *tumidi* subsidite *montes* | et faciles curuis uallibus este, uiae.' Cf. Schol. W. '*tumebit* eleuatur in tumulos.' The student should notice the tense which in accordance with Latin habit gives the point of view of the main action, cf. 495 n. Florus gives as the reason why Curio did not invade Dacia that he '*tenebras saltuum* expauit' 3. 4. 6.

372. **opacas,** as in glens or forests.

373. **debilis** 'unfit,' 'disabled,' cf. Sil. It. 16. 107 'stat tamen una loco perfossis *debilis* armis.'

374. **franget,** so of cavalry swimming. V 440 'aequora *frangit* eques': cf. Shaksp. *Jul. Caes.* 1 2. 107 sqq. 'The torrent roar'd, and we did buffet it | With lusty sinews, throwing it aside | And stemming it with hearts of controversy.'

uiolenti uerticis, for the gen. see 223 n.

375. **tota,** *acc. plur.* a 'transferred' epithet for *totus* 'engrossed in the combat.' Cf. 2 supra n., 449 infr. n., VII 308.

376. **exiget,** 'go thro',' cf. IX 949 '*exegere* hiemem.' So with *noctem* Sen. *Dial.* 10. 16. 4. It is not a mere synonym of *agere*. For the general sense cf. Sen. *Ep.* 80. 3 'patientiam...qua *solem arden-tissimum* in *feruentissimo puluere* et *sanguine suo madens diem ducat.*'

377. **non ullast machina belli,** repeated X 481.

378. **aut** is unusual here; but 11 360 sqq. '*non* timidum nuptae leuiter tectura pudorem | lutea demissos uelarunt flammea uoltus, | balteus *aut* fluxos gemmis astrinxit amictus' is similar.

fossas inplere, to fill up a moat in order to storm the defences. The earth of the *uallum* was usually torn down for this purpose. Lucan here and in VII 326 has this compound for the more usual com*plere*. Cf. Caesar *B. G.* 3. 5. 1 'uallum scindere et *fossas complere.*'

sequenti dat. with **erit** 'will count as a wall'; cf. VII 319 'ciuis, qui fugerit, *esto*' and note on 18 sup.

379. **potest obstare** (cf. 803) is a semi-future expression, the tense being unaccommodated to *erit*; *poterit* would have been the full future (371 n.).

380. **leuis** 'flitting,' the opposite of the Greek σταδίη.

fugax 'runaway,' 'elusive,' of the *fighter*; '*fugax* Parthus' Ov. *Rem. Am.* 155 and elsewhere, '*fugax* Sertorius' VII 16.

381. **cessisse...pellere.** The variation in tense (*cessisse* for *cedere*; cf. *impendisse* VII 617 and note) is purely metrical : had he wished to

invert the expression, he would have used *pepulisse—cedere*, cf. 794 sq.
infr. 'cond*i*—car*uisse*,' IX 55 sqq. 'indigna—accend*isse*—incu b*uisse*—ex-
ur*ere*—compon*ere*,' VII 617, 688 and notes. Tibullus I. 1. 29 sq., Ov.
Am. 3. 7. 25 sq., Stat. Silu. 5. 2. 166 sq., Val. Fl. 3. 626 sq. *tolerare—
quaesiuisse* with Langen's note. Latin is handicapped considerably
through having no separate tense for the perf. and aor. An object,
e.g. *hostem*, is to be supplied in thought with *pellere* (cf. 85 note)
and **loco** has to be carried on from *cessisse.* For the inf. pres. which is
the more usual tense with **melior** compare 482 n.

382. **inlita**, cf. 304 sq. supr.

383. **longe**, i.e. at a safe distance.

tendere, in construction dependent on *ausa* but in thought on a
different word, e.g. *solita*, cf. 610 n.

384*. The order of words appears to be *permittere uentis ferre uolnera quo uelint.* So in 537 *iubere* depends on *permittant* and in 665
aptare on *permittere. uolnera*, of the weapon wounding; Verg. *A.* 2.
529, 10. 140 and elsewhere. The *u*-alliteration in these lines seems
intentional; cf. 367 sq.

385*. **ensis.** For us the bayonet is the test.

habet with a pregnant and difficult sense, such as ἔχει sometimes has
in Greek, 'contains opportunities, affords room for prowess.' Somewhat similar are Sen. *Dial.* 4. 3. 5 'numquam dubium est quin timor
fugam habeat, ira *impetum*,' Ov. *Pont.* 4. 10. 40 'et quae prae-
cipuum sidera *frigus habent*,' Stat. *Silu.* 1. 3. 23 '*habentes carmina
somnos.*'

387. **exarmant** 'disarm,' V 355 sq. 'sperantis omnia dextras | *ex-
armare* datur.'

uacua 'emptied,' a participial use of the adj. not infrequent in Latin;
cf. notes on *diuidui* 465, *mollia* 526, *lacer* 667, *plenus* 752. So *artus
=artatus* in IX 449 'montibus *artum* | aduersis' (*ortum* MSS., *artans*
Mr Anderson with the right sense). Cf. Sil. 6. 194 sq. 'spiris ingenti-
bus *artae* | arboris abstraxit molem,' *Pan. Messall.* 91 '*artis*...habenis'
'tight drawn.'

388. **manus**, the strong right arm. For the gen. cf. 504. These
statements, whether they are to be assigned to the speaker (cf. *Introd.*
p. xiii) or to the poet, are not in agreement with fact. The long pike
(*contus*) and the *acinaces* were both Parthian weapons.

390*. **cum ferro**, with plain steel.

parumst 'is not enough,' i.e. an inadequate equipment.

temptare 'to try for'; cf. 'spem pacis *temptare*' X 468. The reiteration of the *t* sound in these lines 390–3, as in 334 sqq. (n.), is intentional and has a taunting effect. Compare my note on Plautus *Rudens* 494 sqq. in 'Flaws in Classical Research' *Proceedings of British Academy* (1908) p. 202, where I have cited Ennius *Annals* 108 'o Tite tute Tati tibi tanta tyranne tulisti.'

391 sq. So Ovid *Pont.* 1. 9. 48 'aque tuis *toto diuidor orbe* rogis,' cf. ib. 2. 2. 121.

393. **incumbat,** 'is it to lie' or 'press upon you?' This seems to us a very natural expression; but I do not know any Latin parallel save that adduced by Georges s.u. 'ita leuis *incumbat* terra defuncto tibi' Fabretti, *Inscr.* 289, 181 (*Anth. Epigr.* 197. 1).

394. **inuidiosa,** fraught with obloquy.

quaerente, with Crassus in vain quest of sepulture. So v 280 'morti clausuram *quaerere* dextram.'

395. **sors leuior,** cf. 452.

397*. **infando,** except for associations, the equivalent of the Eng. 'unspeakable' Turk 687.

timet 'has to fear'; for the tense cf. *trahitur* 416.

398. **uenus,** lust, as in 413.

399. **leges et foedera** 'terms and compacts'; cf. Prop. 3. 20. 15 sq. '*foedera* sunt ponenda prius signandaque iura | et scribenda mihi *lex* in amore nouo.'

400*. **latent** carries on the sense of *est ignota* 398.

401. **inter mille nurus** signifies Cornelia's position in the harem.

402. **regia,** i.e. *reges* or *rex*; cf. IX 266, X 527.

exceptos 'specially mentioned' in an instrument, a legal term, Pliny *N.H.* 29. 16 '(traduntur), cum Graecos Italia pellerent diu etiam post Catonem, *excepisse* medicos,' i.e. in the decree of banishment against the Greeks they specially mentioned doctors, and elsewhere. Lucan means that the unions permitted by the Parthians were so monstrous that no legislator had prohibited them by name. (There was no law against incest in Great Britain till the present century.) Compare the account of Solon's explanation why he had not forbidden parricide in his code. Cic. *Rosc. Am.* 70 'qui cum interrogaretur cur nullum supplicium constituisset in eum qui parentem necasset respondit se id neminem facturum putasse'; cf. Diogenes Laert. 1. 2. 10. Euripides *Androm.* 174 sqq. l.c. below also says that these unions were not forbidden in the East.

404. **lassat** as in Tibullus 1. 9. 55 and elsewhere.

sorores, Recently discovered documents of the Parthian period confirm this. See Mr E. H. Minns's paper in the *Journal of Hellenic Studies* 35 (1915) p. 39 'Further I. and tablet *n* [date 76 B.C.] tell us that the queen was, again as among the Ptolemies and perhaps among the Seleucids (Bevan *House of Seleucus* II p. 279), the king's sister (so Lucan VIII 404 proves to be true). We know from Herodian (IV 10) that the kings took their wives among the descendants of Arsaces and it might have been expected that they should marry their sisters as this practice, if not enjoined in the Avesta, is certainly approved in Pahlavi literature (J. H. Moulton *Hibbert Lectures* 1913 Early Zoroastrianism pp. 205 sqq.).'

405. **sacrata**, cf. *sacra* 481.

pignora, of near relations VII 324 etc.

matres. This is told of the Magi by Catullus 90 (with Ellis's notes), Strabo 15. 3. 20 (p. 735) in his account of the caste which agrees closely with Catullus, and Diogenes Laertius *Praef.* 6 'They see no impiety in commerce with a mother or daughter as Sotion relates in his twenty-third book.' Euripides *Andromache* 173 sqq. brings it as an accusation against the *barbari* in general τοιοῦτον πᾶν τὸ βάρβαρον γένος | πατήρ τε θυγατρὶ παῖς τε μητρὶ μίγνυται | κόρη τ' ἀδελφῷ διὰ φόνου δ' οἱ φίλτατοι | χωροῦσι καὶ τῶνδ' οὐδὲν ἐξείργει νόμος (the last words, by the way, may have provoked Lucan's artificial expression in 402). As to the Persae Tertullian *Apologet.* 1 325 Migne, cited by Ellis, states 'Ctesias Persas cum suis matribus misceri refert.'

406. **apud gentes,** as 'apud populos' below 420, 'in the eyes of the (whole) world.'

sceleris with **fabula.**

non sponte. So Oedipus himself says *Oed. Col.* 522 ἤνεγκ' οὖν κακότατ', ὦ ξένοι, ἤνεγκ' ἀέκων μὲν θεὸς ἴστω τούτων δ' αὐθαίρετον οὐδέν.

407. **Oedipodionias,** 'Oedipodean,' an adj. formed from *Oedipodion* Οἰδιπόδίων with a patronymic ending, which is cited by the *Etymologicum Magnum*, 544, 48, to illustrate the formation of the Homeric κυλλοποδίων (ὡς ἀπὸ τοῦ Οἰδίπους Οἰδίποδος γίγνεται Οἰδιποδίων οὕτω καὶ παρὰ τὸ κυλλόπους κυλλόποδος γίγνεται κυλλοποδίων), but is otherwise unknown.

This adjective first found here (for Ovid *Met.* 15. 429 is rightly condemned as an interpolation) and again in Statius illustrates the freedom with which the Roman poets coined derivatives from Greek proper names. These massive polysyllables which engross the first two-and-a-half feet of the verse are rare in Greek dactylics. Greek epic has a few patronymics, as Ἀμφιτρυωνιάδης, Ἰαπετιονίδης, Λαομεδοντιάδης, Χαλ-κωδοντιάδης (cited by Priscian), all, with others as *Acrisioniades, Oedi-podionides*, attested for Latin poetry. But the adjectives of corre-sponding length are very difficult to find in Greek verse, whereas in Latin they are a goodly band :

Acrisioneus, Androgeoneus, Arganthoniacus, Bellerophonteus, Deuca-lioneus, Eetioneus, Hellespontiacus (not in Greek *verse*), *Laomedonteus, Polydamanteus, Protesilaeus, Pygmalioneus, Tauromenitanus, Thero-damanteus, Thermodonteus* and *Thermodontiacus, Thiodamanteus*, and very likely others.

They constitute a peculiar class in which Latin imitation of Greek possessives from proper names is pushed much beyond the usage of the models. It is rare to find in Greek absolutely indivisible compounds of this size except from proper names; εἰλαπινάζουσιν *Od.* 17. 536 is perhaps unique. In most of the Homeric compounds the junction is easily perceptible. ἀμφ-αγαπαζόμενος, ἐν-τροπαλιζόμενος, προπρο-κυλιν-δόμενος, ἐξ-ονομακλήδην : αὐτο-κασίγνητος, πατρο-κασίγνητος, χαλκεο-θωράκων : ὀκτω-και-δέκατος, πεντηκοντά-γυος. The εἰνα-ετιζόμεναι of Callimachus *H.* 3. 179 would be another example. (We may here leave out of sight the few examples where the word carries us on to the end of the initial trochee in the third foot as πεντηκοντακάρηνον (-κέφαλλον) Hes. *Theog.* 312 or ἀμφι-περι-στείνωνται, Callimachus *H.* 4. 179, with the rare imitations in Latin of the foreign rhythm, Lucr. 4. 995 *expergefactique*, id. 6. 1158 *intolerabilibusque*.) The instances of native Latin words in this position are scarce enough, and most of those that do occur conform to the practice of Greek. I have noted no examples from Vergil or Lucan. Ovid *Metamorphoses* has three ; *in-tempestiua, in-deploratus* (compare the 'tmesis' of *inque salutatum*), *in-ueniebantur*. Silius Italicus *im-perturbati, in-custoditus, in-dis-pensato*, to which we may add *in-cessebatur*, doubtless felt as a compound though the simple is not extant. Statius has *in-temeratarum* and *ex-ploratores*, although there is no *plorator* or *ploro* in this sense. To get real exceptions you have to go to Lucretius and Juvenal, the first besides *in-satiabiliter, in-sedabiliter, in-tempestiuus, in-numerabilibus, circum-scriptorem, in-duperatorem* having *argumentorum*, and the second *sacramentorum* in addition to *de-clamatoris, in-ritamentum*, and the archaic *induperatorem* of Lucretius.

Less 'sesquipedalian' Graecising formations are naturally more numerous. Let it suffice to cite the following of the six- and five-syllabled adjectives :

Acheronteus, Aganippaeus[1], *Alcmaeonius, Amphrysiacus, Amytha-
onius, Ariadnaeus, Antenoreus* ('Αντηνορίδαι in Greek), *Atalantaeus,
Athamanteus, Eriphylaeus, Erymantheus, Ganymedeus, Hyperionius,
Labyrintheus, Laestrygonius, Meleagreus, Menelaaeus, Mytilenaeus*
(common enough in Greek *prose*), *Nasamoniacus, Perimedaeus, Phae-
thonteus, Phlegethonteus, Polycleteus, Ptolemaeeus, Salaminiacus* (-ιος
normal Greek), *Telamoniacus* (-ιος Greek), *Tritoniacus*.

How far these formations had express warrant in Greek verse and
how far they were only modelled by the Latin Muse on adjectives like
'Αγαμεμνόνιος (*Agamemnonius*), Βερενίκειος (*Bereniceus*), Πολυδεύκειος,
and maybe others it is impossible to say. At all events they form
a noticeable part of the machinery of developed Latin poetry.

409. **Arsacides.** This sweeping charge against the Parthian royal
house seems to lack justification. But Phraataces, the son of Phraates IV
and an Italian slave girl, who attempted with the assistance of his
mother to seize the throne after the old monarch's death, was suspected
of incest, Iosephus *Ant. Iud.* 18. 2. 4 (Rawlinson's *Sixth Oriental
Monarchy*, p. 220).

cui fas 'to whom it is no sin.'

inplere, Ovid *M.* 11. 264 sq. 'confessam amplectitur heros | et
potitur uotis ingentique *inplet* Achille.' So 'fill' in Milton *L'Allegro*
24.

411.   **stabit,** an opprobrious expression; like a slave or captive (43),
'hoc iam non uxoris est *stare* sed paelicis,' Schol. B; 'nudum olido
stans | fornice *mancipium*,' Juv. 11. 173 (Mayor).

barbarico, barbari.

millesima picks up the *mille* of 401.

lecto, dat.

412. **plus...uacabit,** ironical, 'will show more attention'; for the
verb cf. x 185 sq. 'media inter proelia semper | stellarum caelique
plagis superisque *uacaui*,' v 341 sq.

413. **uenus,** 398 n.

414. **portenta** 'horrors'; cf. v 284 sq. 'quid uelut ignaros ad
quae *portenta* paremur | spe trahis?' The alliteration is intentional;
368, 390 and notes.

415.   **et,** as well as of Pompey.

---

1 In the spelling of the adjectives I have given what would be presumably the
correct form if the adjective were borrowed straight from Greek ; see Professor
Housman's paper 'ΑΙΟΣ and ΕΙΟΣ in Latin Poetry,' *Journal of Philology*, 33.
54 sqq. Whether they were thus or otherwise arrived at is another matter.

debita, cf. 91 sq. supr.

416. **trahitur.** For the present cf. 397 'timet.'

417. **haereat** 'cling to thy thoughts,' 'sink into thy soul,' cf. Pliny *Ep.* 10. 20 (31) 'sed et illud *haereat nobis* quam paucissimos milites a signis auocandos esse,' Ov. *Tr.* 3. 4. 36 '*haesura*que fide tempus in omne *mihi*.' But the omission of a dative is exceedingly harsh.

Eoae...sortis 'from our lot in the East.'

418. **funesto** 'murderous,' as 618.

petisse, unless Lucan is thinking of Deiotarus' mission, is for *pet*ere; cf. note on 381. But **gessisse** in the next line is a true perfect.

419. **prius**, 'ante uindictam Crassi,' Schol. C.

422. **perit** (-*it* as in 321), the chance of vengeance has been lost, cf. VII 431 'quod semper saeuas debet tibi Parthia poenas,' Sen. *Dial.* 12. 10. 3 'nec piget a Parthis, a quibus nondum poenas repetiimus, aues petere.'

423. **duces**, i.e. *nostri*. So in 426. See 85 n. on *fortuna*.

uacarent 'be unemployed'; cf. II 56 'nulla *uacet* tibi, Roma, manus.'

424. **Dacis**, cf. II 54 'hinc *Dacus* premat, inde Getes.' The *Daci* (who seem originally to have been called *Da*(*u*)*i*, so that *Dauos* and *Geta* are similar slave names) were a tribe closely allied to the *Getae* of Thrace, from whom they are not always distinguished. At this time, under a powerful monarch Boerebista (Strabo 7. 3. 11 Βοιρεβίστας ἀνὴρ Γέτης), they were a serious menace to Rome and Julius Caesar had planned an expedition against them before he was killed. They seem to have been troublesome also during the reign of Nero (Bury *Roman Empire* pp. 300, 406).

Rheni...cateruis, Germanis.

425. **nudare latus**, expose the frontier; cf. 1 464 sq. 'Rhenique feroces | deseritis ripas et apertum gentibus orbem,' and Florus 3. 5. 4 '*nudum latus imperii* ostendebat' in a slightly different sense.

Susa, the capital of Elymais (Elam), a kingdom conquered by Mithridates I, who was the real founder of the Parthian empire.

427. 'Ne Parthi ulterius haberent pacem nostram,' Schol. C. For the dat. cf. v 273 '*finis* quis quaeritur arm*is*?' 846 infr. and VII 343.

Fortuna apostrophised, as in 600, 793. Sen. *Oed.* 82 '*Fortuna*, credis? aliquis est ex me pius.'

428*. **Thessalia.** The ambiguous abl. means apparently '*at* Pharsalia' rather than '*by* Pharsalia.'

429. **ad Parthos** '*against* the Parthians.' For *ad* in the sense of

aduersus cf. Livy 42. 49. 2 '*ad magnum* nobilemque aut uirtute aut fortuna *hostem euntem.*' So in other writers.

430. **de qua** with **triumphis**, which here takes the construction of *triumphare.*

431. **non,** in the sense of *nonne*; cf. 586.

Araxen. The Araxes of *Armenia,* now the *Eraskh,* is meant; it flowed by Artaxata, the ancient capital. Seneca also calls it *gelidus* and *niueus.*

432. **Scythicis...sagittis** (cf. 302 n.). But the elder Crassus, whom Lucan has confused with his son, was killed at close quarters in a fracas caused by a treacherous attempt of Surenas to carry him off during a parley, Plut. *Crass.* 31. This is a good example of the 'popular' or 'political' syllogism. 'The Parthians usually killed with arrows,' 'Crassus was killed by the Parthians.' 'Therefore Crassus was killed with arrows.' Cf. n. on 388.

confixa. The shade of the unburied Crassus still carries the marks of his death wounds. So the shade of Deiphobus in Verg. *A.* 6. 494 sqq.

433. **ingeret.** This verb, used of frequent and violent assaults (cf. 'ingeris ictus,' 645 inf.), is applied here to the menacing speech and gestures of spectres, cf. VII 785 n.

434. **[quem]...ultorem...sperauimus,** cf. VII 349 'causa iubet melior *superos sperare secundos.*'

funera...cinerum. Unless these words are loosely used, they imply a double duty—to bury as well as to avenge the slain.

nudae, i.e. unburied; cf. IX 64 'o bene *nudi* | Crassorum cineres!' (*cineres* is loosely used here) and Livy 31. 30. 5 'omnia sepulcra monumentaque diruta esse in finibus suis, omnium *nudatos manes,* nullius ossa terra tegi.'

umbrae, nom. plur.

435. **ad foedus,** etc. The fierce indignation here recalls the beginning of the magnificent invective of Constance in Shakespeare *K. John* III 1. 1 'Gone to be married! Gone to swear a peace! | False blood to false blood joined! Gone to be friends!'

Florus 4. 3. 5 imitates Lucan, 'eo denique discriminum uentum est ut *foedus et pax* cum hoste (si modo hostis Pompei filius) tamen *feriretur.*'

436. **monimenta.** We may translate 'reminders.'

trunci...ceruice duces. This does not mean that 'headless bodies of chieftains' were lugged round the walls, an uninstructive and profitless proceeding; the *duces* could only be recognised by their heads (hence the action of the fratricide in VII 626 sqq. 'quis pectora fratris | caedat et, ut notum possit spoliare cadauer, | *abscisum longe mittat caput*'), which, according to a well-known custom, were thus carried on spears, cf. 681 infr. n. Where beheading is in question, *ceruix* differs little from *caput* (see 12 supra n.), and *truncus* 'lopped' is not limited to the trunk; see Ov. *M*. 15. 375 sq. 'ranas...*truncas* pedibus,' Val. Fl. 4. 181 sq. 'hinc *trunca* rotatis | bracchia rapta uiris,' and especially Stat. *Theb*. 1. 276 sq. 'abruptis etiamnum inhumata procerum | reliquiis *trunca ora* rigent,' and ib. 5. 236 sqq. (quoted on 682 inf.) '*truncos*...patris uultus.' The abl. may be either one of the Part Concerned as 1 342 'curuataque *cuspide* pila,' VI 225 'informis *facie*,' 256 'nudum *pectore*,' Val. Fl. 4. 402 'ardua flumina *ripis*,' *or* one of the Instrument, in which case we may compare Prop. 2. 22. 3 'nulla meis frustra *lustrantur* compita *plantis*.'

437. **lustrarunt** 'traversed,' 'made the circuit of'; no doubt with ironical reference to the solemn ceremony of *lustratio*; cf. 1 592 sqq.

nomina tanta, i.e. so many illustrious Romans. For *nomina* cf. VII 584 n. For *tanta* VI 586 'ossaque *nobilium tantosque* adquirere *manes*.'

438. **Euphrates**. On this and the following statement compare Excursus B p. lxxix.

439. **in terras**, i.e. into the bosom of the earth, not very different from '*sub* terras.' Cf. Prop. 2. 6. 31 'a, gemat in *terris*,' Val. Fl. 3. 410 'ille uolens Erebum *terras*que retexit,' the interior of the earth.

reddidit 'gave them up again.' This is explained by III 261 sqq. 'at Tigrim subito tellus absorbet hiatu | occultosque tegit cursus rursusque renatum | fonte nouo flumen pelagi non abnegat undis.' Cf. II 217 'nec iam alueus amnem | nec retinent ripae redditque cadauera campo.' The ancients believed that at one place in its course the Tigris flowed underground, and Pliny, *N. H.* 2. 225, put this in Mesopotamia, which would agree with what Lucan says here.

ista, the sum of all the neuters in the four preceding lines.

440. **sedentem**, sc. *in tribunali*; cf. IX 971 'quo *iudex sederit* antro.'

441. **placare potes**, i.e. you will stoop to appease.

orbem Romanum, 345 n.

442. **proiecta sub Austro** 'stretching out under the south.' Cf. IX 431 sqq. 'ora | sub nimio *proiecta* die uicina perusti | aetheris,' Silius 6. 645 sqq. 'ubi latis | *proiecta* in campis nebulas exhalat inertis,' Val. Fl. 8. 90 sq. 'septem *proiectus* in amnes | Nilus.'

443. **petimus** 'our goal is Pharos.' For the *present ind.*, which presumes the event will occur, cf. 635, 750.

arua...Lagi, cf. 802 and n. on 692.

444. **tuta** 'protected'; cf. 20, 225. Lucan apparently thinks Egypt extended as far as the Syrtes; cf. 540.

445. **septeno**, a collective, 'a group of seven streams,' whereas *septem* would mean *seven separate streams*. See Brugmann's paper *die distributiven und die kollektiven Numeralia* and *Class. Review* 21. 200.

summouet, lit. 'pushes out of the way,' a reference to the formation of the Delta.

446 sq. Egypt is independent both of imports and rain ; cf. Tib. 1. 7. 26 'arida nec Pluuio supplicat herba Ioui.'

448. **tibi debita**, *Introd.* pp. xliii and xlvii.

449—455.

> 'Dost fear a phantom? Youth's a harmless age :
> Of justice, honour and regard for Heaven
> Within the palace of the old despair.
> The veteran sceptre-wielder knows no shame :
> Mildest that kingdom's lot whose king is young.'
> He said no more, to sway them to his mind.
> How large the freedom fate's last hope allows !
> The cause Great Pompey advocates is lost.

449. **tutelae...tuae**, *Introd.* p. xliv.

commissa refers to Ptolemy rather than to the *sceptra* ; cf. 375 n.

nominis umbram 'the phantom of a name.' The words are differently used at 1 135 'stat *magni nominis umbra*,' 'a shadow of greatness.'

450. **iura**, etc. Cf. Verg. *A*. 2. 541 sq. '*iura fidemque* | supplicis erubuit'; Stat. *Ach.* 1. 403 '*iura fidem superos* una calcata rapina.'

451*. **respectum**, cf. 490.

ueteris...aulae. The gen. seems to take the place of a predicative adjective such as we have with *sperare* in 434 n., and means 'belonging to an old (king's) court.' Adjectives and genitives are found side by side elsewhere, e.g. 676 infr.; and we have had harsher uses of the case already, 158 n.

452 sq. **mitissima sors...regnorum.** The sense of this as given in the paraphrase above (cf. Dryden, *The Hind and the Panther*, Part 1 271 'And kind as kings upon their coronation day,' quoted by Haskins) is hardly to the point, since, as Francken saw, Ptolemy's relations with

his own subjects were no concern of a foreigner. The Latin might conceivably mean 'the dispensation, or administration, of a tyranny is least savage when the tyrant is new to his station'; but there is a further confusion between youth and newness to royalty.

454. **animos**, i.e. his hearers' feelings. One of the features of Lucan's Latin is to omit references and determinants, e.g. pronouns, wherever the reader can be deemed capable of supplying them. See 85 n. Here *eorum* would be added in normal prose.

spes ultima, a situation of forlorn hope or despair.

455. **habes.** For the apostrophe to an abstraction cf. 547.

u. s. M., sheer prose and only redeemed from insipidity by the unnatural emphasis on *Magni*, which is used significantly (note on 102 supra) to contrast with *uicta*; cf. Ov. *M.* 15. 825 'et *magnum* Siculis nomen *superabitur* undis' (of Sextus Pompeius). A very different picture in 684 sq.

456. **Cypro.** The dat. of Goal for *ad* with the acc. is poetic and unusual, the more so as it is that of a proper name. Ovid *M.* 8. 178 sq. 'sumptam de fronte coronam | *inmisit* caelo.'

457. **inmisere**, i.e. let them have a free course towards Cyprus.

cui...aras, a 'compendious comparison,' cf. 144 *Lesbo.*

458. **Paphiae.** For the worship of the Paphian Venus see Tacitus *Hist.* 2. 2 sq., who says ch. 3 'conditorem templi regem Aeriam uetus memoria, quidam ipsius deae nomen id perhibent. fama recentior tradit a Cinyra' (cf. 716 inf.) 'sacratum templum deamque ipsam conceptam mari huc adpulsam.'

459. **credimus**, i.e. if it is credible.

coepisse 'have a beginning.' For the absolute use cf. x 265 sq. 'quasdam (sc. aquas) conpage sub ipsa | cum toto *coepisse* reor,' Sen. *Dial.* 11. 1. 1 'ceterum quidquid *coepit* et desinit,' Florus *Praef.* 1. 1.

460. **deseruit**, here simply 'left,' unless Lucan thought that interest in the Cyprian antiquities might have detained Pompey.

totos with **scopulos** here is hardly distinguishable from *omnes* or the Fr. *tous*; cf. 336.

461. **emensus**, i.e. having followed the whole rocky coast line; cf. ix 734 sq. 'has inter pestes duro Cato milite siccum | *emetitur* iter,' Livy 27. 43. 1 'cum per medios hostes totam ferme longitudinem *Italiae emensi* essent,' Sen. *Phaedr.* 948 *longinqua...emetiemur.*

exit, of the promontory Garganus in v 380 'Apulus Hadriacas *exit* Garganus in undas.'

462. **inde**, from the promontory of Curias, *Introd.* pp. xlii, lxxxvii.

transuerso, uertitur. The repetition of the same element would not trouble an ancient writer, cf. e.g. Eur. *Andr.* 652 sq. οὗ πέσημᾶτα | πλεῖσθ' Ἑλλάδος πέπτωκε δοριπετῆ νεκρῶν, Sen. *Dial.* 10. 6. 1 '*dicitur dixisse* uni sibi ne puero quidem umquam ferias contigisse,' Manilius 3. 308 (mundus) 'super trans*uersum uertitur* axem,' of which this place has been thought to be a reminiscence. On the fact recorded here see *Introd.* p. xlii.

463 means he did not 'make' Alexandria or Pharos, with its celebrated lighthouse (whence Fr. *phare*), his destination.

tenuit is almost technical in this sense; cf. v 720, Sen. *Benef.* 2. 31. 3 and elsewhere.

gratum nocturno lumine, sc. nautis. So Suet. *Claud.* 20 of the *pharus* at Ostia 'congestisque pilis super posuit *altissimam turrem* in exemplum Alexandrini *phari* ut *ad nocturnos ignes* cursum nauigia derigerent.' So Val. Fl. 7. 84 sq. of the same lighthouse 'qui iam te, Tiberine, tuens claramque serena | *arce pharon*' e.q.s.

montem. *mons* here, and in 695 which see, has been questioned. The lighthouse at Alexandria was built on a long white calcareous rock, of no great height; but Lucan may have thought otherwise. The alternative is to suppose that the 'mountain' is the huge lighthouse itself. In addition to the passages quoted in illustration above a place of Ammianus Marcellinus is instructive, 'excogitauit in portu Cleopatra (*an error*) *turrim excelsam* quae Pharos a loco ipso cognominatur, *praelucendi nauibus suggerens ministeria* cum quondam ex Parthenio pelago uenientes uel Libyco per pandas oras et patulas, *montium* nullas speculas uel collium signa cernentes, harenarum inlisae glutinosae mollitiae frangerentur,' 22. 16. 9, which shows that the Pharos did the work of a *mons*.

464. **infima.** As a matter of fact, the mouth of the Nile at Pelusium is the one slightly furthest to the south; but we cannot be sure that Lucan intended this.

pugnaci, showing fight, 'struggling'; elsewhere in Lucan applied to combatants or their weapons, vii 232 n. The wind was unfavourable, *Introd.* p. xlii.

465. **diuidui** 'parted,' 'separated'; from *di-uido,* with an old participial sense, preserved also in the simple *uid-uu-s,* Hor. *C.* 1. 10. 11; cf. *in-gen-uu-s* 'native born,' ' free born,' *rig-uu-s* 'watered,' *mort-uu-s, uacuus* 387 above n.

466. **septimus amnis,** its seventh stream or arm, counting from the west. For the use of *amnis* cf. the quotation in Apuleius *Flor.* 6.

p. 19 'Ganges...unus omnium amnium maximus 'Eois regnator aquis in flumina centum...Oceanique fretis *centeno* iungitur *amni*,'' and Val. Fl. quoted on 442.

467-9. 'It was the season when the Balance weighs the hours in even scales, level for but a single day, and the dwindling light pays back to the winter night the losses of the spring tide.' Cf. IV 58 sq. (of the Vernal equinox) 'atque iterum aequatis ad iustae pondera Librae | temporibus uicere dies,' X 227 'ante parem nocti Libra sub iudice Phoebum,' Sen. *Herc. Fur.* 846 sqq. 'quanta cum longae redit hora nocti | crescere et somnos cupiens quietos | Libra Phoebeos tenet aequa currus' e.q.s.

examinat, as in Manilius 2. 795 sqq. 'tertius excelsi signat fastigia caeli | quo defessus equis Phoebus consistit anhelis | declinatque (reclinatque *Housman*) diem mediasque *examinat* umbras'; cf. id. 1. 635.

469. **minor.** So Stat. *Silu.* 3. 2. 79 'paulatim *minor.*'

solacia 'compensation,' cf. Tacitus *Agr.* 44 'festinatae mortis grande *solacium*.'

470. **Casio...monte.** *Introd.* p. xlviii.

se...tenere 'had his quarters,' 'was posted.' 'In Livy *intra Appenninum, loco, finibus, castris, muris, moenibus se tenere* and the like are very common' Munro on Lucr. 1. 508.

471. **nec...languent.** This means that it was still light and that the wind had not dropped as it often does at sunset. After the change of course the wind would be astern.

473. **aduentu...conpleuerat** 'filled with the news of his coming'; Statius, in a passage perhaps inspired by this, is much less curt 'at iam sacrifici subitus per tecta Lycurgi | *nuntius implerat lacrimis* ipsumque domumque' *Theb.* 5. 638 sq.

474. **monstra,** of the Egyptians (as of their gods, Verg. *Aen.* 8. 698, '*portenta*' Juv. 15. 2), 548, 613 inf., Hor. *C.* 1. 37. 21 'fatale *monstrum*,' of Cleopatra.

475*. **Pellaeae,** 298 n.

Acoreus, *Introd.* p. l.

476. **senio,** in the sense of *senecta*, is post-Augustan. The sense was no doubt developed through association with the oblique cases of *senex*.

fractis...annis, cf. Sen. *Phaedra* 1262 'o triste *fractis* orbitas *annis* malum !,' id *Dial.* 10. 4. 6 '*infractam aetatem* territabant.'

modestior, 156 n.

477. **genuit,** cf. Verg. *A.* 4. 366 'duris *genuit* te cautibus
horrens | Caucasus,' Prop. 1. 22. 9 sq. 'Vmbria... | me *genuit* terris
fertilis uberibus,' Ovid *M.* 10. 217 'nec *genuisse* pudet Sparten
Hyacinthon,' and the 'Mantua me *genuit*' and the 'Corduba me
genuit' of the epitaphs on Vergil and Lucan, of persons as of other
produce of a country.

custos Nili, etc. 'watcher of the Nile in his rising to pass upon the
fields,' x 219 sq. 'uana fides ueterum Nilo quod *crescat in arua* |
Aethiopum prodesse niues.' The 'Nile-Observatory' (Νειλοσκοπεῖον
Diod. 1. 36. 7) or Nilometer (Νειλομέτριον Strabo 17. 1. 48 p. 817) in
Memphis, like that in the island off Syene was a well, the rise and fall
of whose waters was an index to the rise and fall of the Nile, Strabo l.c.
Sir G. Wilkinson, describing the latter, says it is a staircase between
two walls descending to the Nile, on one of which is a succession of
graduated scales containing one or two cubits accompanied by inscriptions showing the rise of the river at various periods during the rule of
the Caesars, *Popular Account of the Ancient Egyptians*, 2. p. 257.

478. **Memphis,** the ancient capital of Egypt, whose importance
was recognised even under the Ptolemies who were crowned there
according to Diodorus 33. 13, etc. Its founder was Menes according
to Herodotus 2. 99, but Uchoreus according to Diodorus (*Introd.* p. l).
The mythographers mention Apis, a legendary King of Argos, or
Epaphos, as its founder.

uana sacris 'place of false worship'; for the ablative cf. n. on
ceruice 437.

cultore deorum. This phrase seems to have a more formal and
professional sense than e.g. in Hor. *C.* 1. 34. 1, Cic. *Tusc.* 1. 69, and
one reminding us somewhat of the *collegia cultorum* often mentioned
on inscriptions. The 'gods' must be the objects of the particular
worship, limited as 'deorum' is in Catullus 63. 75, ib. 68 'deum
ministra,' where Cybele only is regarded.

479. **lustra suae Phoebes.** These words seem to mean 'the
period of life assigned to him by his mistress Phoebe,' i.e. the moon-
goddess Isis. Plutarch *de Iside et Osiride* 43 gives 25 years as the life
of the original Apis ὅσων ἐνιαυτῶν ἔζη χρόνον ὁ Ἄπις, the same being
the number of letters in the Egyptian alphabet, whatever this may
mean. Wiedemann, in his edition of Herodotus book II, p. 551, states
that the view of the ancients that the sacred bull was not allowed to
live more than 25 years, being then drowned in a spring, is not borne
out by the Apis monuments, which record 'bulls of all possible ages.'

non unus. This would show its priest's advanced age. Cf. *Introd.*
p. li.

Apis (whose name in Greek was Epaphos according to Herodotus
2. 153) was the name of the sacred and oracular Bull worshipped
in Memphis as an incarnation of Osiris (cf. 833 inf. n.), Plutarch
de Iside et Osiride c. 29 οἱ δὲ πλεῖστοι τῶν ἱερέων εἰς τὸ αὐτό φασι τὸν
Ὄσιριν συμπεπλέχθαι καὶ τὸν Ἄπιν, ἐξηγούμενοι καὶ διδάσκοντες ἡμᾶς ὡς
εὔμορφον εἰκόνα χρὴ νομίζειν τῆς Ὀσίριδος ψυχῆς τὸν Ἄπιν. This
complex of Osiris-Apis is *Serapis*.

480. **uox prima,** i.e. the first speaker; for *uox* applied, though
somewhat differently, to a person cf. 1 269 sq. '(hos) audax uenali
comitatur Curio lingua, | *uox* quondam *populi*,' 'mouthpiece.' For
the noun as predicate, a form of expression of which Lucan is fond,
VII 121 'Pompeius erit miserabile nomen' and note, cf. Sen. *Phaedr.*
851 'malorum *finis Alcides fuit*,' id. *Benef.* 6. 16. 5 'ego illi *potissima
curatio fui*.'

meritumque, etc. 'meritum et fidem Pompei' Schol. a. But probably
the singular is intended to generalize, 'the claims of good service and
honour.'

481. **iactauit,** of insistent presentation, v 799 'talia *iactantes*'
'urging vehemently,' 1 267 'minax *iactatis* curia Gracchis.'

pignora, i.e. the sacred obligations under the will; cf. III 33
'abscidis frustra ferro tua *pignora*.'

482. **melior,** etc. 'better at counselling the bad and reading a
despot's heart.' For the infinitive cf. 381 supr. n.

483*. **Pothinus,** see *Introd.* p. lii. The name is Greek, and means
'desirable,' ποθεινός. A similar one is *Philetus*, that of a favourite
slave in Statius *Siluae*.

484. **nocentes,** that is legally guilty.

485. **laudata,** though formally commended. The word is, like
the Greek ἐπαινεῖν, applied to official expressions of approval; cf.
v 52, 56, IX 166 'sed Cato *laudatam* iuuenis compescuit iram.' For
the turn of the phrase cf. Sen. *Clem.* 1. 2. 1 'condicione temporum
incidunt quaedam quae possint *laudata puniri*,' '*laudata fides*' in
Claud. *Stil.* 1. 236.

486. **premit,** cf. 267.

accede 'join fate and heaven.' Compare the sentiment of 1 127
'uictrix causa deis placuit sed uicta Catoni.'

487. **cole felices,** cf. Eur. *Heraclidae* 25 τοὺς κρείσσονας σέ-
βοντας.

488. There is a mild zeugma, **distant** being first used of distance and then of discord.

flamma mari, cf. Sen. *Thyest.* 480 sqq. ' ante *cum flammis aquae,* | cum morte uita, cum mari uentus *fidem | foedusque iungent*' (Milton, *Par. Regained* IV 412 'Water with Fire | In ruin reconciled '), Lucan III 681 '*pelago diuersa* lues,' i.e. fire, hence we must understand IX 866 sq. '*coeunt ignes* stridentibus *undis* | et premitur natura poli ' (of the topsy-turvy world of the Antipodes) which is explained by the imitation in Florus 2. 17. 12 'cadentem in maria *solem* obrutumque *aquis ignem.*'

490*. **incipit.** The grammatical subject is **sceptrorum uis**; but the real subject is the sceptre-holder. Cf. 166 n., 720 n. There is a harsher shift in Val. Fl. 3. 40 sq. 'cadit inscia clauo | dextera, *demittit*que *oculos.*'

For the sentiments of the whole passage cf. Seneca *Thyest.* 214 sq. 'ubicumque tantum *honesta* dominanti placent, | *precario regnatur,*' e.q.s.

arces, the monarch's stronghold; cf. VII 593 note.

respectus honesti, cf. Sen. *Dial.* 4. 9. 1 'expulso melior*is* aequior*is*que *respectu* ' and the imitation by Claudian *IV Cons. Hon.* 267 ' nec tibi quid liceat sed quid fecisse decebit | occurrat mentemque domet *respectus honesti* '; cf. also 451 supr.

491. ' Free crime' is the despot's cry—as ' free food,' etc., is the mob's—Ov. *F.* 6. 595 '*regia* res *scelus* est.'

inuisa, cf. Seneca *Phoen.* 654 sqq. '*regnare* non uult, esse qui *inuisus* timet. | simul ista mundi conditor posuit deus, | *odium atque regnum.*'

492. **sublatusque modus gladiis** 'and the removal of all restrictions on the sword '; cf. '*perdidit* inde *modum* caedes' VII 532 n., Sen. *Dial.* 11. 11. 6 'quisquis *exempto modo* (Madvig) scripta tua mirabatur.'

facere, etc. This means, ferocity is its own and sole protection or, as he puts it, ' it is not possible to be cruel in all one does, except when doing so habitually.' For the intentional paradox cf. III 145 sq. '*libertas*, inquit, populi quem regna coercent, | *libertate* perit.'

493 sqq.

> Out of the palace ye that would be good !
> Virtue and sovran power mate not together.
> He'll fear for ay whom cruelties revolt.

495. As Seneca says *Dial.* 2. 8. 1 ' non coeunt contraria.'

pudebunt. This personal use of the impersonal was obsolete in the age of Lucan, and seems to show he is borrowing from an old tragedy. If **saeua** is put before **quem**, the maxim falls into trochaic rhythm. Cf. *Classical Review* 18. p. 37. For the tense compare 371 n.

496. **contempserit**, perfect subjunctive. The appeal to the boy's vanity is an effective touch; cf. *Introd.* p. liii n. 4.

497. **nec** 'not even,' as *neque* 206, in 503 'not...either.'

498* sq. The connexion is: 'and that a stranger may not rob our royal house of the sceptre, (reflect) you have those with nearer claims.' The ellipse in the expression of the thought is thoroughly Latin.

nos. The speaker in pleader's fashion associates himself with the King, their interests being identical, so in 5. 18.

499. **pignora**, see above 405, Val. Max. 7. 1. 1 'Metellum...inter oscula complexusque *carissimorum pignorum* extinctum filii et generi, umeris suis per urbem latum, rogo inposuerunt.'

500. **damnatae.** Schol. C. says 'sic enim ei relictum erat regnum a patre < ut Cleopatram sororem sortiretur uxorem, sed > suasu Pompei senatus in hunc contulerat.'

501*. **certe** 'at least,' whatever we do.

503. **toto...orbe**, 336 n.

504. **rerum fiducia** 'reliance on his fortunes.'

505. The emphasis is on **cum qua gente**; *qua* probably has a relative sense, 'quaerit *gentem*, cum qua cadat.'

rapitur ciuilibus umbris apparently means he is hurried to his doom by the shades of citizens slaughtered in the civil war, and now exacting the vengeance due. For the verb we may compare the legal *rapitur in ius* or 'mortuus *rapitur*' (to the tomb) Cic. *de Or.* 2. 283. It is not however clear, whether **umbris** is to be taken as dat. (cf. 301) or abl. as in Juv. 6. 29 'dic *qua* Tisiphone, quibus *exagitare* (-*ere*) colubris?'

506. **fugit ora,** i.e. he cannot look them in the face.

507. **saturat...uolucres.** See VII 830 sqq. especially 842 sqq.

508. **uno**, etc. 'commingled in one field of gore.'

509. **omnia**, subst. 'whose all,' cf. IV 342 sq. 'gerit *omnia uicti* | sed ducis,' Val. Fl. 3. 212 sq. 'perge age *Tartareae* mecum simul *omnia noctis*, | Musa, sequi.'

510. **Thessaliae reus** 'with Pharsalia to his charge,' the usual meaning of *Thessalia* in Lucan, supr. Excursus C p. lxxxix.

nulla tellure. This was substantially true; cf. 250 sqq., *Introd.* p. xxxv.

512. **in Magnum** with **querellae** cf. VII 725 'plurimaque *in
saeuos* populi conuicia *diuos*'; *de*, or the gen., would be more usual with
this subst.

513. **sepositam** 'set apart,' 'remote'; cf. Mart. *Spect.* 3. 1 'quae
tam *seposita*st, quae gens tam barbara, Caesar?' Sen. *Med.* 339 'mare
sepositum.'

semper...quietam. This claim on behalf of the most turbulent
capital of ancient times is as extravagant as the well known lines in
Rejected Addresses 'For dear is the Emerald Isle of the Ocean, | Whose
daughters are fair as the foam of the wave, | Whose sons, *unaccustom'd
to rebel commotion*, | Tho' joyous are sober,—tho' peaceful are brave.'
Only our orator is serious and Moore's parodist was not. For the
expression cf. Tac. *Germ.* 35 'sine cupiditate, sine impotentia quieti
secretique nulla prouocant bella, nullis raptibus aut latrociniis popu-
lantur' (said of the Chauci, a tribe of ancient Germany).

516. **in quam,** etc. For the turn of the thought cf. 92 above.

518. **purgandum gladio** 'to be cleared by the sword'; 'wiped
out in blood' is an inferior metaphor. Cf. Sil. 11. 199 sq. 'et *ferro
purgate* nefas. hic denique solus | eluerit sanguis maculatas crimine
mentes.'

nobis, cf. 498 n.

519*. **te suadente,** *Introd.* p. xlvii.

uotis, with moral support; cf. III 317 sq. 'non tamen auderet
pietas humana uel armis | uel *uotis* prodesse Ioui.' But Egypt gave
Pompey material aid also; *Introd.* p. xlv.

fouimus, of partisan encouragement; cf. Livy 38. 32. 4 'satis
ambitiose partem utramque *fouendo*,' Tac. *H.* 1. 8 'tamquam alias
partes *fouissent.*' It corresponds to *dedit* in the first member of the
quod clause. A similar but harsher juxtaposition of clauses occurs at
772 sqq.

520. **proferre** 'bring out,' 'produce'; so 'ferrum prompserat'
Tac. *A.* 15. 74 ('pugionem templo...detraxerat' ib. 53); but '*detege*
iam ferrum' III 128 'unsheathe.'

521. I.e. I have no personal feeling against you; only you are
beaten.

522. **malueram,** sc. *ferire uiscera*, a common ellipse. This
pluperf. indicative, to which *putaram* 'I should have thought' is
similar, is quoted from only three other places in Latin: Cicero
Att. 2. 19. 3, *Fam.* 7. 3. 6 and Tac. *A.* 15. 2. The sense of unreality
comes from the tense, I 'had once preferred' and did not subsequently.

The use was no doubt colloquial; and in later Latin it was replaced by *maluissem*, first in Livy 1. 5. 6.

rapimur, by irresistible fate, or blind chance; cf. VII 446, 487 '*rapit* omnia casus.' For the sense cf. Sen. *Dial.* 1. 5. 8 'grande solacium est *cum uniuerso rapi*.'

523. The normal order 'dubitasne an uiolare te mihi necesse sit cum liceat' is changed to give prominence to *te mihi*; see *Classical Review* 30. p. 144 *a* (ix). The argument is that the Egyptians will be held responsible if they omit to do what they have the power of doing.

526. **refugo**, for which he might have used *refluo*, reinforces the suggestion of *inermem*.

mollia, i.e. *mollita*, a use of the adj. for which cf. 387 *uacua*, 667 *lacerum* and notes. Compare Cic. *N. D.* 2. 130 'Aegyptum Nilus inrigat et cum tota aestate obrutam oppletamque tenuit tum *recedit mollitos*que et oblimatos *agros* ad serendum relinquit.'

527. **metiri** 'take the measure of,' cf. 346 supr. (The subject (indefinite, hence **sua**) is omitted.) So Sen. *Dial.* 5. 7. 2 'quotiens aliquid conaberis, *te* simul et ea quae paras quibusque pararis ipse *metire*' cf. ib. § 1, id. 4. 21. 7, Hor. *Ep.* 1. 7. 98.

uires, one's real strength, and so one's weakness. So *opes* 'means' may be either riches or poverty, Ovid *F.* 2. 302 'antiquas testificantur *opes*' and elsewhere, and *fides* may mean *failure* in faith.

528. **fulcire ruinam**; for the metaphor of underpropping a falling structure cf. Ovid *Tr.* 1. 6. 5 'te mea supposita ueluti trabe *fulta ruinast*.'

529. **iacet**, is overpowered and prostrate. So in 545 it follows on *premunt*.

bustum is probably a true singular, cf. VII 803 sq. 'petimus non singula busta | discretosque rogos : *unum* da gentibus *ignem*.' The speaker may be *supposed* not to know that the author has said, in VII 797 sqq., that the Pompeians were not burned.

mouere, a perilous impiety, 791 infr. The sense intended is 'to interfere with the issue of the battle of Pharsalia.' This has suggested the phrase of Florus 4. 3. 3 'iterum fuit *mouenda Thessalia*.'

531. **nullis**, loosely put for *neutris*; cf. *quo* 185 n.

accessimus 'joined.' The statement is false, *Introd.* p. xlv. For the argument cf. the address of Curio to his soldiers, Caesar *B. C.* 2. 32. 6 'an qui incolumes resistere non potuerunt, perditi resistant, uos autem, incerta uictoria Caesarem secuti, diiudicata iam belli fortuna *uictum sequamini?*' Contrast Val. Max. 4. 7. 5 'cui gratum animum quia *laeta* in materia exhibere non contigerat in ea quam *inicam* Fortuna esse uoluit cum multa fide praestitit.'

533. Cf. 360 sqq. supr.

534. The other side of the thought is put out in 126 sq.

aduersis, dat. cf. 578 and Cic. *Att.* 3. 27 'te oro ut, quibus in rebus tui mei indigebunt, nostris *miseriis* ne *desis*.'

535 sq. **nulla fides**, no sense of honour however quixotic.

'''Tis base to fail misfortune.' Yes, if we

Have followed fortune ; but the top of honour

Ne'er chose the merely wretched for a friend.

537. **tanta iubere** 'should allow him' (the king!) 'to issue an order so important.' For the construction cf. 384 n. Ptolemy is made formally responsible for the deed; cf. *Introd.* p. liii.

538. **sceleri delectus**, cf. Tac. *A.* 14. 3 'ne quis ill*i* tant*o facinori delectus* iussa sperneret.'

Achillas. *Introd.* pp. xlix, liii. The name (which is found on Egyptian papyri) is Greek, 'Αχιλλᾶς, and formed with a suffix -ᾶς which at least in some words seems to have arisen from colloquial abbreviation like the vulgar *-er* of English slang in ' Rugger,' ' Soccer,' ' bedder ' (for ' bedmaker'). So Μηνᾶς for Μηνόδωρος, Ζηνᾶς for Ζηνόδωρος, Νικανδᾶς for Νικανδρίδας. So 'Αχιλλᾶς may be a popular shortening for the patronymic 'Αχιλλείδης ' Son of Achilles,' a suitable name for a soldier. It seems to have been sometimes confused with 'Αχιλλεύς, and Lucan hence makes the accusative *Achillea* x 523.

539*. **perfida** probably alludes to the dangers of the locality (cf. 566 and Strabo below) as well as to the character of the inhabitants, cf. Prop. 3. 11. 33 'noxia Alexandrea, dolis aptissima tellus' and 823 infr.

excurrit, apparently not as in iv 405 'et tepidum in molles Zephyros *excurrit* Iader ' but = *exultat* (Cr. App.) ' leaps up out of its place ' as Priscian *Perieg.* 499, of a river that dances when you pipe to it, ' hic et Halesinus fons est, mitissimus undis, | tibia quem extollit cantu ; saltare putatur | musicus et ripis laetans *excurrere* plenis.' Compare Solinus 5. 20 on the same ' si insonent tibiae, *exultabundus* ad cantus eleuatur et quasi miretur uocis dulcedinem ultra margines intumescit.' This seems to be clear from the description in Strabo 16. 2. 26 (p. 758). ' Similar phenomena occur near Casium in Egypt. The ground with one sharp shock turns completely round, shifting on two sides at once so that the part elevated forces the sea in and the depressed part receives it. When it reverts, the spot resumes its original position, at times with some alteration and at times with none.'

540. 'And Egypt's shallows bear witness to the Syrtes' neighbourhood.'

iunctas 'adjoining' as in 1 571 'iunctos extremis montibus agros,' Ovid *Pont*. 2. 4. 20 '*iunctis*...locis,' ib. 1. 4. 31 'iunctior Haemoniast Ponto quam Roma sinistro.'

testantur, cf. x 15 sq. 'templa...antiquas Macetum *testantia* uires.'

Syrtes (184, 444 n.), not much less than a thousand miles away.

541* sq. **sociis monstri** 'for his partners in the hideous deed' (cf. VII 464 'factum quae monstra forent') to which **gladiisque** 'and for their swords' is somewhat harshly appended by a sort of afterthought.

543. **Pelusiaci...Canopi.** If Lucan knew, as it appears he did, that the two extreme mouths of the Nile were those at Canopus and Pelusium, this phrase would be a 'fine derangement of epithets' and its reproduction by subsequent writers (see Statius *Silu.* 2. 7. 70, Auienus 3. 34, Sidonius Apollinaris *Carm.* 9. 27) hardly less strange. I have argued (*Proceedings of the British Academy* 1908 pp. 169 sq.) that it means 'Canopus *and* Pelusium,' and compared Ovid *F.* 5. 7. 'Aganippidos Hippocrenes,' that is 'Hippocrene *and* Aganippe.' If so, the four proper names will be an expression for the whole of Egypt from Memphis to the seaboard.

544. **hos animos**, with ellipse of a transitive verb such as *habuit.* Cf. Seneca *Troad.* 347 '*hos* Scyrus *animos*?' Juv. 1. 88 sq. 'alea quando | *hos animos*?' perhaps a scornful echo of Lucan; Val. Max. 4. 7. Ext. 1 '*has*cine *uires* amicitiae?' is slightly different.

ciuilia, with the 'developed' sense of the adj. on which see 604 note.

545. **Romana,** 288 n.

iacent, 529 n.

istis, i.e. *his* 122 n.

547*. **hanc.** But we say 'keep faith *thus far*'; and so in Latin *hactenus.* But cf. Sen. *Herc. Fur.* 1147 sq. 'numquid Hesperii maris | extrema tellus *hunc* dat Oceano *modum*?' where we translate *hunc* 'here.' For the apostrophe cf. 455 n.

548. 'Provide a kindred hand' to strike the blow.

monstra, 474.

550. **Caesaris esse nefas.** Cf. II 264 sqq. 'quis nollet in isto | ense mori, quamuis alieno uolnere labens | et *scelus* esse *tuum*?' Statius *Silu.* 2. 7. 100 sq. in his memorial poem on Lucan adopts the expression 'sic

et tu, rabidi *nefas* tyranni, | iussus praecipitem subire Lethen ' (cf. 139
above n.). For the form of the sentence cf. 480 n.

tanti...ruinam nominis. Cf. Val. Max. 5. 1. Ext. 4 '*tanti uiri*
subitae *ruinae.*' In *nominis* there seems to be an allusion to ' Magnus'
(455 n.).

551*. The thought that this is a conflict of the gods in which no
outsider should intrude occurs again at III 314 sqq. 'tractentur uolnera
nulla | sacra manu: si caelicolis furor arma dedisset, | ' (if there were
civil war in heaven) ' aut si terrigenae temptarent astra Gigantes, | non
tamen *auderet* pietas humana uel *armis* | uel *uotis* prodesse Ioui.'

caelo...tonante, cf. IX 655 '*caelo...timente,*' Sen. *Herc. Fur.* 452.

552. inseruisse ' to interpose (intrude) thy impious hand.' The
verb is used elsewhere of uncalled for interference; IX 1072 '*inseruit*
nostro *sua* tela labori' (cf. VI 504), Tac. *A.* 6. 2 'dum *ignobilitatem
suam* magnis nominibus *inserit.*' For the perf. inf. cf. 1 258 ' non
ausus tim*uisse* palam ' and 381 n.

inpure ac semiuir. These appellations are less suited to Ptolemy
than to Pothinus but are applied again to him by Sextus in IX 130
' *rege* sub *inpuro* ' and 152 '*semiuiri...tyranni.*'

553—556*. This is one sentence with a single verb, *erat,* which is
placed in the emphatic position, but with two contrasted members of
very unequal length. It has another peculiarity, the first part meaning
' *suppose* he was not a conqueror of the world.' For the asyndeton of
the juxtaposition see 118 n.

553. ter (814 n.) **inuectus** substantival ' one who had thrice ridden
into the Capitol.' The acc. is in partial dependence on the preposition
cf. Livy 2. 31. 3 'dictator triumphans urb*em inuehitur.*'

554. regum...potens ' lord of kings,' cf. Tac. *A.* 14. 60 ' mox
mariti *potens.*' For his ' vassal princes ' cf. 207.

uindex...senatus as ' senatus | *assertor*' IV 213 sq.

556 sq. quid uiscera...scr. ' Why dost thou probe our life's seat
with thy sword?' Seneca *Med.* 1021 '*scrutabor ense uiscera* et ferro
extraham,' *Oed.* 986, *Dial.* 1. 6. 9 'non sunt uulnere *penitus* impresso
scrutanda praecordia.' Compare Shakespeare's expression *Jul. Caes.*
V. 3. 41 sq. ' Now be a freeman and with this good sword | That ran
through Caesar *search this bosom.*'

557. nescis...nescis ; cf. Ov. *M.* 1. 514 sq. '*nescis*, temeraria,
nescis | quem fugias.'

559. The argument is, Pompey's overthrow in the civil war has
deprived you of all right over life and death.

560. uela negarat, the opposite of *uela dederat* (185 supr. n.), cf. IX 325 sq. 'frustraque rudentibus ausis | *uela negare Noto.*' Ovid *Met.* 11. 487 (in an episode with which Lucan was plainly familiar) 'pars munire latus, pars *uentis uela negare.*'

561. infanda, 397.

562. quem contra 'to meet him' does not express but may suggest hostility.

non longa…biremi. See *Introd.* p. liv.

563*. adpulerat, if genuine, can only mean 'had come alongside,' an unexampled sense for a verb whose established nautical meaning is 'to come to shore.'

565. malignum 'niggard,' 'inhospitable,' 'forbidding.' Cf. v 651 'oraeque *malignos* | Ambraciae portus.'

566. 'And the surf of meeting seas which the shallows broke'; cf. IX 308 (of the Syrtes) 'aequora *fracta uadis.*'

567*. uetet, i.e. makes it impossible ; the subjunctive is one of Quotation. Either *aduertere* or *adpellere* is possible, but **adpellere** makes the point, the dangers of landing, clearer.

568 sqq. 'Yet had not the laws of doom and death at hand, marking its victim by decree of the everlasting system, not been drawing Pompey to the shore under sentence to die etc.'

intenta, properly 'aimed at' and so 'imminent,' strictly refers to *mortis,* cf. *Consol. Liu.* 361 'ecce *necem intentam* caelo terraeque fretoque,' Val. Fl. 5. 338 sq. 'mox stare pauentes | uiderat *intenta* pueros *nece.*' But as **miserae** is needed to go with *mortis, intenta* is transferred to *uicinia, uicinia mortis* (*u. leti* in v. 224) differing from *mors uicina* 'death in proximity' more in form than substance ; cf. *Pan. Messall.* (Tib. 3. 7.) 167 sq. 'quas similis utrimque tenens *uicinia* caeli | temperat.' This use of the abstract in Latin enables a writer to pack his expression close, e.g. Prop. 3. 2. 17 'pyramidum sumptus ad sidera ducti,' 'the costly pyramids reared to the stars,' ib. 19 'Mausolei diues fortuna sepulcri.' For a variant in the theme cf. IV 737 sqq. 'leti fortuna propinqui | tradiderat fatis iuuenem bellumque trahebat | auctorem ciuile suum.'

ordinis aeterni. The *lex aeterna* of VII 1 note, the *fatorum ordo* of Verg. *A.* 5. 707, the *causarum series* of VI 612 (q.u.), that is, the indissoluble chain of cause and effect of Stoic philosophy.

570. traherent, with tense representing *trahebat,* cf. *peteret* 154 n.

571. derant. 'No one of his company was without forebodings of the crime.' These were 'not absent' (hence the indicative), but they were fruitless, or Pompey 'would have escaped,' which would have furnished a more regular apodosis. Linguistically it is possible to understand the mood as 'they *would not have* been absent' and to regard 572–4 as the reflexions which would have occurred to the 'comites' if they had not been blinded by destiny. In this case there would be formal consistency with 593 sq.

572 sqq. give the tenor of the presentiments.

pura fides is much like the *sincera fides* of Livy 39. 2. 1 'untainted honour.' Compare Ov. *Pont.* 4. 10. 82 'quis labor est *puram* non temerasse *fidem*?'

573. **sceptrorum auctori**, i.e. to whom he owed his throne; cf. 628 infr.

574. **uenturum,** *fuisse* would have been added in classical prose. Val. Max. 4. 7. 1 'se etiam hoc si modo Gracchus *annuisset facturum* respondit' is perhaps the earliest instance of a use which is frequent in the *Annals* of Tacitus.

Pharium...tyrannum again in IX 134.

575*. **classem**, i.e. the protection of his fleet.

576. **letum...timori**, i.e. prefers *risking* death to *showing* fear.

577. **ibat**, i.e. itura erat.

578. **inpatiens**, with inf. as '*inpatiens* uirtus haer*ere* Catonis' IX 371 and *patiens* 637.

egresso, dat. (534 n.), 'when he landed.'

579. **clades**, 'disaster.' It differs little from *caedes*, cf. 541*, III 680 'nulla tamen plures hoc edidit aequore *clades*,' VII 795 'campos sub *clade* latentes,' ib. 651 n.

580*. **nate**, 205 n.

581. **hac,** *mea*. Cf. 315 '*haec*...membra.' For **ceruice** see 12 n.

582*. **explorate**, cf. II 603 '(taurus) in aduersis *explorat* cornua truncis' 'makes trial of,' 'animum explorare' 'ascertain anyone's disposition' Livy 37. 7. 10 al. The word is properly used of scouting or spying work.

surda uetanti, for the dative cf. VI 443 'tot popul*is*, tot *surdas* gent*ibus* aures.'

585. **summota** (445, 689) with an invidious sense here, 'hustled away from' the disastrous field of Pharsalia. For the abl. cf. V 71 sq. 'Hesperio tantum quantum *summotus* Eoo | cardin*e* Parnasos.'

586. **non** goes with **poteras**. For the negative question cf. 431.

587. **alio**, i.e. not to Lesbos.

relinquere, the obj. *nos* is to be anticipated from the next line.

588. **parabas,** with a weak sense, little more than a verbal peri-phrasis ; cf. *parant* 613.

589. ' Or is it for the waves alone that my company is approved?'

590. **prima...puppe,** at its extreme end or edge; cf. '*primo...mucrone*' VII 561 n. Whether *puppis* means 'ship' or 'stern' is hardly determinable ; but Cornelia would naturally be near the gang-way or ladder by which Pompey had just left, and the place for these ladders was the stern ; see e.g. Eur. *Iph. T.* 1349 sqq.

591. For **attonito metu,** which is to be taken with both *nec* clauses, cf. Stat. *Ach.* 1. 613 ' *attonito* stat turba *metu*,' VII 779 'nec magis *attonitos* animi sensere *tumultus*,' all with 'transferred epithets.'

quoquam, anywhere *else* (than in the direction of Pompey), so in V 691 *quemquam =q. alium,* cf. n. on *omnia* 117.

592. **stetit,** i.e. cast anchor ; cf. III 519 'quae *stabat* in undis | classis,' ' in salo stare ' Livy ' to ride at anchor in the offing.' An echo in Val. Fl. 3. 256 ' *stetit anxia* uirtus.'

593. **ad ducis euentum** depends on **anxia** ' waiting in anxiety for what should befall its leader.' For *euentus* cf. Livy 33. 48. 2 ' ita Africa Hannibal excessit saepius patriae quam suum *euentum* miseratus.' This line gives the real reason for their anxiety : the rhetorical one is given in the next line. Cf. note on 571.

594. Cf. Sen. *Herc. F.* 414 sq. 'non ut inflexo genu | *regnantem adores* petimus.' There was no fear of Pompey's ' making obeisance ' to Ptolemy ; but the part he had to play was that of a humble suppli-ant. Cf. Ov. *Pont.* 4. 3. 41 sq. 'quid fuerat Magno maius? tamen ille *rogauit* | *summissa* fugiens *uoce* clientis opem.' Compare the language of his appeal for assistance, as reported by Caesar etc., *Introd.* p. xlviii n. 6.

595. **transire,** elliptical as in 354, to pass into the small boat.

596. **Romanus Pharia,** intentional juxtaposition.

597. **pro superum pudor,** the ordinary exclamation expanded by a gen., cf. Seneca *Dial.* 11. 17. 4 ' pro pudor imperii,' also 605 below.

598. As Septimius was a *tribunus militum,* this is perhaps not to be taken too literally.

deformia, 'dishonouring' (81 n.), cf. Claudian *in Rufin.* 2. 81 sq. 'nec pudet Ausonios currus et iura regentem | sumere *deformes* ritus uestemque Getarum.' The sense is reinforced by the neighbourhood of *posito...pilo.*

599. The asyndeton (for which cf. Hor. *A.P.* 121 ' impiger ira-cundus inexorabilis acer ') increases the emphasis.

nullaque ferarum, etc. ‘There was no beast at all, not even the most savage, than which he was less cruel’; cf. Ovid *Her.* 10. 1 ‘*mitius inueni quam te genus omne ferarum,*’ *Am.* 1. 10. 26 ‘turpe erit ingenium *mitius* esse *feris,*’ Eur. *Alcest.* 310 ἐχίδνης οὐδὲν ἠπιωτέρα. For the turn of the expression cf. Ov. *Pont.* 4. 10. 50 ‘*nullo tardior amne* Tyras.’

601. **parcere te populis** ‘it was a mercy of thine to the nations that’; cf. II 734 ‘parcitur Hesperiae.’

bello, abl., ‘had no part in the fighting.’

602. **noxia** ‘murderous.’

fugasses corresponds to an ind. *fugasti* as *uacaret* to an ind. *uacabat.*

603. **disponis gladios.** Contrast by juxtaposition, compare 118 n. It means ‘whereas the truth is that it was only part of your arrangement of the instruments of slaughter so that no part of the world should be free from “civil” crime.’ For the thought compare the imitation of Claudian *in Rufin.* 2. 24 sqq. ‘et ne qua maneret | inmunis regio, cladem diuisit in orbem | *disposuit*que *nefas*’ and for the expression Sen. *Dial.* 3. 21. 3 ‘per omnem orbem titulos disponere.’

605 sq. **dedecus...fabula** are nominatives in apposition to the sentence *Romanus...ensis*; cf. Tac. *A.* 3. 67 ‘maiestatis crimina subdebantur, *uinclum et necessitas* silendi,’ Pliny *Ep.* 1. 19. 1, Ovid *F.* 6. 277 sq. ‘arte Syracosia suspensus in aere clauso | stat globus, immensi *parua figura* poli.’ Such appositions rarely precede the main verb. But cf. IX 885 sq. ‘aduolat atque, ingens meritum maiusque salute, | contulit in letum uires,’ Ovid *M.* 3. 468 ‘uotum in amante nouum, uellem quod amamus abesset,’ ib. 5. 112 ‘sed qui, pacis opus, citharam cum uoce moueres,’ 10. 278 ‘et, amicum numinis omen, | flamma ter accensast.’ In prose we have ‘*monumentum* eius pugnae, ubi primum ex profunda emersus uoragine equus Curtium in uado statuit, *Curtium lacum appellarunt*’ Livy 1. 13. 5.

606. **Romanus regi,** an invidious antithesis Cic. *de Rep.* 2. 53 ‘(populus Romanus) pulso Tarquinio *nomen regis audire non poterat*’ heightened by the alliteration of the *r*’s and *p*’s; cf. 390 sqq. n.

607. **Pellaeusque puer,** the young Ptolemy (237 n.) who gave the formal order for the murder 537 n.

colla recidit. This is not true of the murder, but it is true of the mutilation 667 sqq. Seneca’s language *Dial.* 9. 16. 1 (*Introd.* p. lvii n. 4) is not less loose.

608. **tuo,** because the army and the general are one; cf. VII 652 n. ‘*suos*...enses’ IV 779 = ‘*suorum e.,*’ ‘Caesare toto’ VI 140 ‘all Caesar’s forces.’

qua, etc. For the turn of the expression cf. 782 below; also X 532 'potuit discrimine summo | Caesaris una dies *in famam et saecula mitti.*'

610. **Bruti,** sc. *factum.* The expression is brief and zeugmatic. If he had written *facinus* for *scelus*, he would have avoided the zeugma.

611. **ablatus** 'hurried off'; cf. Val. Fl. 6. 488 sqq. 'illa nihil contra; nec enim dea passa, *manum*que | implicat et rapidis mirantem passibus *aufert.* | ducitur infelix ad moenia summa, futuri | nescia uirgo mali.' Lucan has given a sinister twist to a very harmless incident, *Introd.* p. xiv. The thought is from Pompey's quotation, ib. p. lvi.

612. **iura sui,** '*ius* sui' as in II 463, '*ius*que *sui* pulso iam *perdidit* Vmbria Thermo,' is more usual. Another phrase is '*iuris sui* non esse' (660 infr.) ' not to be under (of) one's own control.'

613. **monstra,** 474 n.
parant, cf. 588 n.

614*. **inuoluit,** in his *paludamentum*, *Introd.* p. lviii n. 3. The verb usually has an abl. of the covering added, though the participle is used absolutely as in Cic. *Verr.* 2. 5. 157 'capitibus *inuolutis* ciuis Romanos ad necem producere instituit.' This covering of the head when confronted by inevitable death was customary and symbolical.

For the sequence **inuoluit...indignatus** (est) which the editors have tried to remove in various ways cf. IX 11 sqq. ' postquam se lumine uero | inpleuit stellasque uagas miratus et astra | fixa polis, uidit quanta' etc., Val. Fl. 7. 18 sqq. 'felices, mediis qui se dare fluctibus *ausi* | nec tantas *timuere* uias talemque *secuti* | huc qui deinde uirum.' It is carried over into indirect construction, 126 supr. n. Compare *ubi fatus* in 775, *quando...amissus* in 211.

615. **praebere** (1 613 '*praebebat* (uictima) *collum*') and *praestare* are both used in this connexion, v 770 sq. 'fulminibus me, saeue, iubes tantaeque ruinae | absentem *praestare caput*,' cf. Sen. *Dial.* 6. 20. 4 (quoted in *Introd.* p. lvii n. 4) '*caput* satelliti *praestitit.*'

616. **continuit...animam.** So Cic. *de Or.* 1. 261 'deinde cum spiritus eius esset angustior, tantum *continenda anima* in dicendo est adsecutus ut' e.q.s.

uoces 'cries'; Q. Curtius 6. 11. 16 (of Philetas under torture) ' non *uocem* modo sed etiam gemitus habuit in potestate.'

617. **uellet,** with weak force, hardly more than a mere auxiliary (cf. 847 n.) as in Catullus 64. 137 'tibi nulla fuit clementia praesto | inmite ut nostri *uellet miserescere* pectus.'

618. **funestus,** as in 418.

619. **consensit.** This appears to mean 'let no groan of his respond to the strokes,' *consentire* signifying the same as συμπάσχειν : Sen. *N.Q.* 3. 29. 7 'in morbum transeunt sana et ulceri uicina *consentiunt*,' ps.- Quintil. *Declam.* 8. 16 'inde pallor, inde macies quod *ad inferiorem* dolorem super posita *consentiunt*,' Pliny *N. H.* 2. 219 'alter (fons) oceani motibus *consentit*.' So the simple *sentire* is used for 'betraying feeling' 'giving signs of feeling' as Sen. *Dial.* 12. 18. 7 'tua potest efficere pietas ut perdidisse se matrem *doleat* tantum, non *et sentiat*.'

620*. **respexitque** 'nor regarded the outrage.' The negative is carried on to the second clause as in VII 548 sq. n. and often in Lucan. For *respicere* (of emotion) cf. Tibullus 1. 3. 13 sq. 'tamen est deterrita numquam | quin fleret nostras *respiceret*que uias' and my note.

621. **se probat,** makes good or establishes his true character; cf. Claudian *carm. min.* 22 (39) 'in breuibus numquam *sese probat* Aeolus undis' 'shows his strength.' Compare also the use of the verb for making a person out to be someone; Ter. *Eun.* 375 'forma et aetas ipsast, facile ut pro eunucho *probes*,' Cic. *Verr.* 5. 78 'suppositum in eius locum quem pro illo *probare* uelles.'

622. **saecula** 'generations.' At first sight this might appear to be simply an appeal to the verdict of posterity rhetorically imagined to witness the crime. But it is more likely that Lucan is thinking of the spirits of the unborn who are supposed to throng the air, a doctrine which, though not actually Stoic, has a Stoic tinge (cf. Cic. *Diuin.* 1. 64 'quod plenus (sit) aer immortalium animorum') and which may also be traced in the famous passage of Vergil *Aen.* 6. 706 sqq. The same idea appears in VII 389 sqq. (n.) where the carnage of Pharsalia is said to carry off the 'populos aeui uenientis in orbem' by taking away their birthday ('erepto natale'). (The *Elysium* of Vergil's misty topography, which led Dr Henry, *Aeneidea* (on 6. 898), to assert that the poet intended the description of the after world to be regarded as a dream of Aeneas, was placed by some in the lunar circle as is clear from Seruius's note on the obscure phrase '*aeris* in campis' 6. 887 'locutus autem est secundum eos qui putant Elysium lunarem esse circulum'; Macrobius *Comm. in Somn. Scipionis* 1. 11. 6.)

624. **fidem,** as in 311 n., the *Alexandrina perfidia* of Sen. *Dial.* 10. 13. 7 (quoted in *Introd.* p. lvii n. 4).

625. **prospera,** predicate; cf. Cic. *Off.* 3. 90 'in rebus *prosperis* et ad uoluntatem nostram *fluentibus*.'

626. **probaris** passive, or rather middle, so that *in morte probaris* represents *moriens te probas*; cf. 621. For the sense cf. Sen. *Dial.* 11.

6. 1 (perspicit) 'utrumne tu tantum rebus secundis uti dextere scias an et aduersas possis uiriliter ferre'; cf. ib. 1. 4. 3, 6. 5. 5, 12. 3. 2.

627.   This should be added to the exx. of *ignorare an* cited from the two Senecas *Contr.* 7. 8. 6, *Dial.* 10. 12. 7 and Martial 3. 45. 1 sq. in the *Thesaurus* s.u. *an.* (In IX 143 -*ne* has preceded.)

ne cede pudori, etc. 'Do not give way to shame or be distressed at the thought that you die by such unworthy hands; for you must consider your real slayer is Caesar.' Contrast IX 128 sq. 'non Caesaris armis | occubuit *digno*que *perit auctore ruinae.*' Cf. Ov. *M.* 2. 280 sq. 'liceat periturae uiribus ignis | igne perire tuo clademque *auctore* leuare,' Sen. *Dial.* 6. 14. 2 'ut non minus ipsa orbitate *auctor* eius digna res lacrimis esset.'

629.   **spargant.**   The usage of this verb makes it hard to settle whether it means 'fling out' or 'scatter.' See 100 n.   For the latter sense cf. IX 58 '*membra*que *dispersi* pelago *conponere Magni,*' X 22 sq. '*totum spargenda* per orbem | *membra* uiri.'

lacerentque.   This would precede the action in *spargant*; but the Roman writers did not, as too many of their modern interpreters, confuse the order of words and the order of events.   Cf. n. on 324 sq.

630.   '*sum...felix* (quis enim neget hoc?) felixque manebo' is the unhappy boast of Niobe, Ov. *M.* 6. 193.

nullique potestas, etc. because, as Schol. C says, 'quod factum est, fieri infectum non potest'; a common thought in ancient writers, the best known expression of which is Agathon's line quoted by Aristotle *Nic. Eth.* 6. 2. 6.

633.   **meus.**   The student must beware of supposing that this refers only to *Pompeius.*

634.   **claude** 'lock in,' prevent escaping; Stat. *Silu.* 3. 2. 52 sq. 'nequeo, quamuis mouet ominis horror, | *claudere* suspensos oculorum in margine *fletus,*' Martianus Capella 8. 804 'risus circumstantium eo maxime quod *claudebatur* excussus.' *reprime* or *comprime* would have been more usual, ps.-Quintil. *Declam.* 19. 5 '*comprimantur* exclamationes, ora *clauduntur.*'

dolor.   This apostrophe is a favourite one with Seneca, *Ag.* 683, *Med.* 922, 1027, *Thyest.* 948, *Troad.* 604, *Herc. Oct.* 298 sq., 311, 1450.

635.   **si mirantur, amant**, that is, their love will follow on their admiration—a general sentiment but with a particular application.

custodia...mentis 'control over his feelings,' as Sen. *Benef.* 5. 5. 2 'inconsultae adulescentiae diligentem custodiam'; compare id. *Clem.*

1. 1. 4 'sic *me custodio*, tamquam legibus...rationem redditurus sim.' For *mentis* = *animi* cf. 331 n.

636. **ius hoc**, i.e. 'such control,' 'power over.'

morientis, cf. 'morientia ora' VII 609; a 'transferred epithet' (2 n.), as with Lucan the soul does not die but escapes.

637. **patiens**, cf. *inpatiens*, 578.

638*. **perferre**, if right, must mean either (1) to endure *in her own person* (ipsa), or (2) to bear with fortitude *in the future*, both involving harsh ellipses and the second giving a poor sense. This outburst of Cornelia is in express and perhaps in designed contradiction with what is reported in Cicero. See n. on 662.

639. Cf. Ov. *M.* 4. 110 'nostra nocens animast; *ego te, miseranda, peremi*,' Sen. *Phaedr.* 1259 'ego te peremi.'

640. **letiferae**, i.e. that cost your life.

auia, out of your route. But Lesbos was on the direct route to Egypt from Amphipolis (*Introd.* p. xxxviii) and not much out of the way from Tempe.

642*. **ius...sceleris**, right (authority) to command the crime. *ius* here comes close to the sense of 'established power,' possession of force; so in IX 191 'nosse *modum iuris*' 'the proper limits of force' with which *iustum* in the next line is contrasted. It is the opposite of *inmoderatum ius*, Sen. *Dial.* 12. 16. 1 'non est quod utaris excusatione muliebris nominis cui paene concessum est inmoderatum in lacrimas (to command tears) non inmensum tamen.' For the sense cf. Sextus's words in IX 133 sqq. 'uidi ego magnanimi lacerantes pectora patris, | nec credens Pharium tantum potuisse tyrannum | litore Niliaco socerum (*Pompey's* father-in-law) iam stare putaui.'

643. **inmisse** would be *inmissus* in prose. The metrical convenience of the vocative of the second declension led the Roman poets to use it with some latitude. Cf. 338 supra, 767 n., Val. Fl. 2. 485 sq. 'tuque | *ille* ades auguriis *promisse* et sorte deorum,' Sen. *Ag.* 540 sqq. 'quisquis es, nondum malis | satiat*e* tantis caelitum, tandem tuum | numen serena,' *Herc. Oet.* 1 sqq. 'sator deorum—secur*e* regna,' and Ov. *Ars Am.* 1. 145, 2. 254 'iunge tuas ambitiose manus,' quoted in *Pref.* to Bréal's *Semantics*, Eng. ed. p. xxxii. Val. Fl. 1. 391-4 'tu quoque Phrixeos remo, Poeantie, Colchos | bis Lemnon uisur*e* petis, nunc cuspide patris | inclit*us*, Herculeas olim motur*e* sagittas,' Stat. *Theb.* 7. 777 'uetito nud*us* iacitur*e* sepulcro.' There are patterns for the licence in Greek, Eur. *Rhesus* 388 χαῖρ' ἐσθλὸς ἐσθλοῦ παῖ, τύραννε τῆσδε γῆς. For *inmitti* 'to be *sent to kill*' cf. Justin 26. 3. 6 'insidiae

Demetrio comparantur cui. cum in lectum socrus concessisset, *percus-sores inmittuntur*' (cf. id. 9. 7. 1), Sen. *Dial.* 3. 2. 3 'plebem *inmisso milite* contrucidatam.'   Similarly of a massacre, '*inmissa* morte' 11 202.

644*.   **prospicies** = *uis prospicere* to regard (gratify) Caesar's vindictiveness or your own advantage.   For the verb cf. Sen. *Benef.* 6. 35. 2 'qui optat diuitias alicui in hoc ut illarum partem ferat, quamuis pro illo uideatur optare, *sibi prospicit*.'

645*.   **uiscera** 'vital parts.'   We should say 'the very heart of Magnus.'   For the turn of the expression cf. VII 579 'scit, cruor imperii qui sit, quae *uiscera rerum*,' 556 supra.

properas 'art hasty.'

ingeris, 433 n.

646.   **qua uotumst,** elliptical, 'ea qua, ut ingeras, uotum est uicto (uictus optat).'   Cf. 522 n.

647.   **et,** like *que* (note on 1, supra), does not couple but explains, 'that is,' 'and so'; cf. e.g. Lucr. 2. 614 sq. 'numen qui uiolarint | matris et ingrati genitoribus inuenti sint' and Munro's note on *atque* at 3. 993; also 798, 858 below.

ante, 'first.'

caput, with suppression again, 'my severed head,' cf. *ceruix* in X 424 quoted on 12 where compare note.   This pregnant use of nouns is especially frequent after the prepositions *ante* and *post,* cf. Sen. *Dial.* 3. 17. 6 '*post* duorum triumue *sanguinem* occidere desinit,' ib. 5. 30. 5 'aliosque post *Pompeium* demum (after P.'s death) Pompeianos.'

648.   **libera,** sc. sum.

matrum, i.e. matronarum.

649.   **per castra,** Cornelia, or Lucan, has forgotten 41 sqq. and V 723 sqq.   See *Introd.* p. xxix.

650.   **quod...timuere,** in apposition to the general sense.   The allusion is to Ptolemy.

recepi 'harboured,' 'welcomed,' an excited or rhetorical expression without warrant in the facts.

651.   **hoc,** probably abl. neut. 'by so doing.'   But possibly acc., to which the following words are in apposition, Sen. *Med.* 337 sq. 'obici *crimen hoc* solum potest, | Argo reuersa.'

652.   **perfide, parcebas,** ' Traitor to spare me!'   For the alliteration in these lines cf. 368 n.

extrema, 610.

653.   **fui** ' was *I*?'   The *ego* of emphasis is not inserted; cf. 137 n.

nec, 'but not'; for the sense cf. Sen. *Dial.* 6. 20. 4 'quid enim erat turpius quam Pompeium *uiuere beneficio regis* ?'

654. **praecipitem...saltum,** so of suicide by drowning, III 749 sq. 'tamen alta sub aequora tendit | *praecipiti saltu.*'

655. **tortos.** The standing epithet of ropes, as with *funis* in Vergil and Horace.

que, cf. *et* in 647 supr. note.

aptare. The inf. (384 n.) is a necessary change of construction from the verbal noun *saltum*.

656. **Magno dignus,** i.e. as punishing his ' murderess ' (639).

exigat, of thrusting in and out again; X 32 sq. 'gladiumque per omnis | *exegit* gentes,' II 149, IV 565.

657. That is, he can thus pay something (do a service) to Pompey which he may debit to the cause of Caesar, i.e. take credit for with Caesar.

658. **inputet,** a common use of the word in Silver Latin. A good example is Mart. 12. 48. 13 '*inputet* ipse deus nectar mihi, fiet acetum,' i.e. 'let nectar be put down to my account and it will be no better than vinegar.' Lucan has the verb again in a difficult passage VII 325 where see note (in Addendum); compare Mayor on Juv. 5. 14.

After these words Cornelia rushes to the side of the vessel but is caught by the sailors.

660. **iuris...sui,** 'solutus et *sui iuris*' Sen. *Dial.* 10. 5. 3 ; cf. n. on 612.

prohibent. The subject is naturally indefinite and so the verb is equivalent to a passive ; cf. *seruor* 661.

accersere mortem, of suicide ('accersita mors' Plin. *Ep.* 1. 12. 2) 'to fetch death,' Tib. 1. 10. 33 'quis furor est atram bellis *arcessere* mortem?,' and frequent in Silver Latin. So with 'fata' IV 484 '*accersas* dum *fata* manu' (VII 252 is different).

661. **seruor uictori,** cf. IX 213 sq. 'non deprecor *hosti* | *seruari*,' 700 inf. ' *socero seruare*.' In all three passages the dative refers to Caesar.

662. **rapitur,** in the hurried flight of the ship. The narrative is resumed in IX 51. According to Lucan, ib. 117, the fugitives went straight to Cyprus '*prima* ratem *Cypros* spumantibus accipit undis.' But this pointed assertion may only mean that he thrusts aside another and better attested version, cf. *Introd.* p. xxxvi n. 4, for one of his 'synthetic concentrations,' ib. p. x. As we know from Cicero *Tusc.* 3. 66 they fled to Tyre, ' constabat eos qui concidentem uolneribus Cn. Pompeium uidissent, cum in illo ipso acerbissimo miserrimoque spec-

taculo sibi timerent quod se classe hostium circumfusos uiderent, nihil aliud tum egisse nisi ut remiges hortarentur et ut salutem adipiscerentur fuga, postea quam Tyrum uenissent, tum adflictari lamentarique coepisse.' This is confirmed by Dio 42. 49. 2 who says that Caesar removed all the offerings in the temple of the Tyrian Hercules on the ground that the Tyrians had harboured the wife and son of Pompey when they fled. A better reason would have been the sending of the ships mentioned by Appian, *Introd.* p. xxxi n. 3. From Tyre they went to Cyprus, *Introd.* p. lx n. 1.

663. **sonent**, as the swords struck the spine and breastbone; Oudendorp compares Sil. It. 1. 402 'crepitantia dissipat ossa' (of the skull), ib. 4. 632 'pulsati ligno *sonuere* in uolnere dentes.' Perhaps rather as in 'Sen.' *Herc. Oet.* 1169 'nec ullus per meum *stridet* latus | transmissus *ensis'*—what a French writer Jacques Emile Blanche *Cahiers d'un Artiste* calls ' le bruit immonde de l'acier dans la chair.'

664 sqq. For the juxtaposition of the clauses with asyndeton, **permansisse...mutasse**, cf. 118 n.

665*. **iratam**. The effect of anger is to disfigure the face; and there is no trace of anger in Pompey's dying reflexions though there is a certain defiance of the powers above.

faciem opposed to *terga* and *pectora* (663).

ultima mortis, the last death-throes.

666. **habitu**, the set appearance of the face, whereas **uoltu** is its expression. Later on, Lucan says, there was a change IX 1033 sq. 'iam languida morte | effigies *habitum* noti mutauerat oris.'

667. **lacerum**, iam laceratum, cf. IX 57 '*laceros* exurere crines' i.e. lacerare et exurere, Sen. *Oet.* 630 'Bacchis *lacer* | Pentheus,' explained by **nam**, etc.; see also note on 526. For the turn cf. Cic. *Phil.* II 55 'cuius tamen *scelus in scelere* cognoscite,' Sen. *Oed.* 62 'quin *luctu in ipso luctus* exoritur nouus,' Cic. *ad Att.* 9. 10. 2 '*aliud in alio peccare.*'

668. **actu**, cf. II 77 sq. 'primo qui caed*is in actu* | deriguit.'

669. **uelamine**, see 614.

670. **occupat** (cf. II 159 'desilit in flammas et, dum licet, *occupat* ignes'), explained by **spirantia** 'still breathing,' as we might say ' pounces upon.'

671. **obliquo** really refers to the position of the *neck*, 'athwart the bench'; cf. I 220 'primus in *obliquum* sonipes opponitur amnem.'

languentia, i.e. relaxed; cf. III 737 sq. 'ille caput labens et iam *languentia colla* | uiso patre leuat.'

672. **nodosa**, cf. Pliny's description of the neck and its vertebrae,

N.H. 11. 177 'e multis uertebratisque orbiculatim ossibus, flexilis ad circumspectum, articulorum nodis fungitur.'

frangit. On this and the whole incident compare the account which Cicero gives of the treatment of Trebonius by Dolabella *Phil.* XI 7 'post ceruicibus fractis caput abscidit idque adfixum gestari iussit in pilo: reliquum corpus tractum atque laniatum abiecit in mare.'

673. **artis erat,** it had passed into an art; for the gen. cf. Prop. 4. 10. 24 'uincere cum Veios posse *laboris* erat' ('lab*or* erat' Livy), and *moris est* by *mos* est.

Beheading by the sword, instead of the axe (*securi ferire*), had recently been introduced, whether for humanity or despatch, may be doubted; possibly through the encouragement of Caligula, Suet. *Cal.* 32. 3 'miles *decollandi artifex* quibuscumque e custodia capita amputabat.' Caracalla rebuked the executioner of Papinianus for using an axe (Dio Cassius 77. 4. 2, Script. Hist. Aug. *Carac.* 4. 1); cf. Florus 2. 5. 3 'legatos quippe nostros...ne *gladio* quidem sed ut uictimas securi percussit'; Seneca *Dial.* 6. 26. 2 mentions 'nobilissimos uiros clarissimosque ad ictum militaris gladi composita ceruice curuatos.'

rotare, 'whirl off,' as a stone from a sling, IX 826 'quae funda *rotat.*' Claudian copies the use *Bell. Gild.* 465 'tertia iam solito ceruix mucrone *rotetur*,' *Eutrop.* 2. 524 sq.

674. **trunco,** an abl. which may be taken both with **abscisa,** Ov. *M.* 12. 361 sq. 'Crantoris alti | *abscidit iugulo* pectusque umerumque sinistrum' and with **recessit,** 'Ov.' *Her.* 16. 153 'ante *recessisset* caput hoc *ceruice* cruentor.'

675. **hoc** with the gender of *caput* (677) of which *ceruix* is, in this connexion, a synonym, 12 n.

gestare, a harsh inf. which may be the (direct) object of **uindicat** 'claims the carrying of this'; or an inf. of the Complement 'claims this for carrying.'

satelles seems to mean *Achillas* (cf. *Introd.* p. lix n. 3) as in X 418 sq. 'ciuilia bella *satelles* | mouit et *in partem Romani* uenit *Achillas.*'

676. **operae...secundae,** 'in (playing) a second part,' gen. of Description 223 n., coupled by **atque** to **degener.** Cf. Sen. *Benef.* 5. 5. 1 '*non recipiens* ictum lapis *solidus*que et *inuictae* aduersus dura *naturae*,' ib. *Dial.* 6. 21. 3.

For the adj. cf. Hor. *S.* 1. 9. 46 'magnum adiutorem, posset qui ferre *secundas*' (sc. *partes*), play 'second fiddle.'

678. For **ut non** cf. Cic. *Balb.* 46 'potest igitur, iudices, L. Cornelius condemnari *ut non* C. Mari factum condemnetur.'

summi...pudoris, gen. as in 223 (n.).

679. **nosset**, that he might gratify his curiosity. For the sense 'get to know' cf. Ov. *M.* 3. 346 sqq. (of Narcissus) 'de quo consultus an esset | tempora maturae uisurus longa senectae | fatidicus uates 'si se non *nouerit*' inquit.'

uerenda 'awe-inspiring,' 'reverend.' So Plutarch *Pomp.* 2 speaks of the *reverend* and *royal* character transpicuous in his countenance (τὸ γεραρὸν καὶ τὸ βασιλικὸν τοῦ ἤθους).

680. **hirta coma**, of a shaggy fell of hair, such as writers and works of art give to Pompey ; see Sil. It. 13. 861 sq. 'ille, *hirta* cui subrigitur *coma fronte* decorum | et gratum terris Magnus caput' (perhaps a reminiscence of this passage).

generosa fronte 'on his noble brow.' Plutarch *Pomp.* 2 in his description of Pompey's features mentions that some people professed to discover in the expression of his eyes a likeness more apparent than real to portraits of Alexander. As *frons* is the seat of *pudor* with the Romans (cf. IX 207 n.) this may allude to Pompey's habit of blushing in public, Sen. *Ep.* 11. 14, a peculiarity which his enemies did not fail to deride.

681*. **caesaries.** For the conjunction of this with *coma* which offended Bentley cf. Sil. It. 8. 559 'Martia frons facilesque *comae* nec pone retroque | *caesaries* breuior,' also 1 189 sq. 'turrigero canos effundens uertice *crines* | *caesarie* lacera.'

conprensa, *Introd.* p. lix and n. 3.

manu implies violence as *main* in Fr. ; cf. VII 309 'sors quaesita *manu*' (of a violent death).

ueruto. This does not prevent Sextus from saying he saw it on a *pilum*, IX 138 sq. 'ora ducis quae transfixo sublimia *pilo* | *uidimus*.' For the practice cf. II 160 '*colla ducum pilo* trepidam *gestata* per urbem' and 436 supra n.

682. **dum uiuunt uoltus** 'while there is life in the countenance still.'

pulsant in murmura, i.e. stirred to inarticulate sounds ; cf. Sen. *Thyestes* 727 sqq. 'colla percussa amputat, | ceruice caesa truncus in pronum ruit, | querulum cucurrit murmure incerto caput.' Statius *Theb.* 5. 236 sqq. 'ut uero Alcimeden *etiamnum in murmure* truncos | ferre patris *uultus*...conspexi.'

683. **singultus animae.** For the 'sobbing,' or 'gasping breath,' cf. Val. Fl. 2. 211 sq. '*singultantia* gestans | ora manu' (of a head cut off), and Stat. *Theb.* 3. 90 'extremis animae *singultibus*.'

nuda, 'uncovered,' unclosed, heightens the horror. No friendly hand has closed them.

684. **suffixum.** For the force of the preposition cf. Sen. *Dial.* 9. 10. 6 'nec subleuatus is sed *suffixus*.'

numquam, to be taken with **pax fuit.** Pompey's power, not aversion to war, is here in question. Pompey is called by Florus (l.c. on 257) 'belli pacisque moderator.'

iubente, the proper term for a decree of the sovereign populus, is used instead of *suadente* to bring out Pompey's extraordinary power. The order *numquam quo bella iubente* would be clearer but for two adjacent words to exchange places is an extremely common form of hyperbaton, see *Classical Review* 30. 243 sq. (no. *vi*) and compare 384, 367.

685. **mouebat** is used zeugmatically with the accusatives, cf. Sen. *Dial.* 10. 6. 1 'Liuius Drusus cum *leges* nouas et mala Gracchana *mouisset*'; Pompey 'swayed' or 'controlled' legislation, elections and popular meetings. The laws specially referred to are the Gabinian and Manilian rogations.

686. **hac facie,** an ultra-condensed use of the abl. of the Circumstances, 'with this face to look on'; cf. IV 380 sq. '*gurgite puro* | uita redit,' through drinking from the clear stream; it recalls Propertian ablatives, as in 4. 11. 96 '*prole mea* Paullum sic iuuet esse senem.' The sense of the line is that with Pompey at hand the Fortune, or Genius, of Rome was satisfied with itself, 'had no reason for self-upbraiding.'

687. **infando,** 397 n.

688. **uolt sceleris superesse fidem** 'he will have evidence remain.' Cf. IX 139 sq. 'haec fama est oculis uictoris iniqui | seruari *sceleris*que fidem quaesisse tyrannum,' 1037 'utque *fidem* uidit *sceleris*' (both in the same connexion as here).

nefanda, the 'black' art of embalming. Lucan has modelled his description on Herodotus 2. 86 πρῶτα μὲν σκολιῷ σιδήρῳ διὰ τῶν μυξωτήρων ἐξάγουσι τὸν ἐγκέφαλον (*rapto cerebro*), τὰ μὲν αὐτοῦ οὕτω ἐξάγοντες τὰ δὲ ἐγχέοντες φάρμακα (*infuso ueneno*).

689. **capiti,** *dat.* of subject interested, not abl. of place whence as in 585.

tabes verbal; 'decay,' 'putrefaction' as in VII 809, cf. 778 inf.

rapto, hastily removed; cf. 240 n. The removal of the brain was necessary for the preservation of the features. This was omitted in the embalming of Mithridates' body which his son Pharnaces sent to

Pompey and consequently the king's face could only be recognised by its scars, Plut. *Pomp.* 42.

690. adsiccata 'dried up'; a Silver Latin compound, first found in Seneca.

ab alto. As *altus* means both 'high' and 'deep,' the only clue to the sense is that *effluxit* is more natural if the phrase is taken 'from above, i.e. down through the nostrils.

692. Lageae. Lagus was the father, actual or putative, of the first Ptolemy, the founder of the Egyptian line. The expressions *arua Lagi* (443), *rura Lagi* (802) for Egypt are not exact.

peritura. Ptolemy was drowned in the Nile when fleeing after his defeat by Caesar, *Bell. Alexandrinum* 31. 6, Dio Cassius 42. 43, Florus 4. 2. 60.

693. sceptris, an extension of the abl. of place whence (as in *rogo* 750). For the whole construction cf. v 168 sq. 'hominem toto sibi cedere iussit | pectore,' Val. Max. 7. 3. 3 'instrumento suo cupide nostris cessit.' Valerius Flaccus (8. 368) has even 'uirgine cessit ' ' he relinquished the maid.'

694. Macedon, a rhetorician's name for Alexander (Longinus 4. 2) or for Philip, Hor. *C.* 3. 16. 14. Lucan uses the Greek form, while Horace, writing ' *uir* M.,' naturally prefers the customary Latin *Macedo.*

antro, an *underground* chamber or tomb (*conditorium*) Suet. *Aug.* 18, Petronius 111 'descendit...in conditorium.' Visited by Caesar when in Alexandria, x 19 'effossum tumulis cupide descendit in antrum,' and by Augustus (Suet. l.c. with Shuckburgh's note) Caesar's constant imitator. The body which had been removed from Babylon had originally been enclosed in a close-fitting gold case filled with precious spices (Diodorus, 18. 26. 3, where the transportation of the body is described; cf. Lucan IX 10 sq. 'non illuc auro positi nec ture sepulti,' though *ture sepulti* might in itself mean 'burned,' see note on 729), the lid of the coffin being also of gold. But this and the conqueror's arms had long ago been removed by a Syrian usurper (ὁ Κόκκης καὶ Παρείσακτος ἐπικληθεὶς Πτολεμαῖος, Strabo 17. 1. 8 p. 795). It was replaced by a glass lid, Strabo l.c. The Ptolemies were buried in the same Mausoleum.

695. regum, the native kings of Egypt as is shown by IX 155 sq. 'non mihi pyramidum tumulis euolsus Amasis | atque alii reges Nilo torrente natabunt.'

extructo monte. The Pyramids (the 'audacia saxa | Pyramidum' of Stat. *Silu.* 5. 3. 49 sq.) are meant. The sense of *mons* is strange (cf. n. on 463); but there is some evidence for its use for huge masses of stone, Stat. *Theb.* 1. 145 sq. '*montibus* aut alte Grais effulta nitebant | atria,' Amnianus M. 17. 4. 15, where it is applied to the obelisk which Constantius brought from Heliopolis. It would then mean 'in their pile of stone.' Compare Sen. *Thyest.* 641 sqq. 'In arce summa Pelopiae pars est domus | conversa ad Austros cuius extremum latus *aequale monti* crescit.'

696*. **seriemque pudendam** 'in shameful line'; cf. 'Caesareaeque domus *series*' IV 823. For *que* see 1 supra note. After the third Ptolemy the stock rapidly degenerated, Strabo 17. 1. 11 p. 796, Ptolemy Auletes being one of the worst in the line.

697. **indigna,** improper for them, 'undeserved'; cf. Verg. *A.* 12. 811 'digna *indigna* pati.'

mausolea. This passage seems to be the earliest example of *Mausoleum* (originally the name of the magnificent tomb, *Mausolei—sepulcri* Prop. 3. 2. 19, built for Mausolus, prince of Caria, by his widow Artemisia), being used as a common noun. To a Roman it would suggest the 'Mausoleum' of Augustus (Suet. *Aug.* 100, τὸ Μαυσώλειον καλούμενον Strabo 5. p. 236) Florus 4. 11. 11 'in mausoleum se (sepulcra regum sic uocant) recepit.'

698. **feriunt,** a bold use of what I have called the 'inverted passive' (74 n.), like *claudant* just above, as it is the body that strikes the shore, not vice versa. The passive (708) is not so harsh.

truncus, adj.

701. **hac...fide.** There is a grim irony in this. *fides* includes the ideas of 'consistency' and 'punctiliousness.' Fortune kept herself and her favourite to their bond. The repetition of the pronoun emphasizes her persistence.

702. **pertulit** 'carried to the end.' For the compound verb cf. v 605 'nec *perfert* pontum Boreas ad saxa,' Verg. *A.* 12. 907 (lapis) 'nec spatium euasit totum neque *pertulit* ictum' (similarly '*permittat*' in Ov. *M.* 12. 282), ib. 10. 786 (hasta) '*uiris* haud *pertulit*,' ib. 13. 478 '*pertulit* intrepidos ad fata nouissima uoltus,' Sen. *Benef.* 2. 33. 3 'quo uoluit munus suum *pertulit*.' For the general sense cf. v 239 'fatorum tantos per prospera cursus.'

703. **morte petit** apparently means 'aimed at him with a deadly shaft,' 'struck him to death.' For *mors*, 'cause of death,' cf. vi 486 'et *mortibus* instruit artes,' IX 935 sq. 'extractamque potens gelido de corpore *mortem* | expuit.' His fall from the summit of power (8 n.) follows the stroke. The tense will be perfect (*it* as *perit* 422) as Mr

Anderson, *Classical Quarterly* 8. 107, says. For the ablative he compares Verg. *G*. 2. 505 '*petit excidiis* urbem miserosque penates.'

exegit ' required of him,' as the payment due for his past prosperity.

704. **quibus**, with **inmunes**, which means 'free from service' or 'impost,' 'unaffected by.' So IX 541 'nullumque in uertice semper | sidus habes *inmune mari*'; add II 257, VI 764, IX 896.

706. **nullo**, etc. The ablatives qualify the adjectives 'happy (in happiness) with no god to trouble him, wretched with none to spare him.'

707. **inpulit** 'overthrew'; cf. I 149 sq. '*inpellens* quidquid sibi summa petenti | obstaret.'

708. **dilata…manu** 'with stroke deferred.' For *manu* cf. 271 n.

pulsatur harenis, cf. *feriunt* (698) and IX 52 sq.

709. **hausto**, drawn through his wounds; cf. III 660 sq. 'deiectum in pelagus perfosso pectore corpus | *uolneribus transmisit aquas.*'

710. **ludibrium pelagi**, perhaps an echo of VII 380 '*ludibrium* soceri' which Pompey had prayed not to become. Cf. Claudian *VI Cons. Hon.* 139 (of a ship) '*ludibrium pelagi* uento iactatur et unda.' The force is verbal in IX 14 'risitque sui *ludibria* trunci.'

711. **una notast Magno**, 'the one mark (of identity) left to Magnus is the loss of the severed head.' For *nota* cf. 772 where *busti* follows; here however the dat. may be due to a feeling that the body is not quite an inanimate object, or the gen. has been avoided as *capitis* was to follow. *Magno* is probably significant here, cf. Sen. *Dial.* 10. 13. 7 (fin.) quoted in *Introd.* p. lvii n. 4.

712 sqq. **tangat…parauit…iaceat.** In ordinary prose these would have been 'tang*eret*,' 'parau*era*t,' 'iac*eret*'; but the imagination treats the past history as present, 'can touch,' 'has made ready,' 'may lie.' For the perfect doing duty as a preterite (pluperfect) to a historic present cf., e.g., Juv. *S*. 10. 152 sq. '*opposuit* (i.e. op*posuerat*) Natura Alpemque niuemque : | di*ducit* scopulos' and 209 sq. above 'iubet…legit.'

714. **meliore.** Fortune is supposed to have designed that Caesar should show no *pietas* towards the dead, cf. 316.

715. **Cordus.** *Introd.* p. lxii. For **latebris**, hiding place, cf. 780.

716*. **quaestor.** In the Roman view a quaestor of Pompey's would be a very fit person to perform the last rites to him; cf. Cic. *in Q. Caecilium diuin.* 61 'sic enim a maioribus accepimus, praetorem quaestori *parentis loco* esse oportere.'

ab goes with **fuerat comes.** Lucan does not say how he got on shore in Egypt, *Introd.* p. lxii n. 1.

Idalio, from Idalium (now *Dalin*) in Cyprus, seat of a famous worship of Aphrodite.

Cinyreae, from *Cinyras*, an old king of Cyprus, said in legend to have founded the cult of the Paphian Aphrodite, Tacitus quoted on 458.

717. **infaustus** is properly used of things, 'unlucky,' 'disastrous'; of persons it may mean either 'suffering disaster' as in VI 788 sq. 'deplorat Libycis perituram Scipio terris | *infaustam* subolem,' or 'causing it' as in Tac. *A.* 12. 10 'bellis *infaustus*.' How Cordus's company should bring disaster on Pompey is not clear. Hence the first sense is more likely, cf. *Introd.* pp. lxi sq. with the footnotes.

718. **ferre gradum**, a periphrasis which emphasizes the stepping; cf. Ovid *F.* 6. 338 'et *fert* suspensos corde micante *gradus*.' *gressus, passus ferre* are also found.

uictum pietate t. conpulit. Contrast the turn of the expression in 785.

720*. **duceret.** The grammatical subject is *timor*, the real subject is Cordus, cf. 490 n. The shift is the easier, as Lucan uses verbs of 'doing' for allowing to be done (74 n.).

722. **cano...aequore**, i.e. amid the surf, with **conspicitur.**

723. **artis** 'tightened,' explained by the following words: *arte conplexa* in a metaphorical sense occurs at IX 111.

724. **eripiente**, present of action attempted, Cic. *de Sen.* 11 'Q. Fabius Maximus C. Flaminio...restitit agrum Picentem et Gallicum... *diuidenti*,' Verg. *A.* 2. 111 sq. 'saepe illos aspera ponti | interclusit hiemps et terruit Auster *euntis*,' Sen. *Dial.* 12. 7. 1 'non hominum ingenia ad similitudinem caeli sui horrentia *transferentibus* (transferre uolentibus) domos suas obstiterunt.' Cf. 797 n.

mari, the ebbing water, opposed to **fluctus** (725).

726. **sedit** from *sido*, the subject being of course *cadauer*; the word is specially used of vessels coming to shore or grounding 'high and dry' as we say. Livy 26. 45. 7 'piscatores Tarraconenses nunc leuibus cumbis, nunc, ubi eae *siderent*, uadis peruagatos stagnum,' Tac. *A.* 2. 6 (naues) 'planae carinis ut sine noxa *siderent*' (cf. ib. 1. 70), Livy 2. 5. 4 'ita in uadis haesitantis frumenti aceruos *sedisse* inlitos limo,' Val. Fl. 2. 445 sq. 'Thessala Dardaniis tunc primum puppis harenis | adpulit et fatis Sigeo *litore sedit*.'

728. **obscura**, explained by 721.

729. **sepulcra**, 'a pyre,' as in 750, III 11 and VI 526 'accenso... *sepulcro*'; compare Ter. *Andr.* 128 sq. 'ad *sepulcrum* uenimus; | *in ignem* inpositast; fletur.' So *sepelire* of cremating, as in Manilius quoted on 755 and elsewhere.

730. Pompeius, Fortuna, tuus. Cf. Florus 3. 5. 21 'perque omnia et decus et nomen et titulos gloriae *Pompeio suo Fortuna* quaerebat.'

pinguis 'rich'; cf. Sen. *Herc. Fur.* 913 sqq. 'quicquid Indorum seges | Arabesque odoris quicquid arboribus legunt | conferte in **aras.** *pinguis* exundet *uapor.*'

732. Romana...pia, in accordance with Latin usage which permits two adjectives with one substantive, if one defines and the other describes.

suum...parentem. An allusion to the title *pater patriae*, or sometimes (e.g. Cic. *Phil.* 11 31, and *Off.* 3. 83 of Caesar, Plin. *N.H.* 7. 117 of Cicero) *parens patriae* or *parens Vrbis* (as in Cic. *Att.* 9. 10. 3, of Cicero, Livy 1. 16. 3, 6, of Romulus and so Prop. 4. 10. 17 'Vrbis uirtutumque (·isque) *parens*') conferred in compliment on several personages but officially on Augustus in B.C. 2 (see Mayor's n. on Juvenal 8. 244). The best comment on it is the fine passage of Ennius *Annales* 115 sqq. 'o Romule, Romule die, | qualem te patriae custodem di genuerunt! | o *pater*, o genitor, o sanguen dis oriundum, | tu produxisti nos intra luminis oras.' Whether it was ever applied to Pompey we do not know. Lucan's words do not imply this, cf. IX 601 'ecce parens uerus patriae' of Cato.

colla, rather *ceruices* or *umeri*. So it is said was Coriolanus carried on his bier to the funeral pyre, Dionys. Halic. 8. 59. 3 πρὸ τῆς κλίνης αὐτοῦ φέρεσθαι κελεύσαντες λάφυρά τε καὶ σκῦλα καὶ στεφάνους ὧν εἶλε πόλεων ἤραντο τὴν κλίνην οἱ λαμπρότατοι τῶν νέων ἐν τοῖς κατὰ πολέμους ἔργοις, and Aemilius Paullus (by a Macedonian embassy) Val. Max. 2. 10. 3, while a similar honour was asked for Augustus, Tac. *A.* 1. 8 'conclamant patres corpus ad rogum *umeris* senatorum ferendum.' Cf. also Verg. *A.* 6. 222 (quoted below), Val. Max. 7. 1. 1.

733. praeferat, bear in front of the bier, cf. Dionysius quoted above.

triumphos, the marks or insignia of his triumphs, a pregnant use with which we may compare VII 234 'totos consume triumphos' 'the whole stuff of triumphs,' and note there. Tacitus l.c. supra mentions amongst the special marks of respect voted to the memory of Augustus 'ut legum latarum tituli, uictarum ab eo gentium uocabula ante ferrentur.'

734. cantu, of the flute-players in particular, cf. Ovid *F.* 6. 660 'cantabat maestis *tibia funeribus*,' *Tr.* 5. 148 '*tibia* funeribus conuenit ista meis,'

fora. The *laudatio funebris* was delivered in the Forum; the plural is generic.

735*. proiectis...armis. This is obscure. It can hardly mean 'after throwing away their arms'; an incident like that which occurred at the funeral of Iulius Caesar, Suet. *Iul.* 84 'deinde tibicines et scaenici artifices uestem quam ex triumphorum instrumento ad praesentem usum induerant detractam sibi atque discissam *iniecere flammae*, et ueteranorum militum legionarii *arma sua quibus exculti funus celebrabant.*' Perhaps it means 'with weapons advanced, pushed forward,' a sense which *proicere* sometimes has, as in Nepos *Chabrias* 1. 2 'obnixo genu scuto, *proiecta hasta* impetum excipere hostium docuit.' Compare IV 755 'oraque *proiecta* squalent arentia *lingua*,' that is *exserta*.

ambiat. Compare Quint. *Decl.* 329 p. 296 (Ritter) 'universus populus lustret atque *ambiat* rogum.' The ceremony is the *decursio* or *decursus* which formed part of the funeral rites of Iulius Caesar (see above) and Drusus (Dio Cass. 56. 42. 2, *Consol. Liu.* 461). Hannibal is said to have paid this honour to Gracchus, Livy 25. 17. 5. See also Verg. *A.* 11. 92, Stat. *Theb.* 6. 213 sqq., Val. Fl. 3. 347 sqq. The custom is as old as Homer, *Il.* 23. 13, *Od.* 24. 68 sqq.

736. plebei funeris, cf. Prop. 2. 13. 23 sq. 'desit odoriferis ordo mihi lancibus: adsint | *plebei* paruae *funeris* exequiae.'

arcam, the coffin, in such cases of wood, on which the corpses of the poor were carried on the bier (*sandapila, capulus*) to be burned, cf. Hor. *S.* 1. 8. 8 sq. 'huc prius angustis eiecta cadauera cellis | conseruus *uili* portanda locabat in *arca*'; cf. Val. Max. 2. 6. 7 'duae etiam ante portas eorum (the people of Marseilles) *arcae* iacent, altera qua liberorum, altera qua seruorum corpora ad sepulturae locum deuehuntur sine lamentatione, sine planctu.'

737. quae...effundat, to 'pitch out,' as we might say; VII 856 sq. (of tombs split by the wild fig) 'qui radice uetusta | *effudere* suas uictis compagibus urnas.'

siccos.. ignes, unfed by unguents.

738. sordidus ustor 'a grimy cremator'; the *ustor* was the person set to watch and 'stoke' the lighted pyre.

739. sit satis, i.e. let Cornelia's enforced absence be penalty enough.

non of course covers **imperat.**

740. subici, with the scansion of *subicit*, VII 574, and *obici* inf. 796. For the action cf. Verg. *A.* 6. 222 sqq. 'pars ingenti subiere feretro, | triste ministerium, et *subiectam* more parentum | auersi tenuere *facem*.'

741*. **munere busti**, with the same meaning of *munus* as in Sil. It. 2. 264 sq. 'at Nomadum furiosa cohors miserabile *humandi* | deproperat *munus*, tumulique adiungit honorem.'

742. **nec adhuc**, etc. So near and yet so far. The two clauses are contrasted in the Greek manner.

743. **iuuenis**, though apparently the same person whom Plutarch calls an old man ; see *Introd.* p. lxi.

744. **uile suis**, explained by 746 sq. 'nec ulli | cara tuo'; cf. IV 276 'en, *sibi uilis* adest inuisa luce iuuentus.'

748. **iam conpositum**. This does not mean so much 'put together' as 'arranged,' with the body laid out on it. The word is also used of laying the body on the *lectus* or *feretrum* which was placed on the pyre, Ovid *M.* 9. 905, Pers. *S.* 3. 104 and often, e.g. in Ovid *F.* 3. 547, of placing the remains in the urn, or tomb, after the burning.

uiolat, etc. Cf. an epitaph in verse 'ne qua *manus bustum uiolet*' *Carm. Epigr.* 1432. 9.

749. Compare the similar line III 39 'aut nihil est sensus animis a morte relictum, | aut mors ipsa nihil.' Val. Max. 4. 6. 3 'si quis modo extinctis sensus inest.' In VII 470 sq. sensation after death is doubted but existence is presumed.

750. **sepulcri**, 729 n.

751. **sparsis**, here apparently not 'proiectis' (100 n.) but 'scattered' IX 1092 sq. 'cineresque in litore fusos | colligite atque unam *sparsis* date manibus urnam.'

752. **plenusq. sinus**. *plenus* is practically a perfect part. =*impletus*; cf. IX 60 'ossibus et *tepida uestes implere fauilla.*' So Verg. *G.* 4. 180 sq. 'at fessae multa referunt se nocte minores | crura thymo *plenae*'; and it may be thus taken in all the places where it is construed with the acc. of Part Concerned, Val. Fl. 1. 298, 2. 506, Sil. It. 10. 14 and also in other connexions as Hor. *Ep.* 1. 20. 8, 2. 1. 100. The description is outrageously loose. Schol. W saw this and endeavoured to reconcile it with probabilities but without success : '*sinus* i. gremio; non habebat quomodo aliter prunas ferret atque ideo additum est *peruolat* ne uestis exureretur (!)' cf. *Introd.* p. lxii n. 2.

753*. **peruolat**. The preposition implies that he got 'through' the distance in time to rescue the body.

relatus. Compare IX 53 'ne forte repulsus | litoribus Phariis remearet in aequora truncus.'

754. **pendebat**, hung swaying.

755. Compare the account in Manilius 4. 50 sqq. 'quis te Niliaco

periturum litore, Magne, | ...crederet, ut corpus sepeliret naufragus ignis | eiectaeque rogum facerent *fragmenta carinae?*' and Val. Max. 1. 8. 9 (*Introd.* p. lxi n. 2).

756. exigua scrobe, of the shallowness of the trench, cf. 867 ; it would be of the same length as the corpse. Compare Tac. *A.* 15. 67 'scrobem...humilem et angustam' and Suet. *Nero* 49 init., where *scrobes* are made for still living persons. On the gender (reprehended by some of the grammarians) see Neue-Wagener, *Formenlehre* 1. 1004 sq.

757*. premit 'loads,' 'rests on.'

strue, sc. *lignorum.* Cf. '*struem* rogi' Tac. *Germ.* 27, 'funebrem *struem*' Sen. *Oed. Fr.* (*Phoen.*) 112.

758*. subditus, as was usual, cf. *subici* 740 n.

accipit. The fire is half-personified. This helps us to understand Prop. 2. 28. 56 'has omnes *ignis* auarus *habet*' (of the dead, where *habet = accepit*).

760. Hesperii...nominis. Cf. 1 359 sq. ' *Romani* maxime rector *nominis*' (addressed to Caesar) and note on 798, VII 392 sq.

maiestas, 'eminence.' This word, an abstract noun from the comparative stem *maies-*, and so 'greaterness,' properly expresses dignity, precedence or higher station. Hence in VII 378 'imperii *salua* si *maiestate* liceret' is 'without lowering my position as general.' The Romans were aware of the origin of the word, as may be seen from a highly instructive passage of Ovid *Fasti* 5. 25–52 'hinc sata *Maiestas,* quae mundum temperat omnem, | quaque die partust edita, *magna* fuit | ...protinus intrauit mentes suspectus honorum ; | fit pretium dignis, nec sibi quisque placet.' It is worth noting that Latin has formed abstracts from all the degrees of *magnus, magnitudo, maiestas, maximitas.*

Lucan is right in claiming that Pompey had held a unique position in Rome, which entitled him to his name of ' Great' to which there is a clear allusion in *maxime* and *maiestas*; cf. 94 n. and Ovid quoted on 594.

761*. iactatu pelagi, cf. *iactatus* of the sea Plin. *N.H.* 14. 118.

funere nullo, cf. 714 and the well-known epigram quoted in *Introd.* p. lxviii. See also Cr. App.

762. iste, clearly for *hic*; cf. 122 n. *est* is to be supplied with *tristior*, cf. 51 n.

manes, etc. the attention and so the formidable vengeance of thy departed spirit.

763. officiis. If abl., then *ab* would be inserted in prose ; but cf.

1 65 'Bacchumque *auertere* Nysa,' Verg. *A*. 1. 38 'Italia Teucrorum *auertere* regem.' It might however be *dat*., the action being fused with the agent. There is the same doubt about Sen. *Phoen.* 540 sq. 'nefandas moen*ibus* patriis faces | *auerte*' and Verg. *G*. 2. 172.

764. **hoc fas esse iubet,** sanctifies this inadequate rite.

766*. **audeat quidquam** is euphemistic.

quantum potes is most simply taken as 'all that you can receive, or I can give.' Its more usual sense is 'with all your might.' So Sen. *Dial*. 11. 8. 2, 12. 19. 3.

767*. **succense.** The voc. is in accordance with poetical usage, cf. 643 note and Stat. *Silu*. 2. 6. 82 'quo domini clamat*e* sono,' quoted on 319.

recursus, like *reditus*, is not unfrequently used in the plural of a single returning, especially where this is not definitely presented to the mind. Cf. Ovid *Her*. 6. 59 'sed dent modo fata *recursus*,' ib. *M*. 11. 576 '*reditus*que sibi promittit inanes.'

770*. **nostro...sinu** (cf. 843) abl. of the place whence; so with the simple verb Ov. *Ars* 1. 287 'lacrimis quas arbore *fudit* odora,' *M*. 9. 161 'patera *fundebat*.'

transfundet in the same connexion Stat. *Theb*. 5. 633 sq. 'hocne ferens onus inlaetabile matris | *transfundam* gremio?'

772. **nota,** 711 n.

sit...inueniat (744) correspond, with a harsh asyndeton; cf. 519 n. There is no contrast here as in most of the juxtapositions of clauses cited on 118 n.

773. **plenos,** 'complete,' 'full,' for which the presence of all the body was necessary; so with *piacula* II 305. This is what Caesar is said by Lucan IX 1090 sqq., quoted in *Introd.* p. lxvi, to have ordered to secure a *iustum sepulcrum* for his dead rival.

775. **fatus,** sc. *est*. Compare note on 614 supra, III 372 'sic postquam *fatus*.'

776. **admoto,** as in 758.

777. **carpitur,** of piecemeal destruction by fire, as in IX 741 sq. of the fiery venom in the bite of a *dipsas* 'ecce subit uirus tacitum, *carpit*que medullas | *ignis* edax *calida*que *incendit* uiscera *tabe*.'

lentum a 'slow' fire, as we say.

destillat 'drips.' For the metaphor cf. Sen. *Ep*. 24. 5 '(Mucius) spectator *destillantis* in hostili foculo dexterae stetit nec ante remouit nudis ossibus fluentem manum quam ignis illi ab hoste subductus est' and again of the same, ib. 66. 51; so too the simple verb IX 783 '*parua* *loquor, corpus* sanie *stillasse* perustum; | hoc et flamma potest.' So in Sen. *Thyest.* 1065 sq. ' illa *lentis ignibus* | *stillare* iussi' (cf. ib. 765 sq.), *Med.* 845, *Benef.* 4. 21. 6.

778. **tabe,** 689 n.

fouens bustum. 'stillante pinguedine flamma iuuatur; et rogum dicere debuit. nam "bustum" est ubi ustum est cadauer' Schol. C. The remark is just; but *bustum* is used elsewhere not merely of the lighted (748) but also of the unlighted *rogus* Stat. *Silu.* 5. 1. 218.

percusserat, cf. VI 744 ' subito *feriere* die.'

779. **Aurorae praemissa dies.** Inasmuch as *aurorae dies* is an unmeaning expression, *aurorae* must be the dat. and we have to choose between the translations 'sent on by the Dawn' and 'before the Dawn.' In either case *dies* would have to be understood as the *diluculum,* or *prima lux* (*albente caelo,* Caesar). The white light preceding the dawn is associated with the morning star; which is elsewhere called the harbinger of the Dawn Ovid *M.* 15. 189 sqq. ' cumque *albo* Lucifer exit | clarus equo, rursusque alius cum praeuia lucis | tradendum Phoebo Pallantias inficit orbem'; cf. Val. Fl. 2. 72 sq., Cic. *ap. Non.* 65. 7 ' Cicero Alcyonibus : hunc genuit claris delapsus ab astris | *praeuius Aurorae,* solis noctisque satelles,' cf. ' Ov.' *Her.* 18. 111 sq. ' iamque fugatura Tithoni coniuge noctem | *praeuius Aurorae* Lucifer ortus erat,' cf. Ov. *M.* 4. 629. In this sense Lucifer is said to drive the day before him, Verg. *Eclog.* 8. 17 ' nascere *prae*que diem ueniens *age,* Lucifer, almum.'

ordine rupto funeris means ' breaking off the due course' or ' progress of the funeral rites'; cf. Ovid *Tr.* 1. 7. 14 ' infelix domini quod fuga *rupit* opus.'

780. **attonitus,** of fear, 591 supr.

781. **crimine,** cf. *scelus* 842.

782. **quo** (crimine); for the abl. and the general expression, cf. 608 note.

loquax ' chattering,' i.e. many-voiced; cf. Catullus 78. 9 sq. ' nam te omnia saecla | noscent et qui sis Fama loquetur anus.' ' fama loquax' of rumour Ovid *Pont.* 2. 9. 3.

accepit. On the significance of the tense see *Introd.* lxii n. 1.

783. **condita,** without an abl. IX 151 ' inhumatos condere manes.'

784. **sepulcrum,** as used here, hardly differs from *sepultura*; cf. 394.

785. **cogit pietas,** cf. 718 n.

786. The order is 'semiusta ossa rapit neruisque nondum satis resoluta et inustis medullis plena aequorea aqua restinguit.'

semiusta. The incompleteness of the burning was regarded as an injury to the dead. Hence the taunt in Cicero's words to Antony on the 'half-burning' of Caesar's corpse *Phil.* II. 91 'illas faces incendisti et eas quibus *semustulatus* ille est,' etc.

787. **neruis**, the construction as in II 145 '*resoluta*que legum | fren*is* ira ruit.'

inustis 'unburned,' elsewhere the part. of *inuro*. There are a considerable number of these ambiguous forms in Latin, *inauditus*, *inauratus*, *incinctus* ('ungirded' [Tib.] 3. 2. 18), *incoctus*, *indictus*, *infectus*, *inminutus*, *inmixtus*, *inmorsus* ('unbitten' in Prop. 3. 8. 21), *innutritus*, *inquisitus*, *intectus*, *inuocatus*.

788. **aequorea...aqua**. Contrast Stat. *Silu.* 5. 5. 17 'ardentes restinxit *lacte* fauillas,' the usual practice.

789. **clausit**, an intentional change of tense to give the climax, *claudit* being just as convenient metrically.

791. Compare VII 860 sqq. 'nullus ab Emathio religasset litore funem | nauita, nec terram quisquam mouisset arator, | Romani bustum populi.'

793. **placet hoc**, with bitter emphasis: 'are you satisfied with a decision like this?' Cf. Martial 4. 40. 10 '*hoc*, Fortuna, *placet*?' VII 58 '*hoc placet*, o superi, cum uobis uertere cuncta | propositum, nostris erroribus addere crimen?' For the thought cf. Val. Max. 1. 8. 9 'ipsi Fortunae erubescendum rogum' quoted in *Introd.* p. lxii n. 1.

794–5. **condi...caruisse**. See note on 381.

796. **obicis** is here the equivalent of *opponis* (cf. Juvenal *S.* 10. 151 '*opposuit* Natura Alpemque niuemque'); 'wouldst block his path with a grave mound.' Compare *obicere portas, fores*, of closing a gate, or door, against a person. Verg. *Aen.* 9. 45, Livy 5. 13. 13, 28. 6. 5.

Magno, the repeated use of this surname in this context is designed.

797. **includis**, cf. *inclusum* 864. Both presents express actions only purposed or attempted; cf. n. on 724.

situs est picks up and corrects 'hic situs est' of *v.* 793.

For the interpretation of the next words we must consider the passage of Vergil which Lucan is imitating, *Aen.* 7. 225 sqq. (The battles of Greece and Troy) 'audiit, et siquem tellus extrema **refuso** | submouet Oceano et siquem extenta plagarum | quattuor in medio dirimit plaga Solis iniqui': another imitation of which is Seneca *Phaedra* 938 sqq. 'te licet terra ultimo | summota mundo dirimat Oceani plagis, | orbem-que nostris pedibus obuersum colas.' Dr Henry (*Aeneidea*, ad loc.) has made out that *refuso* in both places does not refer to the sea's being

'poured (thrown) back' by the land, as e.g. in 11 617 sq. 'si non
uiolentos insula Coros | exciperet saxis lassasque *refunderet* undas,' but
that it means 'wide-spreading' (from the notion of 'overflowing'), the
sense being that seen in other compounds of *fusus*, '*effusi* late maris'
(Hor.), '*diffuso*...in aequore' (11 654), *circumfusus* Rutil. 1 55 sq.
'nam solis radiis aequalia munera tendis, | qua *circumfusus* fluctuat
Oceanus.' He supposes further that Lucan (like Vergil) viewed the
terra extrema as surrounded by the Ocean, so Schol. W '*pendet* insulas
dicit in Oceano sitas' which can hardly be reconciled with the sense of
pendet or Lucan's use of it elsewhere, cf. IX 335 'has uada destituunt,
atque interruptâ profundo | terra ferit puppes, dubioque obnoxia fato |
pars sedet una ratis, pars altera *pendet* in undis,' and 754 supr. ('trun-
cum qui, fluctu paene relatus, | litore *pendebat*') suggests rather that it
means 'overhangs.' **in** need cause no difficulty; cf. '*in* aequore' 862
below and note.

qua. *quacumque* would be clearer, as in 'Sen.' *Herc. Oet.* 3 sq.
'protuli pacem tibi | *quacumque* Nereus porrigi terras uetat,' as Lucan
is precluded from thinking of a particular country, e.g. Spain.

798 sq. **R. nomen...imperium** 'the Roman race's entire dominions.' The **et** does not couple but unites the two conceptions,
which thus make a spatial whole to which **tumuli modus** may be
applied.

For *nomen* cf. Cic. *de Diu.* 1. 20 'hic siluestris erat *Romani
nominis* altrix' (of the She-wolf) and 760 n. For the thought 'Sen.'
Herc. Oet. 1831 sq. 'quae tibi sepulcra, gnate, quis tumulus sat est ? | *hic
totus orbis*, fama erit titulus tibi,' is a close parallel : but its source is
Greek; cf. Thucydides in the famous phrase attributed to Pericles 2. 43. 3
ἀνδρῶν γὰρ ἐπιφανῶν πᾶσα γῆ **τάφος**. A bolder use is found in *Anth.
Pal.* 7. 137 (of Hector) Ἰλιὰς αὐτὸς Ὅμηρος ἐμοὶ **τάφος** Ἑλλὰς Ἀχαιοὶ ·
φεύγοντες· τούτοις πᾶσιν **ἐχωννύμεθα**.

799. **obrue,** addressed to the *temeraria dextra* of 795, contains a
point that may easily be missed. Lucan would say 'Why bury Pompey?
Better bury a stone which reflects so severely on Providence.' For
obruere in this absolute sense see Tac. *A.* 1. 29 and Festus s.u. *statua*
p. 290, 19 Mueller quoted in *Cl. Quarterly* 1. p. 222; also Suet. *Cal.* 59
'cadauer eius clam in hortos Lamianos asportatum et tumultuario rogo
semiambustum leui caespite *obrutum* est, postea per sorores ab exilio
reuersas erutum et crematum sepultumque,' Cic. *N.D.* 2. 129 'testudines
autem et crocodilos dicunt, cum in terra partum ediderint, *obruere*
oua, deinde discedere.'

saxa, a generic plural.

800. **crimine...deum**, cf. 55 supr.

801. **uacant**, 'are open' or 'free' to Bromius, i.e. at his entire disposal. Compare X 442 'nec tota *uacabat* | regia compresso; minima collegerat arma | parte domus': also VII 205 sq. 'o summos hominum, quorum Fortuna per orbem | signa dedit, quorum fat*is* caelum omne *uacauit*' 'found space for'; see note there.

Bromio. This name of Bacchus occurs also at V 73.

Nyseia. On *Nysa* see I 65 'Bacchumque auertere *Nysa*' and note on *Nysaeus* 227 supr.

802*. **Lagi**, n. on *Lageae* 692.

803*. **tenere potest**, a variant for the future or the present subj. in apodosis, 'His might be all the land of Lagus'; cf. e.g. Cic. *de Fin.* 1. 54 'ne ipsarum quidem uirtutum laus *reperire potest* exitum... nisi derigatur ad uoluptatem,' Ov. *M.* 10. 621 sq. 'tibi nubere nulla | *nolet* et *optari potes* a sapiente puella,' cf. 379 supra n.

caespite. This is a most unsuitable word for the actual burying-place of Pompey; but Lucan's account is curiously like that of the burial of Caligula upon which that of Suetonius *Cal.* 59, quoted above on 799, is founded.

nomen, the name of the dead. The word would seem to have had this association, to judge from Prop. 3. 16. 30 'non iuuat in media *nomen habere* uia,' of being buried on a highroad.

804. **haeserit**, 'were fixed.'

erremus, 'be at fault,' 'be at a loss to know'; cf. Plautus *Mil.* 786 '*erro* quam insistas uiam.'

populi, cf. VII 400 'toto *populi* qui *nascimur* orbe.'

805. **nullas...harenas**, in artificial contrast to *nullo caespite*.

806. **dignaris**, continuing the address to the *temeraria dextra*. The intervening apostrophe to Magnus is merely grammatical. We have had the verb in 113.

807. **monimenta maxuma rerum**, i.e. *maxumarum rerum* with an epithet 'transferred' for obvious reasons. *monimenta* here of noteworthy memorable deeds as in IV 497 sq. 'quaecumque per aeuum | exhibuit *monimenta* fides.'

808. **trucis Lepidi** like *truces Marii* VI 794.

M. Aemilius Lepidus, consul, largely through the support of Pompey, in 78 and proconsul of Transalpine Gaul in 77 took up arms to overthrow the constitution of Sulla but was defeated in the battle of the Mulvian Bridge by Q. Lutatius Catulus, his colleague, Florus 3. 23. 6

adds 'and by Pompey.' But this appears to be an error. Pompey was at the time engaged in Cisalpine Gaul reducing Lepidus's lieutenant, M. Iunius Brutus, who had occupied Mutina. Pompey admitted Brutus to a surrender but afterwards (Plut. *Pomp.* 16) sent an agent of his, named Geminius, to put him to death. The allusion however in **Alpina bella** seems to be to some opposition encountered by Pompey in the neighbourhood of the Alps when on his route from Italy to conduct the campaign against Sertorius which is referred to in exaggerated language in his letter to the Senate given by Sallust in his *Histories*, § 4 'diebus XL. exercitum paraui hostisque in ceruicibus iam Italiae agentis et *Alpibus* in Hispaniam submoui.' Mommsen *Hist. of Rome* 4. p. 28 assigns to this time the reduction of the Volcae Areocomici and Heluii mentioned in connexion with Pompey by Caesar *B.C.* 1. 35.

809. **reuocato** 'recalled' (more fully '*ex prouincia* reuocato' cf. Suet. *Claud.* 1) is inaccurate. Metellus was not recalled, but Pompey was associated with him in the command with 'proconsular imperium' (Val. Max. 8. 15. 8). The mistake may be a confused reminiscence of another Pompeius, Q. Pompeius Rufus cons. 141, who succeeded Q. Caecilius Metellus Macedonicus, cons. 146 and 143, in the government of Spain, Val. Max. 9. 3. 7.

consule should in strictness be *pro consule* (which however a poet could hardly use). A similar laxity occurs in Livy 31. 49. 4 (of Scipio Africanus in Africa), also id. 26. 33. 4, 7 (the correct title is given in § 12) and Florus 2. 6. 43.

810. **currus,** the car of the triumph proper (Val. Max. 2. 8. 7 'aut *ouans* aut *curru* triumphauit,' VII 18 n.), plural because Pompey triumphed twice as a simple *eques* in 81 and 71.

811. **pauidos maris** 'frightened of the sea,' as applied to pirates, is an effective exaggeration. For the gen. cf. Seneca *Herc. F.* 297 'luci*s*que *pauidos* ante te populos age,' II 578 'omne fretum *metuens* pelag*i pirata* reliquit.'

812. **quidquid...regnorum.** For the partitive gen. cf. VII 363 sq. '*quidquid* signiferi comprensum limite caeli | sub Noton et Borean homin*um* sumus,' n.

in Euro...Boreaque. The employment of the names of the winds for the quarters or the regions from which they blow is not uncommon in verse with prepositions like *ab* ('*ab* extremo...*Aquilone*' II 51, 'extremo...*ab Euro*' Claudian *Stil.* 2. 417, even '*immenso...ab* Euro' Val. Fl. 1. 538) or *sub* (VII 36 above, '*sub* Austro' 442 supra) or *in* with *accus.* ('*in* Austrum' 461 supra). But *in* with the *abl.* carries the licence further. The prose expression is seen in Cic. *Rep.* 6. 22 'quis in reliquis orientis aut obeuntis solis ultimis aut Aquilonis Austriue *partibus* tuum nomen audiet?' The transition of the sense of 'wind' into that of 'quarter' is well illustrated by IX 417-20. It is complete in e.g. Stat. *Silu.* 5. 1. 81 sq.

813. **iacet,** 102 n.

814. **ter,** a 'record' number which had deeply impressed the Roman imagination; see 553 sup., IX 178, 599, Prop. 3. 11. 35 '*tres* ubi Pompeio detraxit harena *triumphos* | una,' Vell. 2. 53. 4 'post *tres* consulatus *totidem*que *triumphos*' etc.

815. **donasse** 'gave away,' 'waived,' did not claim; cf. III 243 sq. 'iniecisse manum fatis uitaque repletos, | quod superest *donasse* deis.' On Lucan's other uses of this verb see note on VII 784. For the idea see Ovid *M.* 15. 757 'et multos meruisse, aliquos egisse triumphos' (applied to Caesar). Valerius Maximus also extols Pompey's moderation 8. 15. 8 'de Mithridate et Tigrane de multis praeterea regibus plurimisque ciuitatibus et gentibus et praedonibus *unum* duxit *triumphum*.'

816*. **surgit,** is erected, not necessarily to any height; it is used of corn VII 851, 865. Compare IX 180 sq. 'toto litore busta | *surgunt* Thessalicis reddentia manibus ignem.'

817* sq. **illis,** those referred to in the previous context.

ordine tanto fastorum, so long a roll of records in the Fasti.

818 sq. **solitum,** cf. the ναοῖς βρίθοντι of the inscription placed over Pompey's tomb, *Introd.* p. lxiv.

super alta deorum culmina. Inscriptions on temples were usually placed over the architrave, a fact of which we cannot suppose Lucan ignorant; and so with the ordinary use of the words the phrase is false and extravagant. If it is not to be viewed as merely loose writing, its credit may be saved by supposing that *super* here does not mean 'above' but 'high up on,' a use which is not attested for *super* but is similar to an occasional use of *pro*, e.g. in *pro rostris* which does not mean 'in front of the rostra' *but* 'on the rostra in front,' 'on the forepart of the rostra'; so *pro rupe* Val. Fl. 4. 110 'on' or 'from the front part of the cliff,' and other phrases.

It would be another way out of the difficulty if we could suppose that *culmina* (properly the plural of *columen* syncopated, and so only admissible into dactylic verse) could mean *columnas*, the supports on which the architrave rested. There are traces of overlapping in the usage of the two words. Cicero *de Diuin.* 1. 18 (fax) 'quae *magnum* ad *columen* flammato ardore uolabat' seems to refer to the same 'pillars of fire' called by Lucan VII 155 '*immenso*que igne *columnas.*' In Horace *C.* 2. 17. 3 sq. 'mearum | grande decus *columen*que rerum' seems to have the idea of 'support.' Cf. Donatus on Terence *Phorm.* 287 *columen familiae* and the passages quoted by him.

For the sense cf. Val. Max. 6. 9. 5 (of Q. Catulus) 'quae quidem ei impedimento non fuerunt quominus patriae princeps existeret *no-men*que eius *in Capitolino fastigio* fulgeret.' The most celebrated of Pompey's temples was the *delubrum Mineruae,* which was built from the proceeds of his victories, with its vainglorious inscription, that he had subdued the earth *a Maeotis ad Rubrum Mare,* Pliny *N.H.* 7. 97. Another was that of *Venus Victrix* (whose name was the Pompeian watchword at Pharsalia) dedicated in Pompey's second consulship, id. 8. 20.

820. **ima...harena,** cf. Ovid *Pont.* 3. 3. 102 'utque latens *ima* uipera serpit *humo,*' Sen. *Troad.* 1114 '*imam* pondus ad *terram* datum' (of falling from a height), cf. id. *Med.* 691. We should say 'close to the ground.' IX 470 sq. '*ima*que *tellus* | stat, quia summa fugit' is different.

821. **depressum tumulo** 'sunk low on the grave.' The abl. is a rather strained one of place; II 669 'nulla *uado* tenuit sua pondera moles.'

rectus, without bending. Compare Martial 8. 53. 8 'si tua non *rectus* tecta subire potes' and the humorous phrase of 11. 18. 10 sq. 'in quo nec cucumis iacere *rectus* | nec serpens habitare tota possit.'

822. **monstratum,** pointed out by the guides to the tourists; cf. 870 and elsewhere, e.g. Verg. *A.* 8. 337, 343, 345, Sen. *Dial.* 6. 25. 2 'ignotarum urbium *monstrator*' and *monstrator* a guide, Lucan IX 979.

transeat 'pass by'; for *trans* 'past' see 184 n.

823. **noxia,** etc. An apostrophe perhaps suggested by Prop. 3. 11. 33 quoted on 539 supra.

ciuili...fato, cf. 544 and note on 604.

824. **equidem** with a negative, as in the other place where Lucan has it, VI 777.

Cumanae c. uatis. Cf. Claud. *Eutrop.* 1. 11 'pandite pontifices *Cumanae carmina uatis.*' On this Sibylline oracle Schol. C has: 'quoniam cum Publius Lentulus sortitus Aegyptum prouinciam proficisci uellet, Tiberis effusus in tantum inundauit ut transgressum prohiberet, unde inspectis Sibyllinis inuentum est piaculum ne in

Aegyptum exercitus transisset.' According to Dio C. 39. 15 the intrigues of Ptolemy Auletes to get restored to his throne (*Introd.* p. xliii) were frustrated by means of a consultation of the Sibylline books when the statue of Iuppiter on the Alban Mount was struck by lightning and the production of an oracle which declared that 'if the king of Egypt came to ask for help, friendship should not be refused him, but that he should not be aided with numbers; else toil and peril would ensue.' This agrees with the reference to it in Cic. *Fam.* 1. 7. 4.

825. **Pelusia,** because Lucan has the end of Pompey in view. The prohibition of course referred to Egypt in general.

ora. Both the word and its number are poetical; the prose expression is *ostium.* In Livy 1. 33. 9 'in *ore* Tiberis Ostia urbs condita' *os* is used for stylistic reasons. At X 213 sq. 'Nili | *ora* latent' means the *sources,* or the source, of the Nile.

826. **ripas** has a slightly extended sense, being not so much the bank itself as the stream's edge, as **tumentis** shows; cf. III 28 'Lethaeae...obliuia *ripae*,' Val. Fl. 6. 149 'maestaque *suspectae* mater stupet aggere *ripae*' (of a frozen stream), Sil. 10. 89 'stagnantis... *ripas.*'

The peculiarity of not swelling in winter ('leges aliarum nescit aquarum | nec tumet hibernus') is discussed by Lucan in X 219 sqq. (put in the mouth of Acoreus).

828. **uertat aquas,** change its course; cf. Tibullus 1. 2. 44 (of a witch) 'fluminis haec rapidi carmine *uertit* iter.' The words cannot be pressed; cf. *retentus.*

orbe, *part* of the world; so in 289, 603 supra.

829. **egeant,** and so be parched all the year round.

830. **Aethiopum,** such as Aethiopia has; cf. IX 599 sq. 'ter Capitolia *curru* | scandere *Pompei*,' 'like Pompey's.'

putres...harenas, the crumbling desert soil; so '*putri...harenae*' IX 699. Prop. 4. 3. 39 'quae tellus sit lenta gelu, quae *putris* ab aestu.' For **soluaris in** cf. 106 supra.

831. **in templa,** in sharp contrast to *in puluere* 834.

832. The 'demigod dogs' is a gibe at the *latrator Anubis* Verg. *A.* 8. 698, the Egyptian god of the dead, who was figured with the head of a jackal which the Romans mistook for a dog.

sistra, σεῖστρα, the Egyptian rattles, which would appear to have been used to give the signal for the wailing for Osiris (833) = Apis 479 n.

iubentia luctus, cf. 1 297 sq. 'tumultum | conposuit uoltu dextraque *silentia iussit.*' Cf. T. Campbell's *Hohenlinden* 'But Linden saw another sight, | When *the drum* beat at dead of night, | *Commanding* fires of death to light | The darkness of her scenery.'

833. **testaris.** For the construction cf. Ovid *M.* 14. 306 'nec uerba locuti | ulla priora sumus quam *nos testantia gratos*' and 540.

Osirim. Osiris and Isis were associated as the two chief divinities of the Egyptians (Herodotus 2. 42). According to the legend Osiris was cut to pieces by Typhon, the jealous husband of Isis. Isis, with the aid of Anubis, found the remains on the banks of the Nile and solemnly mourned and buried the dead. This was commemorated in her worship; cf. the account in the Christian writer Minucius Felix 22 'Isis perditum filium (i.e. *Osiris*) cum Cynocephalo (*Anubis*) suo et caluis sacerdotibus luget, plangit, inquirit, et Isiaci miseri caedunt pectora et dolorem infelicissimae matris imitantur, mox inuento paruulo gaudet Isis, exultant sacerdotes, Cynocephalus inuentor gloriatur, nec desinunt annis omnibus uel perdere quod inueniunt uel inuenire quod perdunt. nonne ridiculum est lugere quod colas uel colere quod lugeas? haec tamen Aegyptia numina quondam, nunc et sacra Romana sunt' (from Mayor's n. on Iuv. 8. 29 which see for other references). The criticism in the last words exactly agrees with Lucan's here and with that of Xenophanes (quoted by Plutarch *De Iside et Osiride* c. 70 p. 379 B) εὖ μὲν οὖν ὁ Ξενοφάνης ὁ Κολοφώνιος ἠξίωσε τοὺς Αἰγυπτίους εἰ θεοὺς νομίζουσι, μὴ θρηνεῖν, εἰ δὲ θρηνοῦσι, θεοὺς μὴ νομίζειν. Cf. Seneca's gibe at Caligula *Dial.* 11. 17. 5 'incertus utrum *lugeri* uellet an *coli* sororem.'

On the connexion of the three associated divinities see an instructive passage of Ovid *Am.* 2. 13. 7—14.

834. **nostros...manes,** a spirit of ours, viz. Pompey's remains.

835. **tyranno,** Iulius Caesar, as in X 343 '*Romani* poena *tyranni*' and more than once in Cicero; **templa,** the 'aedes diui Iuli' built by Augustus (*Mon. Ancyran.* c. 19) and dedicated in 29 B.C., adjoining the Sacra Via, opposite the temple of Castor.

836*. **o Roma** 'Oh, Rome,' not 'O Rome' which is translators' English for '*Roma*' though Latin and English agree in not using the interjection (as Greek does) for a sign of the vocative. *o* always conveys some emotion and is not an address but an appeal. The student may easily see this by considering the passages where it occurs in this book, 94, 222 n., 542 and 630 *o superi* 'ye gods,' 639, 658, 759, 843; see also Cr. App.

837. **exul a. i. umbra.** On this see *Introd.* pp. lxviii sqq.

saecula. The plural is poetical (cf. *templa* 835) and the phrase extravagant for the three years or so which were to elapse before the death of the *uictor*.

839.   **subruta**, of the sapping action of the sea; cf. Vitruuius 5. 12. 4 'harena fluctibus subruta.'

840*.   **sedent**, 'remain unmoved' or 'undisturbed'; cf. Ovid *M.* 1. 267 'fronte *sedent* nebulae,' and 15. 336 sqq. 'tempusque fuit quo nauit in undis, | nunc *sedet* Ortygie.'

busta timebit, *mouisse* is to be supplied from the next line; cf. 529, 791.

841.   **sacris** (478) **dignam** 'worthy of worship,' cf. IX 601 'parens uerus patriae, *dignissimus aris.*'

mouisse; for the tense see 381 n.

842.   **scelus**, of course ironical; cf. 781.

843*.   **sinu**, to carry the ashes in.   See note in Crit. App. on 770.

satis o...beatus.   The exclamatory statement does not require a verb; cf. IX 64 sq. 'o bene nudi | Crassorum cineres!,' Hor. *Epod.* 12. 25 'o, ego non felix quam tu fugis!' Cic. *Phil.* 13. 34 'o miser cum re, tum hoc ipso, quod non sentis quam miser sis.'   But the omission of the subject *ego* here is very harsh.

845.   **Ausoniam**, for the acc. cf. 170 n.

846.   **sulco sterili**, failure of crops; cf. IV 90 sq. 'non pabula mersi | ulla ferunt *sulci.*'   For the dat. after *finem poscere* cf. 427 n.

847.   **uolet**, almost an auxiliary (like the English *will*); cf. Ennius *Ann.* 82 sq. 'exspectant ueluti, consul cum mittere signum | *uolt*, omnes auidi spectant ad carceris oras,' 'is about to,' Juvenal 10. 282 'cum de Teutonico *uellet* descendere curru,' i.e. descensurus esset, cf. also 617 n.

feralibus, i.e. *funestis*, of the deadly scirocco; so '*feralia* dona' Ovid *M.* 9. 213 of the poisoned shirt that killed Hercules.

848.   **ignibus...nimiis**, of the sun's heat; cf. IX 375 'et spes imber erat *nimios* metuentibus *ignes.*'   In a similar catalogue of catastrophes VII 412 sqq. 'it refers to conflagrations; *nimius* is used in the same connexion in 164 supra, IX 383 *nimius Titan* and 432 'sub *nimio...die.*'

tecta mouenti.   Cf. the fuller description of this effect of an earthquake in Lucr. 6. 561 sqq.

850.   **busta**, here 'ashes,' a most unusual sense, perhaps found in Ovid *Tr.* 4. 10. 80 '*matris* proxima *busta* tuli' (*al.* '*matri...iusta*'); though Statius has it even of *unburned* corpses *Theb.* 12. 247 'egena sepulcri | *busta.*'

summus...sacerdos, the *pontifex maximus*, the head of a priestly

9—2

corporation, of which Dionysius says *Ant. Rom.* 2. 73 that it had the most important functions of the priesthoods of Rome and that its members in the sphere of religious rites were responsible neither to the senate nor the people. The *pontifex maximus* was not allowed even to look on a corpse, Sen. *Dial.* 6. 15. 3; but the fire of cremation would have purged the taint.

851*. **nam.** The connexion of thought is: Sooner or later you must be brought back, since your memory will be kept alive by pilgrimages to your grave.

Syenen, now *Assouan,* only a little to the north of the tropic of Cancer.

852. **siccas,** which the Pleiads (collective singular as in Verg. l.c. inf.) 'leave dry,' i.e. parched even in the rainy season, the beginning of which was associated with the setting of the Pleiades; Columella V Kal. Nou. = Oct. 28 *Vergiliae occidunt* (true morning setting), id. VI Id. Nou. = Nov. 8 *Vergiliae mane occidunt* (apparent morning setting), IV Id. Nou. = Nov. 10 *hiemis initium.* (These dates are correct enough for the latitude of Rome in the time of Lucan, see Smith's *Dict. of Antiquities* s.u. *Astronomia,* vol. 1 p. 227.) The setting of the Pleiades was often attended by storms; cf. Verg. *G.* 4. 234 sq. 'aut eadem [Plias] sidus fugiens ubi Piscis aquosi | *tristior hibernas* caelo descendit in undas,' Hor. *C.* 4. 14. 20 sqq. 'indomitas prope qualis undas | exercet Auster Pleiadum choro | scindente nubes,' Claud. *IV Cons. Hon.* 437 sq. '*madida*que *cadente* | *Pliade* Gaetulas intrabit nauita Syrtes,' and elsewhere.

The abl. appears to be a 'mixed' one of time and cause, cf. *Thessalia* in 108* if that is the right reading.

853. **spectator Nili,** like Germanicus, Tac. *A.* 2. 60 sq. He visited all the places mentioned by Lucan here. *spectator* supplies the place of a verbal subst. of the agent to *uiso* which is the verb usually applied to sightseers, as in Tacitus l.c., Val. Max. 8. 11 Ext. 3 'tenet *uisentis* Athenis Volcanus Alcamenis manibus fabricatus.'

Rubri...profundi, n. on 293.

854. **mercis,** a collective sing.; cf. Quint. 1. 12. 17 'sordidae *mercis* negotiator.'

mutator, also in X 212 'uarii *mutator* circulus anni' (of the zodiac); and after Lucan in Val. Fl. 6. 161, Stat. *Silu.* 5. 2. 135 and Arnobius. In his liking for this formation in *-tor* Lucan follows in the steps of Livy.

855. **uenerabile saxum,** to be read as a correction of *miserabile bustum* of 816.

856. **forsan,** with a participle also in Sen. *Thyest.* 747 sq. 'obiecit feris | *lanianda forsan* corpora atque igne arcuit.' This word with *forsitan* and *fortasse* appears for some reason or other to be practically confined to books VIII and IX (*forsitan* once in X 364).

turbatus, scattered in confusion; cf. Verg. *A.* 6. 74 sq. 'foliis tantum ne carmina manda, | ne *turbata* uolent rapidis ludibria uentis.'

857. **auertet,** turn from his path, and so 'attract,' with a sense of the preposition that reminds us of the Greek ἀποβλέπειν 'to gaze (away) at something.' So Livy 1. 12. 10 '*auerterat*que ea res etiam Sabinos tanti periculo uiri,' 28. 6. 4 'cum omnium animos oculosque id certamen *auertisset.*' So *auocet* absolutely in the sense of 'distract,' Sen. *Dial.* 1. 3. 10. The ind. fut. for the pres. subjunctive is unusual. The desire for emphasis has weakened the grammatical nexus between the relative and principal clauses. Accius *Fr.* 458 'quis *erit* qui non me spernens, incilans probris, | sermone indecorans turpi fama *differet*?' The road to the Red Sea lay through Mt Casius, *Introd.* p. lxiv.

iubebit, of suggesting insistently some thought or action, cf. VII 349 'causa *iubet* melior superos sperare secundos,' and 387 supra.

858. **et** adds another view of the action, 'putting them before' the famous temple of Zeus on Mt Casius, a day's march from the mouth of the Nile at Pelusium and about the same distance from Ostracine (cf. *Introd.* p. lxiv n. 3), Iosephus *Bell. Iud.* 4. 11. 5. The god was a youthful figure holding the mysterious pomegranate, Achilles Tat. 3. 6, and his worshippers were not allowed to eat onions, Sextus Empiricus *Pyrrhoniae Hypotyposes* 3. 224. There were temples to Iuppiter Casius elsewhere, in Syria and at Cassiope in Corcyra.

859. **auro,** of an urn or coffin of gold; cf. IX 10 'non illuc (i.e. to where Pompey is) *auro positi* ueniunt nec ture sepulti | perueniunt.'

860*. **pro numine summo** = 'summi numinis instar' *Priap.* 40. 4.

861. **fortuna** appears to be used in a sense resembling that in Hor. *Ep.* 2. 1. 191 'mox trahitur manibus *regum fortuna* retortis,' a periphrasis with which we may compare Prop. 3. 2. 19 'nec Mausolei diues *fortuna* sepulcri,' Sen. *Dial.* 12. 7. 10 'ita fato placuit nullius rei eodem semper loco stare *fortunam,*' and **iacens** means 'quae iacet hoc tumulo.' The whole phrase signifies: 'he whose portion it is to lie in so poor. a grave.' *iacentis* would certainly have made the meaning clearer, but the nominative is a shift like that in *tota* 375. Cf. 459 *commissa.*

augustius, the real predicate; 'More revered than the conqueror's altars is the surf-beaten stone above the Libyan seas.'

aris, cf. 835.

862. **in** 'on' or 'over'; of what is close to, on the banks of, rivers or other stretches of water; '*in* oceano' 798 supra, '*in* herboso concidit Apidano' Prop. 1. 3. 6. 'canes currentes bibere *in* Nilo flumine | ...traditum est' Phaedrus 1. 25. 3.

863 sq. The point of these lines is that the humbleness of a place does nothing to prejudice the worship accorded to the divinity.

Tarpeis...deis, the three august deities housed in the magnificent temple of Iuppiter Capitolinus.

sua, the incense they claim.

864. **inclusum**, etc. The reference is to the sacred places called by the name of *bidental* from the victim sacrificed in the *fulminis procuratio*, as described in 1 606 sqq. The remains and traces of the fallen thunderbolt were buried in the earth by the Etruscan *uates* according to the native ritual and the spot fenced off.

865. **proderit h. olim.** Cf. Ov. *Am.* 3. 11. 7 'perfer et obdura; dolor *hic* tibi *proderit olim.*'

futuris, dat. masc. (as in X 270) with **mansura**.

866. **marmoreo...pondere** 'with a load of marble.' The adj. represents a gen. Cf. 'marmoreas moles' Sen. *Dial.* 11. 18. 2 (in a passage verbally similar to the present one).

867. **uetustas**, length of years, lapse of time; cf. VII 850, 'quod nulla consumat *uetustas*' Sen. *Dial.* l.c.

868. **mortis...peribunt**, apparently an intentional conceit.

869. Cf. Sil. It. 11. 123 sq. '*ueniet* quondam *felicior aetas* | cum pia Campano gaudebit consule Roma.'

870. **monstrantibus**, 822 n.

871. **erit**, the 'subjective' use of *esse*, 18 n.

populis...nepotum. Compare VII 207 'apud seras gentes *populos-que nepotum.*' *Romans* are perhaps meant in the first instance by this plural which is very frequent in Lucan, cf. 420 supra and VII 28 (with note in the *Addenda*). But its limitation to this sense would be incidental as it is also used of non-Italian peoples; thus IX 163 sq. 'solusque tenebis | Aegyptum, genitor (Pompey's son is speaking), *populis* superisque fugatis,' ib. 597 'quis tantum meruit *populorum* sanguine nomen?' X 34 sq. '*omnis*—populos' of the nations subjugated by Alexander. The truth is that from the time of Ovid the meaning of *populus* both in singular and plural was approaching that of 'multitude,' 'numbers,' Ovid *Am.* 3. 13. 29 'ore fauent *populi*' (of a crowd), *Fast.* 1. 381 (of early Rome) 'moenia iam *stabant populis* angusta futuris,' 4. 640

'luce Palis *populos* purget ut ille cinis.'   Hence exactly like our 'people'
in Aulus Gellius 3. 13. 2 'Demosthenes domo egressus, ut ei mos
erat, cum ad Platonem pergeret *compluris*que *populos* (a number of
people) concurrentis uideret, percontatur eius rei causam.'   For the
singular cf. Ovid *M.* 3. 340 'irreprehensa dabat *populo* responsa petenti'
(in the similar passage of Lucan IX 544 '*populi* quos miserat Eos'),
Sen. *Dial.* 7. 2. 4 'quam magnus mirantium tam magnus inuidentium
populus est,' ib. 9. 9. 3 'cenare posse sine *populo*,' id. *Ep.* 77. 13
'quantus te *populus* moriturorum sequetur.'   Cf. n. on 253 above.

872.   **Magni tumulo,** by (claiming) Magnus' grave; a condensed
expression to which we have already had several parallels.   See note
on 113.

Creta.   Ovid *Ars Am.* 1. 297 sq.   'non hoc centum quae sustinet
urbes, | quamuis sit mendax, Creta negare potest.'   The charge of
mendacity without doubt rested in part on the claim of the Cretans
that Zeus was buried in Crete, Callimachus *H. in Iouem* 8, Statius
Theb. 1. 278 sq. 'placet Ida nocens mentitaque manes | Creta tuos,'
Ovid *Am.* 3. 10. 19 sq. 'Cretes erunt testes; nec fingunt omnia Cretes; |
Crete nutrito terra superba Ioue.'

Tonantis, sc. *tumulo.*   Cf. 1 446 'et Taranis *Scythicae* non mitior
ara *Dianae*' (sc. *arā*).   Greek has an advantage over Latin here as it
could say τῷ Διός.

NOTES TO BOOK IX

1—18

4. degenerem, genere ipsius indignum, cf. x 441 (of Caesar in hiding) '*degeneres* passus latebras.'

conuexa Tonantis. 'The sphere of the Thunderer' is a Roman Stoic's expression, as we may infer from Seneca *Benef.* 4. 7. 1 'Natura' inquit 'haec mihi praestat.' non intellegis te, cum hoc dicis, mutare nomen deo? quid enim aliud est natura quam deus et diuina ratio toti mundo partibusque eius inserta? quotiens uoles, tibi licet aliter hunc auctorem rerum nostrarum conpellare et Iouem illum Optimum ac Maximum rite dices et Tonantem et Statorem.'

5. astriferis...axibus, the ether where are the stars, the hollow sphere enclosing that of the cloudy atmosphere (niger aer).

6, 7. The construction appears to be 'semideique manes habitant quod patet inter terras lunaeque meatus.'

8. uita, an extension of the abl. of Part Concerned, 'of harmless (blameless) life.'

imi, lowest part of the *aether* adjoining the *aer*.

9. aeternos...orbes, explained by the Stoic doctrine for which the Schol. on Hom. *Il.* Ψ 65 quotes Chrysippus: 'Chrysippus teaches that souls assume the spherical form after separation from the body' (μετὰ τὸν χωρισμὸν τοῦ σώματος σφαιροειδεῖς γενέσθαι δογματίζει). Our whole passage is inspired by Stoicism.

collegit, appropriate of the compact globular form, cf. Columella 10. 391 (cucumis) 'semper *collectus in orbem.*' **animam** is a distributive singular.

10. i.e. conquerors like Alexander or Caesar. Cf. 859.

12. miratus, 614 n.

16. classes, the Pompeian fleet.

18. inuicti. Hor. *C.* 2. 1. 23 sq. 'et cuncta terrarum subacta | praeter atrocem animum Catonis.'

169—214

The scene is the camp of Cato in Africa where the vessel carrying Cornelia and Sextus has just arrived.

170. **potentis**, 'a ruler's,' after **mortem**.

175 sq. It is not clear where these **uestes** etc. were got from.

178. **Ioui**, i.e. Capitolino.

179. **fuit**, 'counted as' Pompey's ashes; cf. VIII 18 n.
omnis, i.e. ceterorum omnium.

181. **Thessalicis**, of the killed at Pharsalia.

182. **depastis** 'eaten down,' 'grazed bare' (Haskins).
summittere 'let (or make) the grass spring up.'

183. **hibernas**, proleptic, 'for the winter,' cf. VIII 4 n.

184. **fouet** 'treats with fire.'

187. Cf. VII 725.

188. **Pompeium**, 'the end of Pompey' (cf. VIII 113 n.), which is a *crimen deum*, VIII 55.

191. **modum iuris**, see VIII 642 n.

193 sq. i.e. solus priuatus, parata plebe seruire sibi.

195. **regnantis**, remaining sovereign.

197. **possedit**, from *possido*. **retentis**, sc. sibi.

198. **intulit**, i.e. into the State's coffers.

200. **iuuit**, 'was a pleasure to.'

203. **gentibus**, dat., the outside nations.

204. **uera fides**, i.e. genuine safeguards.

205. **rebus**, the conduct of affairs, the 'world.'

206. **perit**, perfect proper, whereas *obit* is aor.

207. **color**, 'palliation,' 'pretence of excuse' on the part of our rulers. (*imperii = imperantium*, in antithesis to *senatus*.) **frons**, 'blush,' as we should say.

209. **quaerendos**, 'to be sought for' if not offered.

212 sq. **fatis**, 'by fate's decree.'
talem mihi Iubam, qualis erat Pompeio Ptolemaeus.

214. **seruari**, cf. VIII 661.

INDEX

*References by arabic numerals are to the **lines** commented on in the notes (* indicating a note in the Critical Apparatus) and by small roman numerals to pages of the Introduction.*

*References printed thus **108** are to notes where other references are collected.*

I. LATIN AND GENERAL

Ablative, ultra-condensed use of 686
abruptus with dat. 293
abstract subst. with genitive 569
accersere mortem 660
Achillas xlix, liii, liv, lv, lvii, lxvii
Achillas, formation of 541
Acoreus (*Ach.*) 475*
Acoreus, or Achoreus, high priest of Memphis l, li
ad 'against' 429
adjectives as past participles **387**
adstrictus 'rigid' 67
Aegyptos, -on 501*, 871*
agitare (*fata*) 138
Alani lxxx, lxxxi
    and Albani confused lxxx and note
Alanus spelling 223*
Albani lxxx
Alexandria, Pompey's objective xlii
alliteration **368**
Alpina bella, Pompey's 808
ambiguous compounds with *in-* 787
ambire rogum 735
amnis, arm of a river 466

Amphipolis, Caesar at xxviii
    Pompey at xxviii
'Annaean inaccuracy,' the xxii
Antioch hostile to Pompey xli
Apis 479
apostrophe to an abstraction 455, 547
Appian and Lucan xvi n.
Araxes 431
arbor 'mast' 179
Arctophylax and *Cynosura* 180
Arctous formation 363
Armenia and Parthia lxxix
Armenius of the Parthians 221
Arsacidae 218
    accused of incest 404, 409
artus = artatus 387
Asine (Asina) 195*
ast 151
astringere (*foedus*) 220
asyndeton in contrasts **118**
Attalia, Pompey at xxxvi
auditu 'at hearing' 342
auertere 'attract' 857
aula 239
authorities for Pompey's last days xv sq.
auxilium 'remedy' 334

II. PASSAGES COMMENTED ON OR EMENDED (†)

A. LATIN.

B. GREEK.

III. LITERARY PARALLELS

IV. LUCAN AS A WITNESS

(Places in the *Introduction* and *Notes* where Lucan's recording of fact is considered, those favourable to the author being printed in italics) :

NOTE ON THE MAP OF POMPEY'S ROUTE OF FLIGHT

This map does not profess, as the reader will readily understand, to give the exact line pursued by Pompey. Even where the points of departure and arrival are known, the course pursued between these points may be nothing more than conjectural. Thus, while the direction which Pompey took after leaving Lesbos can be determined with certainty, there is room for difference of opinion as to his course past the sea-board and islands of Ionia. The marking of the route here and elsewhere has been made as far as possible to conform to the require-ments of the evidence, and failing evidence to those of probability. But it cannot claim implicit acceptance for its details and it is possible that in some respects as in the case of the coasting along the southern portion of Cyprus (460 sq., Excursus B p. lxxxvii) it may really be committed to an error. In one case the data are so uncertain that I have felt bound to mark an alternative route. When Lucan makes Pompey go past the cliffs of Icaria and also 'shave' the rocks of Samos, 244–6, this may only mean that he thought the islands were closer together than they are. But, apart from this, one does not see why Pompey should have passed to seaward of Samos.

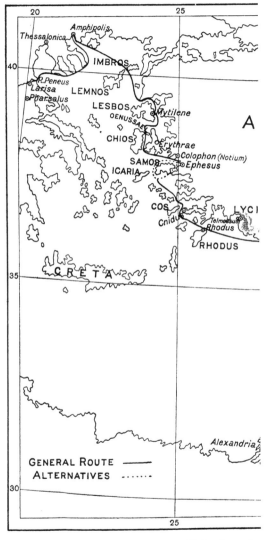

Pompey's flight from La

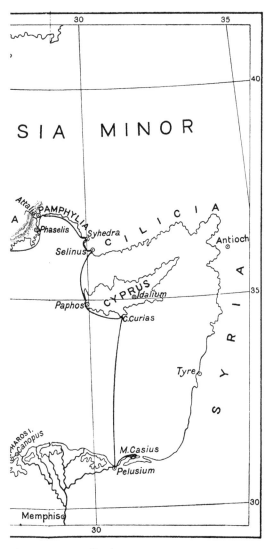

...risa to Mount Casius

For EU product safety concerns, contact us at Calle de José Abascal, 56–1°, 28003 Madrid, Spain or eugpsr@cambridge.org.

www.ingramcontent.com/pod-product-compliance
Ingram Content Group UK Ltd.
Pitfield, Milton Keynes, MK11 3LW, UK
UKHW020310140625
459647UK00018B/1818